The Roots of the Synoptic Gospels

The Roots of the Synoptic Gospels

Bo Reicke

FORTRESS PRESS PHILADELPHIA

Library of Congress Cataloging-in-Publication Data

Reicke, Bo Ivar, 1914–
The roots of the synoptic gospels.

1. Synoptic problem. 2. Bible. N.T. Gospels—Criticism, interpretation, etc. I. Title.
BS2555.2.R39 1986 226′.0663 85–45485
ISBN 0–8006–0766–X

1835A86 Printed in the United States of America 1–766

Contents

Preface

The aim of this study is to illustrate the origin and formation of Christian traditions behind the Gospels of Matthew, Mark, and Luke, called "synoptic" because they can be studied in parallel columns showing various degrees of similarity. Special attention will be paid to preliterary factors which are reflected in the written Gospels and related texts.

Consequently the exposition will concentrate on points of view rarely taken into account in the modern synoptic discussion, which is mainly concerned with the reconstruction of literary sources. This may be explained in two short comments.

First, since the middle of the nineteenth century, most scholars have based their synoptic investigations on the assumption that texts were used by the evangelists as literary *sources.* (1) Widely dominant today is the two-source theory, according to which Mark and a presumed document called Q were the common sources of Matthew and Luke. (2) Some contemporary scholars, however, reject this position and return to an older tradition which reserved a priority for Matthew. (3) Others prefer to reconstruct a number of different sources behind the Gospels by separating a proto-Luke from Luke, a pre-Mark from Mark, or by dividing the so-called Q into various documents. These literary approaches contradict each other, and their advocates have not yet been able to convince the adherents of the other theories.

Second, in this study the question will be raised from which historical *roots* the material had grown up that was used by the evangelists in their books and under which circumstances these authors or redactors had elaborated it. As a correlate to any higher criticism, the basic development of the synoptic traditions is to be considered by paying regard to how the traditionists may have handled the reminiscences before the material was collected and ordered by the evangelists in writing.

Certainly students of the New Testament in general, and even contributors to different assumptions of literary sources, realize that oral traditions circulated

among the early Christians long before the Gospels were composed. But this vague recognition seldom involves any effort to explain how, where, and when those early traditions later used in written texts were fashioned and developed. There are exceptions, to be sure. In our first chapter we review attempts to shed light on the oral traditions behind the written Gospels by drawing attention to form categories, to rabbinic analogies, or to folklore experiences.

Nevertheless there is still room for an *internal* analysis of the *entire* synoptic material with regard to possible influences of living oral traditions upon the structures of the written texts. Inquiries may be made to explain in particular on which basis early oral traditions were formed and spread; from which persons the evangelists took over their material; and in what regions they may have been active.

These are fundamental questions, and they can only be treated with the aid of indications given by the Gospels themselves, by other books of the New Testament, and by writings produced shortly after the New Testament period. It is not fair to reject or neglect such ancient witnesses in favor of theoretic literary genealogies. A positive attitude toward the documents available will characterize this attempt to find the living roots of the Gospels according to Matthew, Mark, and Luke.

Since the study does not follow the general trend of modern scholarship, there has not been great reason for references to literature. Only the history of the debate, treated in the first chapter, will include a detailed bibliography.

The following abbreviations have been used in connection with biblical quotations:

etc. (= et cetera) means: similar examples are found in the subsequent context;
e.p. (= et passim) means: scattered examples are found in different contexts;
with par. (= with parallels) means: analogies to the passage quoted are found in the same context of the other synoptic Gospels, so that a triple contextual parallelism is formed;
the sign // is used between two such contextual parallels.

The author is responsible for the English text of this book, which he wrote on the basis of a German manuscript. A helpful partial translation had been made by Mrs. D. Richardson and Mr. K. Richardson, Basel. For valuable corrections the author thanks John A. Hollar and Stephanie D. Egnotovich of Fortress Press. The text was completed in March 1985.

Bo Reicke

Basel
July 31, 1986

Chapter One

History of the Synoptic Discussion

The three Gospels according to Matthew, Mark, and Luke are called "synoptic" because their texts can be studied in parallel columns in a so-called synopsis (in Greek, σύνοψις, "survey"), which discloses their similarities and differences. Any adequate synopsis must present the units of each Gospel in their own sequence. The first Greek synopsis of this kind was published in 1774 by Johann Jakob Griesbach in Halle,[1] and the expression "synoptic" was used thereafter for the Gospels in question.

Reading the Gospels in a synopsis facilitates the study of the "synoptic problem," the discussion of the historical, literary, and theological relationships between Matthew, Mark, and Luke. Although the present investigation of the "roots" of the synoptic texts will concentrate on the historical circumstances that were in the background of the literary compositions and theological expositions of the evangelists, our overview of the scholarly discussion will also deal with other aspects of the problem.

Several attempts to compare and harmonize the Gospels were already made in antiquity. One notes especially the lists of analogous passages constructed by Eusebius which received general attention.[2] But a more detailed analysis of synoptic analogies or differences was possible only after the publication of Griesbach's Synopsis and its successors.

1. Originally the presentation of Matthew, Mark, and Luke in parallel columns was part of Griesbach's general New Testament text edition: J. J. Griesbach, *Libri historici Novi Testamenti graece*, 1 (Halle, 1774). Two years later Griesbach printed the text of the first three Gospels in separate form: *Synopsis evangeliorum Matthaei, Marci et Lucae* (Halle, 1776). Numerous new editions and revisions have appeared in various languages.

2. Reprinted in K. and B. Aland, *Novum Testamentum graece*, 26th ed. (Stuttgart: Deutsche Bibelstiftung, 1979), 73–78.

Four Theories

During the decades before and after 1800, Protestant theologians in Germany developed four theories to answer the synoptic question with regard to the genealogy of traditions: the utilization hypothesis; the proto-gospel theory; the tradition hypothesis; and the multiple-source theory. With some variations, and sometimes in combination with each other, these four theories are still of importance for the scholarly discussion, which has now become international and interconfessional.

The Utilization Hypothesis

Implying that one evangelist was dependent upon another, the utilization theory is an option that has mostly been regarded as the least complicated. The order in which the utilization took place, however, could always be pictured in different manners.

1. In the early church and later, Matthew was granted priority because his Gospel introduces the canon and because he is mentioned among the apostles. Thus the sequence Matthew → Mark → Luke was represented by Origen and Ammonius in the third century and by Augustine around the year 400.[3] In later centuries this order was accepted, for instance, by the Dutch scholar Hugo Grotius in 1641.[4]

2. In publications of the years 1783 and 1789–90, Griesbach suggested the sequence Matthew → Luke → Mark.[5] On the basis of his Synopsis he saw the

3. Origen, quoted by Eusebius in *EH* VI.25.3,6. Ammonius Alexandrinus, quoted by Eusebius in his *Epistula ad Carpianum,* reprinted in Aland, *Novum Testamentum graece,* 73–74: a synopsis beginning with Matthew. Augustine, *De consensu evangelistarum* I.23, Corpus scriptorum ecclesiasticorum latinorum 43 (Vienna, 1904), 3–6: Mark the successor and abbreviator of Matthew. In IV.10.11, however, Mark was also said partly to follow Luke: D. Peabody, "Augustine and the Augustinian Hypothesis," in *New Synoptic Studies: The Cambridge Gospel Conference and Beyond,* ed. W. R. Farmer (Macon, Ga.: Mercer Univ. Press, 1983), 37–64.

4. H. Grotius, *Annotationes in libros evangeliorum* (Amsterdam, 1641), 5–8: Hebrew Matthew → Greek Mark; 594: Matthew → Mark → Luke.

5. J. J. Griesbach, *Fontes unde evangelistae suas de resurrectione Domini narrationes hauserint,* Osterprogramm der Universität Jena, 1783; reprinted in Griesbach's *Opuscula academica* (Jena: Fromann, 1825), 2:241–56; idem, *Commentatio qua Marci evangelium totum e Matthaei et Lucae commentariis decerptum esse monstratur, scripta nomine Academiae Jenensis 1789–1790 jam recognita multisque argumentis locupletata,* printed in the work edited by J. C. Velthusen et al., *Commentationes theologicae* (Leipzig, 1794), 1:360ff.; reprinted in Griesbach's *Opuscula academica* 2:358–425. Reprint and English translation in *J. J. Griesbach: Synoptic and Text Critical Studies 1776–1976,* ed. J. B. Orchard and T. R. W. Longstaff, SNTSMS 34 (New York and Cambridge: Cambridge Univ. Press, 1978), 74–102.

Earlier suggestions to place Mark historically after Matthew and Luke are known (1) from the patristic time and (2) from the eighteenth century, though Griesbach did not mention this. (1) Around the year 200, Clement of Alexandria said in his *Hypotyposeis* that Matthew and Luke had preceded Mark (quotation of Eusebius, *EH* VI.14.5–7). Two hundred years later, Augustine declared a similar view to be a considerable alternative, partly correcting the position taken earlier in his *De consensu evangelistarum.* (2) Shortly before Griesbach's time, the order Matthew → Luke → Mark had been proposed by Henry Owen in *Observations on the Four Gospels, Tending*

possibility of regarding the Second Gospel (Mark) as a short recapitulation of the two others. Because he presented the Synoptic Gospels in parallel columns without changing the order of each text, Mark's consistently intermediate position became evident to him. Mark's arrangement of the material is sometimes in simultaneous correspondence with that of Matthew and Luke, and at other times in alternating correspondence with that of Matthew or that of Luke.

Griesbach's important student Professor Wilhelm Martin Leberecht de Wette of Basel supported his theory by analyzing numerous passages that could further demonstrate the alternating dependence of Mark upon the two other evangelists.[6]

During the second third of the nineteenth century, Griesbach's theory was also represented by Ferdinand Christian Baur in Tübingen and the members of his school. But since they applied Georg Wilhelm Friedrich Hegel's dialectic process of thesis, antithesis, and synthesis to the synoptic material, their expositions became rigorously schematic and brought the historical views of Griesbach and de Wette into discredit.[7]

3. In 1786, exactly between the two studies of Griesbach quoted above, the priority of Mark in relation to Matthew and Luke was suggested by Gottlob Christian Storr.[8] At that time Storr was a professor in Tübingen, and later became a chaplain of the court in Stuttgart. In spite of Storr's great renown, his suggestion of the priority of Mark did not find many adherents in his lifetime, because his contemporaries were still partial either to Matthew or to the oral tradition.

After the political revolution of 1830, however, German Protestants began to develop a predilection for Mark. The homely reports of Mark pleased a generation that was stamped by bourgeois liberalism and realism and that insisted upon empirical immanence and historical reliability in written documents. Matthew and Luke were regarded as more encumbered with speculative theology. Thus the philologist Karl Lachmann in Berlin declared in a famous paper of 1835 that

Chiefly to Ascertain the Times of their Publication, and to Illustrate the Form and Manner of their Composition (London, 1764), 32; and the order Luke → Matthew → Mark by Anton Friedrich Büsching in *Die vier Evangelisten mit ihren eigenen Worten zusammengesetzt und mit Erklärungen versehen* (Hamburg, 1766), 99, 108, 118–20. Circumstances which indicate that Griesbach knew of Owen's and Büsching's studies have been pointed out by F. Neirynck, "The Griesbach Hypothesis: The Phenomenon of Order," *Ephemerides Theologicae Lovanienses* 58/1 (1982): 111–22, esp. 116–17 (in n. 24, a reference to observations of H. Marsh made in A.D. 1789); and D. Dungan, "The Purpose and Provenance of the Gospel of Mark According to the Two-Gospel (Owen-Griesbach) Hypothesis," in *New Synoptic Studies*, 411–40, esp. 412–14. Yet even if Griesbach knew of Owen's and Büsching's studies, he did not quote them.

6. W. M. L. de Wette, *Lehrbuch der historisch kritischen Einleitung in die kanonischen Bücher des Neuen Testaments* (Berlin: Reimer, 1826), 128–71; 5th enl. ed. (1848), 131–79.

7. On the synoptic theory of Griesbach and its later development: W. R. Farmer, *The Synoptic Problem: A Critical Analysis* (New York: Macmillan, 1964; 3d ed., Macon, Ga.: Mercer Univ. Press, 1976), 5–9; B. Reicke, "Griesbach's Answer to the Synoptic Question," and "Introduction" (to his Commentatio) in *J. J. Griesbach*, 50–73.

8. G. C. Storr, *Über den Zweck der evangelischen Geschichte und der Briefe des Johannes* (Tübingen: Osiander, 1786), 2d ed. (1810), 274–307.

early traditions on the life of Jesus had included five "corpuscles" of a report already structured, which the synoptic evangelists had been able to use. Lachmann claimed that Mark had preserved the preestablished order in a more pure form than either Matthew or Luke.[9] He did not regard Mark as the source of Matthew and Luke, for he based his thinking on the tradition hypothesis (see below); but because Lachmann found the Second Gospel most in harmony with preliterary traditions, he claimed respect for Mark and caution against Matthew.

The two-document theory. It was the same bourgeois realism, implying an inclination to seek the foundations of the Gospel literature in historical documents unencumbered by advanced theology, that led Karl August Credner of Giessen in 1836 to go one step farther than Lachmann and assume that Mark was a source used by Matthew and Luke.[10] Storr had made the same suggestion fifty years earlier, but, independently of him, Credner gave the priority of Mark a new support that was soon amplified by others. At the same time, Credner supposed that Matthew and Luke had used a second written source, containing sayings of Jesus (Logia). Like Friedrich Schleiermacher, he believed that Bishop Papias of Hierapolis (ca. A.D. 110), when treating the compilation of the **λόγια** in Hebrew by Matthew, used this Greek word to signify only "sayings" of Jesus—although Papias spoke about the **λόγια** of Matthew and especially Mark in the broader sense of "reports" on the Lord (cf. below, p. 8). Credner thus became the father of the rapidly growing two-source theory, according to which Matthew and Luke had been using Mark and what has later been called Q in the sense of an unknown document containing sayings of Jesus.

In 1838 the philosopher Christian Hermann Weisse of Leipzig delivered further inducement to regard the presumed sayings or Logia of Matthew and the Gospel of Mark as the two sources of Matthew and Luke, which he did with extensive references to Schleiermacher and Lachmann.[11] Like several contemporaries, Weisse was eager to use written documents as sources for his portrait of Jesus, and since he felt bound to see the Son of Man merely under human aspects, Mark and the Logia suited his purpose best. In particular, Weisse was afraid that David Friedrich Strauss, whose radical portrait of Jesus had just appeared in a second edition, would lead people to replace history with mythology.[12] He therefore alluded to Strauss in the title of his book ("kritisch . . . bearbeitet") and

9. K. Lachmann, "De ordine narrationum in evangeliis synopticis" in *Theologische Studien und Kritiken* 8 (Hamburg, 1835): 570–90.

10. K. A. Credner, *Einleitung in das Neue Testament* (Halle: Waisenhaus, 1836), 201–5.

11. C. H. Weisse, *Die evangelische Geschichte kritisch und philosophisch bearbeitet,* 1–2 (Leipzig: Breitkopf & Härtel, 1938). Volume 1 refers to Schleiermacher on pp. 34–38, Lachmann on pp. 38–40, Mark on pp. 56–83, and the Logia on pp. 83–87.

12. D. F. Strauss, *Das Leben Jesu kritisch bearbeitet,* 1–2 (Tübingen: Osiander, 1835–36; 2d ed. 1837). [Eng. trans. G. Eliot: *The Life of Jesus Critically Examined,* ed. with introduction by Peter C. Hodgson, Lives of Jesus Series (Philadelphia: Fortress Press, 1972; London: SCM Press, 1973).]

started his discussion by rejecting the hypothesis of an oral tradition which Strauss represented.[13]

A second proclamation of Mark's priority happened to appear simultaneously with Weisse's book of 1838. Its author was a pastor in Dresden by the name of Christian Gottlob Wilke, and without knowing Lachmann's and Weisse's works in favor of Markan priority, he published his rather polemical book after ten years of struggle with the synoptic problem.[14] While he was occupied with this book, numerous and important theologians still preferred to derive the synoptic material either from Matthew or from an oral tradition. In sharp opposition to his contemporaries, Wilke alleged that a written report on the life of Jesus must have existed from the very beginning and that Mark must be identified with this document because of its historical orientation. It followed that Luke was based on Mark and Matthew on Luke.[15] Wilke's purely literary analysis yielded an extreme form of the utilization hypothesis, implying the sequence Mark → Luke → Matthew.

It took some time until Weisse's and Wilke's preferences for Mark became influential; but the triumph of liberal theology after the revolution of 1848 concentrated the interest on Mark again.

The first scholar of importance who adopted the two-document theory in this period was the orientalist Heinrich Georg August Ewald in Göttingen, a forceful representative of liberal Protestantism. In his papers on the subject printed from 1848 to 1851, Ewald went one step farther and introduced the distinction of a proto-Mark from Mark.[16] In a commentary on the Synoptic Gospels of the year 1850, Ewald was so confident of his scheme that he distributed the pretended sources on different script types, and in the preface expressed a conviction that his literary analysis would both enable the public to realize the value of true religion demonstrated by him in this way and bring about the unity of all Germans.[17] Afterward a unification of the Germans may at least be said to have been established in the field of synoptic criticism, for the successes of liberal theologians made the two-document hypothesis a generally accepted principle.

In 1863, Heinrich Julius Holtzmann's *Die synoptischen Evangelien* secured the final victory of this hypothesis in Protestant Germany. Referring to Weisse, Wilke, and Ewald, Holtzmann stated the priority of a proto-Mark named Alpha

13. Weisse, *Die evangelische Geschichte,* 3–16.

14. C. G. Wilke, *Der Urevangelist oder exegetisch kritische Untersuchung über das Verwandtschaftsverhältnis der drei ersten Evangelien* (Dresden and Leipzig: G. Fleischer, 1838).

15. Ibid., 4–17 (a synopsis proceeding from Mark to Luke and further to Matthew); 656–85 (Mark used by Luke and Matthew); 685–92 (Luke used by Matthew).

16. H. G. A. Ewald, "Ursprung und Wesen der Evangelien," *Jahrbücher der biblischen Wissenschaft* 1 (Göttingen, 1848): 113–54; 2 (1849): 180–224; 3 (1851): 140–74; 1:138–47; 2:191–95.

17. H. G. A. Ewald, *Die drei ersten Evangelien übersetzt und erklärt* (Göttingen: Dietrich, 1850), xviii–xix.

and of a proto-Matthew symbolized by the letter Lambda.[18] The symbol Lambda was used for the presumed collection of sayings called Logia, which Schleiermacher had ascribed to Matthew by means of a peculiar interpretation of Papias, and it corresponds to what has later been standardized with the letter Q.

Holtzmann's theory and similar presentations of the utilization hypothesis were accepted by a growing number of scholars in Germany and other countries, either with various simplifications or with further complications. From the Protestant quarter it also spread to Catholic scholars. Thus generations of students were told by their professors that Mark and the Logia, or some predecessors of them, were the literary sources of the synoptic material.

As to other countries, this German theory was especially cultivated in England at the University of Oxford, where members of a seminar on the synoptic problem held regular meetings beginning in 1894. Some of their studies were published in 1911 by William Sanday of Christ Church, and he introduced his article by this declaration: "We assume what is commonly known as the 'Two-Document Hypothesis.'"[19] Among the contributors were several renowned scholars: Charles Allen Willoughby, Sir John Hawkins, and Burnett Hillman Streeter.

In 1924, the last-mentioned contributor to Sanday's collection, B. H. Streeter, published an impressive volume that was to receive decisive importance for the whole English-speaking world. Rejecting any suggestion of a proto-Mark, he called the use of Mark's present Gospel by Matthew and Luke "a fundamental discovery."[20] He also found the Logia source, now called Q, an indispensable assumption, but since he also combined Q with a proto-Luke (called L) and a proto-Matthew (called M), the result was a four-document hypothesis.[21] At any rate, the self-confident exposition of Streeter has led many scholars in England and America to regard the two-document theory as indispensable.

Today the dependence of Matthew and Luke upon Mark and the unknown document called Q is accepted by innumerable theologians and lay people of every nationality and confession. It is generally taken for granted without any discussion. Although detailed investigations of the literary relationships between Matthew, Mark, and Luke have inspired several experts of higher criticism to more complicated stemmata, including a proto-Matthew, a proto-Mark, or a proto-Luke as well as different levels of a Q, most theologians are satisfied with a simple pattern: Mark + Q = the substance of Matthew and Luke. This common opinion also provides the basis for numerous theological expositions, in which

18. H. J. Holtzmann, *Die synoptischen Evangelien. Ihr Ursprung und geschichtlicher Charakter* (Leipzig: Engelmann, 1863), on predecessors, pp. 29–33, 36–38; on Alpha, pp. 56–111; on Lambda, pp. 126–57; summary, pp. 162–68.

19. W. Sanday, ed., *Studies in the Synoptic Problem, by Members of the University of Oxford* (Oxford: Clarendon Press, 1911), 3.

20. B. H. Streeter, *The Four Gospels: A Study of Origins Treating of the Manuscript Tradition, Sources, Authorship, & Dates* (London: Macmillan, 1924; 2d ed., 1926), on the synoptic problem, pp. 149–360; on Mark's basic function, pp. 157–201.

21. Ibid., 199–270.

Matthew and Luke are treated as secondary in comparison with Mark and Q. Matthew and Luke are thus supposed to have altered given documents in a very subjective way, but the adherents of the two-source hypothesis have normally avoided the inconvenience of explaining this circumstance.

The Proto-Gospel Theory

From the attempts to reconstruct a proto-Matthew and the like, there is but a step to the second form of the classical synoptic theories presented in Protestant Germany toward the end of the eighteenth century, that is, the so-called proto-gospel theory. It was developed by Gottfried Ephraim Lessing at Wolfenbüttel in 1779, and implies than an unknown document is regarded as the common source of the four Gospels or at least of three or two of them.

Lessing started from information offered by patristic writers about the original language of the First Gospel. Around A.D. 110, Papias of Hierapolis in Phrygia had found out that Matthew had collected in Hebrew what Papias called the λόγια (Eusebius, *Ecclesiastical History* III.39.16 [hereafter, *EH*]). In antiquity this statement was not referred to any collection of sayings like the hypothetical Q but to a Gospel report written by Matthew in Hebrew or perhaps in Aramaic. Further comments by Epiphanius and Jerome from the end of the fourth century led to an identification of this Hebrew Matthew with the so-called Gospel of the Hebrews or that of the Nazareans, used by Jewish-Christians in Syria.[22] In 1689, Richard Simon of Normandy, the pioneer of biblical criticism, took these patristic indications into account when he stated that the Aramaic proto-Matthew of the Nazareans had been the source of the first Gospel in the canon.[23] Lessing, who was then a librarian in Wolfenbüttel, used these patristic traditions as a point of departure while endeavoring to bridge the chronological distance between the life of Jesus and the redaction of the canonical Gospels. With great élan he wrote some theses on the subject in 1779 which, after his death, were published by his brother in 1784. According to Lessing, the Aramaic Matthew of the Nazareans was the original document from which all canonical and apocryphal Gospels had emerged.[24]

Some scholars found this explanation much too simple. One reaction was that of the Göttingen polyhistor Johann Gottfried Eichhorn, who endeavored to improve the proto-gospel hypothesis in 1794 by inserting several intermediate stages.[25] He took over his theory of auxiliary sources from a colleague in

22. Quotations of Epiphanius and Jerome in W. Schneemelcher, *Neutestamentliche Apokryphen* (Tübingen: Mohr/Siebeck, 1959), 1:90–100, 104–8; Eng. trans. E. Hennecke-W. Schneemelcher, *New Testament Apocrypha* (Philadelphia: Westminster Press; London: Lutterworth Press, 1963), 1:123–36.

23. R. Simon, *Histoire critique de texte du Nouveau Testament* (Rotterdam, 1689), 71–100.

24. G. E. Lessing, "Neue Hypothesen über die Evangelisten als bloss menschliche Geschichtsschreiber betrachtet," *Theologischer Nachlass* (Berlin, 1784): 45–72, esp. 68; idem, "Theses aus der Kirchengeschichte," 73–82, esp. 80.

25. J. G. Eichhorn, "Über die drei ersten Evangelien," *Allgemeine Bibliothek der biblischen*

Göttingen, Johann Benjamin Koppe, who had suggested a plurality of shorter and longer sources now lost, thus inaugurating the multiple-source theory, discussed below.

Eichhorn's eclecticism resulted in an extraordinarily complicated picture of a development on several levels, and few of his contemporaries found it convincing.

In 1832, a limited form of the proto-gospel theory, also based on Papias's declaration concerning Matthew, was introduced by Friedrich Schleiermacher in Berlin. His suggestion gradually brought about the widespread conception of a specific Logia source or Q.[26] Schleiermacher's innovation consisted in a particular interpretation of Papias's information that Matthew had put together the λόγια in Hebrew (Eusebius, *EH* III.39.16). He explained λόγια in this passage as "sayings" and believed Papias had referred to a document containing sayings of Jesus, which should be understood as the source of material found in Matthew but not Mark.

Schleiermacher's translation of λόγια as "sayings" was conventional and influenced by New Testament passages (e.g., Rom. 3:2). But as will be demonstrated in chapter 7, it was not in accordance with the technical meaning in which Papias used the word λόγια, judging from the fragments of his book available in patristic quotations. The word is found three times in the extant fragments of Papias, and the context makes it obvious that Papias used λόγια in the technical sense of "reports" or "traditions," including quotational elements as well as narrative units. He called his book "Investigation of the λόγια κυριακά" (Eusebius, *EH* III.39.1), and by this Greek expression meant the canonical Gospels whether they contain sayings or narratives. Papias then used the same expression, λόγια κυριακά, with reference to all units of tradition contained in the Gospel of Mark (*EH* III.39.15). By defining these units as dealing with "things either said or done by Christ" (*EH* III.39.1), Papias made it evident that for him the λόγια written down by Mark included both types of tradition: quotations as well as narratives. There is every reason to give those λόγια which Papias mentioned as collected by Matthew the same technical meaning of tradition units, including both sayings and narratives. According to what Papias declared, the Hebrew composition of Matthew was not a collection of quotations but a Gospel like Mark, and he added that it had been translated into Greek by others (*EH* III.39.16). Papias was also understood to have spoken of a whole Gospel by those patristic authors, who referred to the Gospel of the Hebrews or that of the Nazareans.

On this account Schleiermacher must be said to have misinterpreted the words of Papias about Matthew. In the same arbitrary way he did not understand the notice of Papias on Mark as referring to the Second Gospel, which ought to have

Litteratur 5 (Leipzig, 1794): 759–996.

26. F. Schleiermacher, "Über die Zeugnisse des Papias von unseren beiden ersten Evangelien," *Theologische Studien und Kritiken* 5 (Hamburg, 1832): 735–68, esp. 738–58.

been natural, but to a proto-Mark supposed to have been a preliminary report containing narratives.[27]

In spite of these deficiencies Schleiermacher's suggestions of 1832 were, soon after his death in 1834, taken over by Credner in 1836 and then used in the powerful two-document hypothesis. Only the assumption of a proto-Mark has not generally been preserved by later advocates of the Logia source. In fact, many scholars or students, who have regarded a Logia document or what is called Q as the one source, have acquiesced in the extant text of Mark as being the other source. An influential representative of this position, partly inspired by William Wrede in Breslau, was Rudolf Bultmann in his *History of the Synoptic Tradition* (discussed below in connection with form criticism, pp. 14–16). Without permitting any questioning of the sources, Bultmann treated Mark and Q as two source documents absolutely established and universally accepted, and he emphatically denied the existence of any Gospel before Mark.[28]

Actually the powerful two-source theory implies a combination of the utilization hypothesis in the Markan form with the proto-gospel theory in a limited form. A background is found in two of the classical theories inaugurated before 1800, as mentioned above. For when the assumption of Mark's priority was prepared by Lachmann in 1835, further proposed by Credner in 1836, and firmly contended by Weisse and Wilke in 1838, it meant a reincarnation of the utilization hypothesis according to that Markan alternative which had been presented by Storr in 1786. And when Schleiermacher suggested the existence of a Logia source in 1832, he created a limited analogy to the unknown proto-gospel which had been presupposed by Lessing in 1784.

The Tradition Hypothesis

A third attempt to answer the synoptic question was the tradition hypothesis, by which the similarities and deviations of the synoptic reports were ascribed to an oral tradition represented by the apostles and the evangelists. This theory was developed in Weimar by Johann Gottfried von Herder and made public in 1796–97.[29]

Herder rejected both the utilization hypothesis and the proto-gospel theory. Instead, he conjectured that a proto-Mark in Aramaic had been the "protoplasm"

27. Ibid., 758–67.

28. R. Bultmann, *Geschichte der synoptischen Tradition,* FRLANT, N.F. 12 (Göttingen: Vandenhoeck & Ruprecht, 1921; 2d ed., 1931; 3d ed., 1957; with appendix, 1958, the latter in a 2d ed., 1962; Eng. trans. J. Marsh: *The History of the Synoptic Tradition* [New York: Harper & Row; Oxford: Basil Blackwell, 1963]). Bultmann declared about Mark and Q (1st ed., p. 194; 2d and 3d eds., p. 347): "Ich setze nur die sog. Zwei-Quellen-Theorie voraus"; and concerning Mark (1st ed., p. 226; 2d and 3d eds., p. 394): "Auf keinen Fall ist eine seiner Quellen als Evangelium zu bezeichnen. . . . Denn beide (Mt und Luk) legen den Mk-Aufriss zugrunde." In this regard the impact of the scribal tradition in question was strong enough to entail leaving out any motivation.

29. J. G. Herder, *Christliche Schriften* 2 (Riga, 1796): 149–233; 3 (1797): 301–416; reprinted in *Sämtliche Werke,* ed. B. Suphan (Berlin: Weidmann, 1880), 19:194–225, 380–424.

of a living "Gospel Saga," by which expression he meant the common oral tradition of the early church. Based on the preaching of the apostles and the expositions of evangelists such as Philip and others (Acts 21:8; Eph. 4:11), this proto-Mark had been developed in oral form between A.D. 34 and 40. Later it had also been written down but not officially disseminated. Some thirty years later a messianic elaboration of proto-Mark had been written and published, and this was the Aramaic proto-Matthew or the Gospel of the Nazareans. When the Christian message was spread among the nations and translated into Greek, these two Palestinian sources gave rise to our Gospels: Mark in the 60s on the basis of proto-Mark; Luke in the same years on the basis of proto-Matthew.

Herder's reference to a proto-Mark and a proto-Matthew partly anticipated the later two-document hypothesis. But since he referred to a living oral tradition, Herder's theory was basically different, and he rejected all ideas of redactional activity on literary terms such as would be done in a chancellery. His observations are still noteworthy, because an oral tradition was absolutely the first stage and has certainly influenced the literary products. This is also realized in our days since the inauguration of the form-critical approach.

More specifically, the judgment of Herder on the Gospel traditions was based upon the following principles: Each of the first apostles and their assistants, the evangelists, transmitted the oral message in his own way. They offered a living report, not dead letters written by hand (Rom. 10:8–18; 2 Cor. 3:7).[30] A fundamental unity was guaranteed by their common task, which consisted of historical information about Jesus as the Messiah. Paul also emphasized that nobody can lay another ground for belief than what had been done by Jesus Christ (1 Cor. 3:11).[31] However, the report on the events was always given form in a personal way. It is anachronistic to find the extant plurality disturbing and to attempt to reconstruct homogeneous sources.

Herder rejected current methods of literary criticism by these frank declarations:

> Considering the manner in which Gospels were understood at the time in question, namely that Gospels contain oral records in written form, there was no objection to adding new oral communications, thus supplementing extant Gospels. . . .[32] It was only natural that several Gospels were composed. . . .[33] The whole idea that our Evangelists had been like scribes (scribae) who collected treatises and supplemented, improved, collated and compared each with the other, is . . . extraordinarily inconsistent and unnatural with regard to their situation and intention, also to the purpose of their respective Gospels. . . . Assumptions of this kind lead to such a confusion that all points of contradiction between the Evangelists become even more conspicuous. Ultimately, one does not know which Evangelist would have copied the

30. Herder, 2:190, 196; 3:306.
31. Ibid., 2:185–88.
32. Ibid., 180 n. 1.
33. Ibid., 186–87.

other, or supplemented, abbreviated, disrupted, improved, corrupted him or even stolen from him. . . . In fact, not one of them endeavored to surpass and subdue the other, but each simply presented his report. Perhaps none of them had seen the Gospel of another, and even if this had been possible for one author, he did not make use of it when he wrote his own Gospel.[34]

While the synoptic problem continued to be discussed, however, Herder's ironical observations were suppressed by eager representatives of literary criticism. In modern synoptic research a picture may still be found of the muddle deplored by him.

Herder's accentuation of the oral tradition was in any case clarified and substantiated in 1818 by the young grammar school master Johann Carl Ludwig Gieseler, a mediating theologian who became a well-known church historian in Bonn and Göttingen.[35] Gieseler suggested a more distinct separation of the oral and written stages than Herder had indicated.[36] He wanted to explain similarities and differences between the Gospels under practical and psychological aspects. Even if this approach was generally neglected in the nineteenth century, it proved valuable again in the twentieth century when form criticism began to pay attention to the life setting and the structures of the oral traditions.

A statement of Gieseler, which is especially instructive, should be quoted here:

Assuming a common oral source is the most convenient means to explain how the following state of things has emerged: The more the stories appeared important to the disciples, the more they were told in a congruous way. It was these units that were most often presented, and being frequently repeated they preserved their original form in a more pure way than did other stories. Concerning the latter it was the matter and not so much the form that was recalled by the individuals. But here, too, the noticeable expressions are more or less identical, while before and after those expressions there is variation in the form of synonyms. This exactly had to be the natural consequence of an oral prototype.[37]

Gieseler did not exclude a theoretical possibility that some traditions were recorded in written form rather early, although no evidence for this is available.[38] But he emphasized that oral teaching remained an essential practice for a considerable length of time, after written documents had appeared.[39] Gieseler pointed out three general characteristics of this oral teaching: (1) Memorizing was a living reality in antiquity. It was cultivated successfully and was often regarded as more reliable than fixed documents. (2) An oral paradosis is close in harmony with the intellectual standard of the Palestinian believers and the

34. Ibid., 191–93.
35. J. C. L. Gieseler, *Historisch-kritischer Versuch über die Entstehung und die frühesten Schicksale der schriftlichen Evangelien* (Leipzig: Engelmann, 1818).
36. Ibid., 55, 83.
37. Ibid., 90.
38. Ibid., 91.
39. Ibid., 116–18.

Hebraizing diction of the Synoptic Gospels.[40] (3) For a long time the canon was fluctuating, and this also confirms the relative indifference of the early church to written documents as long as living traditions existed.[41]

Among the examples quoted by Gieseler, the reference to a letter of Ignatius written in A.D. 114 is especially instructive (*Letter to the Philadelphians* VIII.2).[42] Opposing contemporary literalists who required written documents (ἀρχεῖα) in order to believe the preaching of the church, Ignatius remarked that documents were easy to falsify (*Philadelphians* VIII.2). In his eyes, the only authentic testimonies were Christ's cross, death, and resurrection as well as the belief in these facts. Thus, like Paul, Ignatius referred to items of the orally transmitted kerygma (1 Cor. 15:1–8).

When these observations were published by Gieseler in 1818, romanticism was dominant in literature, and German scholars were still inclined to prefer oral traditions. In the bourgeois period after 1830, however, literary documents were required again, and twenty years after Gieseler's book a new reasoning in terms of records and offices broke through when Weisse and Wilke ascribed priority to Mark and inaugurated the triumph of the two-document theory.

The Multiple-Source Theory

The fourth synoptic theory to be considered here implies the assumption of multiple sources. Its pioneer was a professor in Göttingen, Johann Benjamin Koppe, later a chaplain at the court of Hannover.

Koppe thought of the "numerous" writers to whom Luke has alluded in 1:1 and suggested in an essay of 1782 that a plurality of shorter and longer units should be sought behind the extant Gospels.[43] It was supposed that these multiple sources were spread among the Christians in oral and written form and molded into narratives, speeches, parables, sayings of Jesus, and other form categories. By his reference to such units, Koppe anticipated two important theories of later date: the fragment theory of Schleiermacher and the form-critical insights of Martin Dibelius (below, pp. 13–14).

As mentioned above, Koppe's productive colleague Johann Gottfried Eichhorn in Göttingen combined Lessing's proto-gospel theory with this multiple-source theory in a paper of 1794, but his contemporaries found the pedigree designed by Eichhorn too complicated.

Yet the hypothesis of multiple sources was taken up again in a book on Luke published by Schleiermacher in 1817, that is, several years before the above-mentioned Logia source was averred in his article of 1832. Unlike what he was

40. Ibid., 88, 93–111.
41. Ibid., 142–203.
42. Ibid., 160–64.
43. J. B. Koppe, *Marcus non epitomator Matthaei* (Programm der Universität Göttingen, 1783); reprinted in *Sylloge commentationum theologicarum,* ed. D. J. Pott and G. A. Ruperti (Göttingen: Vandenhoeck & Ruprecht, 1800), 1:35–69, esp. 66.

going to do when dealing with the Logia source, Schleiermacher rejected in that earlier work the anachronisms of the utilization and proto-gospel theories. He characterized his reactions in this way: "I find myself in a German book factory of the eighteenth or nineteenth centuries, not in the very beginnings of Christianity.[44] Schleiermacher preferred to assume there were a number of written sources, which he called notes or reports, and in principle his version of the multiple-source theory was a multiple-fragment hypothesis. More precisely, Schleiermacher suggested that after the dispersion of the disciples in Jerusalem their oral reports had been written down by auditors. This material developed into smaller and greater collections of topical reports, such as speeches, stories, and the narrative of Christ's passion and resurrection. Independently of each other the synoptic redactors then used such collections.[45] Although this reconstruction of the process involved a background in the oral traditions, Schleiermacher did not pay much attention to the activity of the apostles but concentrated his interest on circumstances in the Diaspora. On the whole, he did not find the oral reports of the early disciples as important as the written notes of the auditors, which he postulated. This centrifugal and pluralizing tendency, as well as the assumption of fragmentary notes, involved several uncertain factors, and so Schleiermacher's multiple-source theory of 1817 did not convince his contemporaries who preferred more documentary evidence.

A hundred years later, however, Schleiermacher's fragment hypothesis of 1817 was partly recalled to life by the pioneers of form criticism, who championed a multiple-source theory. To be sure, form criticism is not only a modern counterpart to Schleiermacher's fragment hypothesis insofar as it represents a modified version of the multiple-source theory, for the new approach is also related to Herder's tradition hypothesis. Similar to what has been observed about the two-document theory—that it represents a combination of the utilization hypothesis in its Markan form with a limited form of the proto-gospel theory—form criticism has adjusted Herder's tradition hypothesis to Schleiermacher's fragment theory. This compromise implies restrictions on both sides. On the one hand, form criticism wants to study preliterary traditions like Herder but is concerned only with short elements and not with comprehensive structures. On the other hand, the material collected by the evangelists is supposed to have consisted of numerous isolated fragments such as those of Schleiermacher, but they are conceived as oral units and not as written notes.

Later the Heidelberg professor Martin Dibelius presented the program of form criticism in 1919, elaborating impressions incurred during his studies in Leipzig and Berlin. Among his teachers in Leipzig was Georg Heinrici, who

44. F. Schleiermacher, *Über die Schriften des Lukas. Ein kritischer Versuch* (Berlin: Reimer, 1817), 6.

45. Ibid., 7–14; cf. his *Einleitung ins Neue Testament,* ed. G. Wolde (Berlin: Reimer, 1845), 315. On his exegesis in general, see H. Weisweiler, *Schleiermachers Arbeiten zum Neuen Testament* (Diss.; Bonn, 1972).

published a book on New Testament literature in 1908 and traced its roots back to early Christian mission and oral form categories such as teaching, prophecy, hymnology, and prayer.[46] Three esteemed teachers of Dibelius in Berlin were the theologians Hermann Gunkel and Adolf Deissmann, who emphasized folklore aspects of the Old and New Testament traditions, and the philologist Eduard Norden, who published a classical work on *Formgeschichte* ("form history," although the standard English term has become "form criticism").[47]

Dibelius wanted to discontinue regarding the Synoptic Gospels as compositions of authors displaying literary material, and instead to regard them as compilations of popular microliterature elements. The practical basis or "life setting" *(Sitz im Leben)* of the elements called pericopes was defined as early Christian "preaching," which Dibelius understood to include both sermons and teaching. He distributed the pericopes in different categories, and the most important of those suggested by Dibelius were "paradigm" (short narrative ending in a point); "novel story" (longer narrative with several details); "parenesis" (admonition based on words of Jesus); and "myth" (revelation of his messianic sovereignty).

Just after the First World War this new approach to the Synoptic Gospels was embraced as a refreshing renewal among German scholars. Already in the year 1919, Dibelius was followed by his former student Karl Ludwig Schmidt, who declared the individual pericopes of the Gospels as the original material and the general itinerary as redactional arrangement.[48] Other young scholars in Germany, in turn, applied the form-critical program to the disputation pericopes and the passion narrative.[49]

In 1921, Bultmann submitted the whole synoptic material to a similar criticism in a book that has been authoritative since then.[50] He adopted two principles of Dibelius's form criticism, first by starting with smaller units of the synoptic tradition and then by asking for their life setting in the church. In practice, however, Bultmann degraded the form-critical method to an instrument which he used in order to carry out certain ideas about the development of the original message into a Hellenistic cult-myth. The analysis of the forms was thus used for several alterations or transpositions of the material that he needed. Bultmann

46. G. Heinrici, *Der literarische Charakter der neutestamentlichen Schriften* (Leipzig: Dürr, 1908), 23–48, 100–127.

47. M. Dibelius, *Die Formgeschichte des Evangeliums* (Tübingen: Mohr/Siebeck, 1919), 2–15; enl. 2d ed. (1933), 1–34.

48. K. L. Schmidt, *Der Rahmen der Geschichte Jesu. Literarkritische Untersuchungen zur ältesten Jesusüberlieferung* (Berlin: Trowitzsch & Sohn, 1919), v, 317.

49. M. Albertz, *Die synoptischen Streitgespräche. Ein Beitrag zur Formgeschichte des Urchristentums* (Berlin: Trowitzsch & Sohn, 1921); G. Bertram, *Die Leidensgeschichte Jesu und der Christuskult. Eine formgeschichtliche Untersuchung,* FRLANT, N.F. 15 (Göttingen: Vandenhoeck & Ruprecht, 1922).

50. R. Bultmann, *Geschichte der synoptischen Tradition.*

actually started with the result to which he wanted to come, and summarized the process assumed in the following words:[51]

> The type of a Gospel meets us first in Mark, and one may say that Mark has created it. By no means is any of his sources to be called a Gospel. . . . For neither Matthew nor Luke has used such a product: both are based on Mark's outline. In any case, the Gospel is a creation of Hellenistic Christianity. . . . There was need of a cult-legend for the Kyrios of the Christian cult. Since the pattern of the Christ-myth had to be illustrated, it needed to be combined with traditions about the history of Jesus. . . . Thus the Gospels are cult-legends. Mark has created this type. The myth of Christ gives his book . . . a unity which is not biographical, but simply based on the myth. Matthew and Luke have . . . enforced the other aspect by taking up historical traditions not found in Mark, yet available to them.[52]

The goal determined in this quotation was reached in three steps: (1) Form-critical principles were used to show that Mark had only isolated pericopes at his disposal, no coherent information on the life of Jesus. (2) Literary criticism was added on the basis of the two-document hypothesis in order to illustrate changes of the pericopes supposed to have taken place in connection with a centrifugal movement from Jerusalem to Hellenism, which Bultmann found essential. (3) From religiohistorical points of view, this dislocation of the material from the center to the periphery implied that Bultmann dispossessed the Palestinian church described in Acts of any productive importance. Instead, he associated the material collected by Mark with the so-called Hellenistic community. By the latter he meant pre-Pauline churches in Syria and elsewhere which he, under the influence of Wilhelm Bousset, had promoted to a decisive historical factor and equipped with a cult-legend and Christ-myth, although no such complexes are described in relevant texts. At last Matthew and Luke were assumed to have supplemented Mark by particular material in order to give the reports a more historical appearance, and in this case Bultmann alluded to the source called Q.

For a long time Bultmann's monumental work has deeply affected form criticism and synoptic discussion in Germany along with other countries. His keen jump from a form-critical analysis to manipulations with the two sources and his violent move of the data to the Hellenistic periphery did not disturb the experts, but was eagerly imitated.

A similar use of form criticism in combination with the two-source theory has dominated synoptic research since 1921, and the primary form-critical impulses have therefore gone off the rails. In principle, the analysis of microstructural forms and the determination of their categories were meant to illustrate oral traditions but, in analogy to Bultmann, numerous scholars have presented form-critical preliminaries merely in order to sort out written texts of supposed earlier

51. Ibid., 1st ed., pp. 226–27.

52. In the 2d and 3d editions, Bultmann gave this summary an expanded form, pp. 394–97. He also replaced the radical term "Christ-myth" with the milder expression "kerygma of Christ" (p. 396) but the religiohistorical pattern remained the same.

or later origin, and to confirm their conceptions of a doctrinal evolution within early Christianity. In reality the deductions have moved backward from the literary results desired, so that form criticism has not been practiced for its own sake. Until and even after the Second World War the synoptic discussion has been waning, because the patterns of form criticism and the two-source theory have been widely understood as representing final truth. Certainly, new outlines have also been drawn up since the war, as will be indicated below, but textbooks and commentaries are still dominated by faithfulness to this mixture of two approaches that represent widely differing levels of the material contained in the Synoptic Gospels.[53]

Modern Attitudes and Recent Contributions

After the Second World War, new attitudes to the synoptic material and new discussions of the synoptic problem may be observed. The perspectives have developed in two opposite directions.

1. On the one hand, inherited synoptic questions have sometimes been relinquished by modern expositors. Some believe that all historical factors of interest have already been explained by the two-source theory; others feel that such background circumstances are of no hermeneutical relevance. Two new synoptic programs have thus appeared on the stage, and their representatives are in both cases occupied with analysis of the extant texts without discussing the sources. One of the schools presents itself as "redaction criticism," since it wants to establish what the Gospel redactors had intended to make of their material. The other movement is known as "structural linguistics," which means that a so-called linguistic analysis is used to display logical structures within given textual units. In the present treatment, it will be enough to recall a few details concerning the origins and the principles of these two attempts, which seek to interpret the Synoptic Gospels on levels above the genealogy of their traditions.

Redaction criticism, or what German scholars call *Redaktionsgeschichte*, became an important approach in connection with the revival of theological studies in Germany after the last war. Among its pioneers were Günther Bornkamm, Hans Conzelmann, and Willi Marxsen—former students of Bultmann's—who also based their conceptions on the two-source theory but desired to find out more about the contents and the structure of each Synoptic Gospel in its present form.[54] Younger scholars of different nationalities have followed them

53. Examples of textbooks in German representing form criticism together with the two-source theory: W. G. Kümmel, *Einleitung in das Neue Testament* (Heidelberg: Quelle & Meyer, 1963, and later editions), 20–44; J. Schmid, *Einleitung in das Neue Testament* (Freiburg: Herder, 1973), 279–96; Ph. Vielhauer, *Geschichte der urchristlichen Literatur* (Berlin: Walter de Gruyter, 1975), 268–80.

54. G. Bornkamm, "Die Sturmstillung im Matthäusevangelium," *Wort und Dienst*, N.F. 1 (Bielefeld, 1948), 49–54; H. Conzelmann, *Die Mitte der Zeit. Studien zur Theologie des Lukas*, Beiträge zur historischen Theologie 17 (Tübingen: Mohr/Siebeck, 1954); W. Marxsen,

with a multitude of dissertations and monographs. In spite of the general enthusiasm, redaction criticism does not represent a new method but the resumption of an old endeavor in biblical theology to search for peculiarities within each of the Gospels.[55] No doubt the new contributions of redaction criticism have also clarified the message of the synoptic evangelists. But on the other hand a serious restraint is placed on several monographs and commentaries practicing redaction criticism, because some form of the two-document hypothesis is forced upon the individual witness of each Gospel in a mechanical way. The outcome is that what Matthew and Luke have written is relativized and deprived of its own life and value. Primary attention is not drawn to the actual message of each one in objective comparison with that of the other evangelists, but to his presumed manipulations of Mark and Q. Right or wrong, the two-source theory has thus become an obstacle to a consistent development of redaction criticism, because it does not always permit Matthew and Luke to speak for themselves.

Adherents of the approach called structural linguistics avoid this dependence on a literary source theory. They follow an international and interdisciplinary program developed by philologists for the interpretation of texts in general, and its application to biblical documents is only secondary. Inspiration for the program called "linguistics" came from a book, published in 1916 and based on lectures delivered in Geneva by the comparative philologist Ferdinand de Saussure. He drew up methodological differences between "diachronic" and "synchronic" investigations of language and literature, emphasizing that philology does not only have to illustrate the historical development of given units but also has to analyze their logical composition independently of historical circumstances.[56] The linguistic method of de Saussure has later been called "structural semantics" because of a textbook which is representative of the method's current form and was published in 1964 by the Russian scholar Algirdas Greimas in Paris.[57] Avoiding so-called diachronic questions, the structuralists analyze given texts in a synchronic framework with the aid of rather complicated philosophical or sociological terminology.

Structuralistic liberation from the preoccupation with historical problems has also inspired New Testament scholars to apply linguistic hermeneutics to the synoptic material. A need was felt to get beyond the stereotyped combination of form criticism with the two-source theory which had been dominant for several

"Redaktionsgeschichtliche Erklärung der sogenannten Parabeltheorie des Markus," *Zeitschrift für Theologie und Kirche* 52 (1952): 255–71.

55. The title of J. Rohde's *Die redaktionsgeschichtliche Methode. Einführung und Sichtung des Forschungsstandes* (Hamburg: Furche, 1966) gives the impression of a special method. But on p. 13 the author has observed that redaction criticism is rather an expansion of form-critical perspectives.

56. F. de Saussure, *Cours de linguistique générale, publié par Ch. Bally & A. Riedlinger* (Lausanne: Payot, 1916), 139–44. Several later editions; see ed. with introduction and notes by T. de Mauro (Paris: Payot, 1972).

57. A. J. Greimas, *Sémantique structurale. Recherche de méthode* (Paris: Larousse, 1964).

decades.[58] Thus linguistic schedules were rapidly disseminated from Paris over the entire theological world, and presently the movement is popular in France, North America, and South Africa. It is also possible that some of the linguistic experiments with technical conceptions and distinctions will yield permanent results in biblical studies.[59] Of course the synoptic problem itself has not been promoted by the structuralists, because their methodology prescribes that historical questions are left aside. Nevertheless this movement is also of interest within the history of the synoptic discussion, since it represents dissatisfaction with the routine subjection of synoptic exegesis to an established pattern of Gospel sources.

Redaction criticism and structural linguistics are thus connected with different inclinations to let the inherited discussion of synoptic problems rest in peace.

2. In other contexts a forceful revival of the synoptic discussion is noticeable after the Second World War. Essentially the new drives are due to modifications and modernizations of the four alternatives that were elaborated in the eighteenth and nineteenth centuries, although the perspectives have also been widened. Some distinguished scholars can thus be mentioned as examples of modern analogies to the classical theories. Among them are representatives of a utilization hypothesis who plead either for the priority of Matthew in analogy to Griesbach or for that of Mark in analogy to Storr (above, pp. 2–3); of a proto-gospel theory in essential analogy to that of Lessing (p. 7); of a multiple-source theory comparable to suggestions by Koppe and Eichhorn (p. 12); and of an oral tradition hypothesis reminiscent of Herder's view (pp. 9–12). Evidence for the permanent impact of the four alternatives is offered by the fact that eminent proponents of each view were invited to defend their options at the international and interconfessional symposium on the synoptic problem held in Jerusalem during two weeks before Easter 1984.

Only a few names and data connected with the renewal of the four approaches in question will be recalled here.

Utilization hypothesis. After the last war the dominant Markan form of the utilization hypothesis was first criticized by Basil Christopher Butler in London, who took up the Augustinian theory in 1951 and defended the sequence Matthew → Mark → Luke.[60] This thrust did not find great support.

More successful was the campaign against the established consensus which

58. A general stagnation of form criticism was observed by E. Güttgemanns, *Offene Fragen zur Formgeschichte des Evangeliums. Eine methodologische Skizze der Grundproblematik der Form- und Redaktionsgeschichte,* Beiträge zur evangelischen Theologie 54 (Munich: Kaiser, 1970), 35–39.

59. Summary and support of linguistic hermeneutics in biblical contexts: R. Kieffer, *Die Bedeutung der modernen Linguistik für die Auslegung biblischer Texte,* Theologische Zeitschrift 30 (Basel, 1974), 223–33.

60. B. C. Butler, *The Originality of St. Matthew: A Critique of the Two-Document Hypothesis* (Cambridge: Cambridge Univ. Press, 1951), 170.

William R. Farmer of Dallas began in a book of 1964, stating that Griesbach's subordination of Mark to Matthew and Luke is the simplest answer to the synoptic question.[61] Several scholars have welcomed this form of the utilization theory, which avoids the assumption of unknown sources, and have supported it by informative publications and conferences.[62] Certainly most adherents of Markan priority and the source called Q have not been willing to give up their convictions. In the main, they do not even find it necessary to discuss the synoptic problem anymore. A laudable exception is Frans Neirynck of Louvain, who has deeply felt the challenge of theories based on Matthew's priority and developed an immense erudition in order to secure the leading position of Mark. He did it first in a monograph of 1972 on dual phrases in Mark, and then in numerous later studies.[63]

Proto-gospel theory. It was nevertheless in Louvain, where Neirynck had studied, that a revival of Lessing's proto-gospel theory had been developed by leading Roman Catholic professors. In a lecture given there in 1952, Léon Vaganay of Lyon suggested that one should begin with Papias's indication of the Aramaic Matthew, a source that he supposed to have been a collection of speeches, and in addition think of another source behind Luke.[64] At the same time, Lucien Cerfaux of Louvain supported Vaganay but also characterized Greek versions of this Aramaic Matthew as intermediary sources of the canonical Matthew, whereas Mark and Luke were regarded as later compositions.[65] Somewhat later, Xavier Léon-Dufour, then active in Lyon, expressed fundamental agreement with Cerfaux in a well-known textbook, although he added the assumption that preliterary traditions have determined the form of the Aramaic Matthew as well as of intermediary Greek predecessors to Matthew, Mark, and Luke.[66]

Multiple-source theory. Since the last-mentioned Roman Catholic scholars did not see the canonical Gospels as deriving immediately from the proto-Gospel of Matthew, but added several intermediary sources, their synoptic genealogies were reincarnations not only of Lessing's proto-gospel theory but also of the

61. Farmer, *The Synoptic Problem,* 211.

62. Of special importance was the symposium held at the University of Münster in 1976 to celebrate the bicentenary of Griesbach's Synopsis, *J. J. Griesbach: Synoptic and Text Critical Studies 1776–1976.*

63. F. Neirynck, *Duality in Mark: Contributions to the Study of the Markan Redaction,* BETL 21 (Louvain: Louvain Univ. Press, 1972); in collaboration with Th. Hansen and F. van Segbroeck, *The Minor Agreements of Matthew and Luke Against Mark, with a Cumulative List,* BETL 37 (1974); a great many later critiques of theories starting from Matthew.

64. L. Vaganay, *La question synoptique,* ALBO II/31 (Louvain: Louvain Univ. Press, 1952), 7.

65. L. Cerfaux, *La mission de Galilée dans la tradition synoptique,* ALBO II/36 (Louvain: 1952), 5, 42. Cf. idem, *Luc, Dictionnaire de la Bible,* Supplement 5 (Paris: Letouzey, 1957), col. 565.

66. X. Léon-Dufour, in *Les évangiles synoptiques,* ed. A. Robert and A. Feuillet, Introduction à la Bible (Tournai: Desclée, 1959), 2:143–320, esp. 293–95 and 319–20.

multiple-source theory inaugurated by Koppe. They combined two of the classical alternatives, corresponding to what Eichhorn had done in 1794 (above, pp. 7–8).

A further step toward an elaborate multiple-source theory was taken in 1972 by Marie-Émile Boismard at the École Biblique of the Dominicans in Jerusalem. Without the aid of a hypothetical proto-gospel, Boismard started with preliminary stages of the canonical Gospels corresponding to those presumed by the scholars mentioned at the end of the foregoing paragraph.[67] He first called them A, B, C, and Q, but later simplified his terminology by referring only to a pre-Matthew, a pre-Mark, and a pre-Luke.[68] These three sources were treated as earlier redactions of the extant Gospels and were supposed to have been edited independently of each other, except that pre-Matthew had inspired pre-Luke. What is called pre-Matthew and pre-Mark would therefore have been two independent sources behind three of the extant Gospels, whereas pre-Luke would have contributed only to Mark and Luke.

Recently, a former student of the same Jerusalem school has developed a similar multiple-source theory. This is Philippe Rolland, who teaches at a Sulpician seminary in France. Starting with a "Gospel of the Twelve" in Jerusalem he advances three intermediary sources treated as documents and localized to Caesarea, Antioch, and to later Pauline centers as well. By combining two of these intermediary documents in different ways he constructs sources of each Synoptic Gospel.[69] His theory is based on studies of double phrases in Mark, which correspond to single phrases either in Matthew or Luke. These double phrases have been observed and discussed in the past, especially by Neirynck (above, n. 63), but Rolland has set their number at no fewer than 174. In contrast to Neirynck, he understands them as evidence for a Markan conflation of sources behind Matthew and Luke, thus approaching Griesbach's theory without subscribing to it.[70]

Oral tradition hypothesis. Besides the modernizations of different utilization and source theories mentioned above, a renascence of Herder's and Gieseler's oral tradition hypothesis is also discernible in contemporary synoptic discussions. To support this view, analogies have been collected from contexts outside the New Testament, partly from Judaism and partly from folklore.

Oral traditions found in Judaism have been emphasized by Swedish scholars

67. M.-E. Boismard, "Introduction," in Pierre Benoit and M.-E. Boismard, *Synopse des quatre Evangiles en français avec parallèles des Apocryphes et des Pères* 2 (Paris: Cerf, 1972), 15–59.

68. Boismard, in a paper of 1983 submitted to participants of the Jerusalem symposium on the interrelations of the Gospels arranged in 1984.

69. Ph. Rolland, "Les évangiles des premières communautés chrétiennes," *RB* 90 (1983): 161–201.

70. Ph. Rolland, "Les prédécesseurs de Marc. Les sources présynoptiques de Mc II,18–22 et parallèles," *RB* 89 (1982): 370–405; idem, "Marc, première harmonie évangélique?" *RB* 90 (1983): 23–79.

who have studied in Uppsala. Their inspiration came from the orientalist Henrik Samuel Nyberg, who analyzed the prophecies of Hosea in 1935.[71] Drawing attention to the dominant function of living traditions in oriental literature, Nyberg rejected the mechanical dissection of texts which has often been practiced in biblical criticism. Similar principles were applied to the Gospels in 1957 by the Uppsala theologian Harald Riesenfeld in a lecture with which he inaugurated a congress at Oxford.[72] According to him, the oral teaching of Jesus was the direct source of the Gospel tradition. To illustrate such dependence of the Gospels on Christ's oral teaching, the Uppsala theologian Birger Gerhardsson, later professor in Lund, wrote a dissertation in which he ascribed the oral traditions of the rabbis to an elaborate memorization practice, and then presumed a corresponding practice behind the Jesus traditions of the apostles,[73] though he admitted that private notes were sometimes a support to memorization. In subsequent publications Gerhardsson has defended his comparison of the rabbinic and the apostolic traditions and clarified his views.[74]

The use of folklore to illustrate oral traditions behind the written Gospels was a starting point for pioneers of form-critical studies but remained in the background and was actually neglected in favor of the two-source theory (above, pp. 14–16). In recent years some American theologians have again found it valuable to apply folkloristic observations to the synoptic problem. Research work done by scholars at Harvard University have made New Testament scholars acquainted with the way in which great epics have been orally transmitted from generation to generation in regions now belonging to Yugoslavia. Impressive material was recorded as early as 1913–1919 by Mathias Murko in Vienna[75] and has been supplemented in campaigns undertaken since 1930 by Milmam Parry[76] and

71. H. S. Nyberg, *Studien zum Hoseabuch. Zugleich ein Beitrag zur Klärung des Problems der alttestamentlichen Textkritik,* Uppsala universitets årsskrift 1935, 6 (Uppsala: Lundequistska, 1935).

72. H. Riesenfeld, *The Gospel Tradition and Its Beginnings: A Study in the Limits of "Formgeschichte"* (London: Mowbray, 1957); reprinted in Texte und Untersuchungen zur Geschichte der altchristlichen Literatur 73 (Berlin: Akademie-Verlag, 1959), 43–65; and in *The Gospel Tradition* (Philadelphia: Fortress Press, 1970), 1–29.

73. B. Gerhardsson, *Memory and Manuscript: Oral Tradition and Written Transmission in Rabbinic Judaism and Early Christianity,* Acta Seminarii neotestamentici upsaliensis 20 (Lund: Gleerup, 1961), conclusions pp. 328–35.

74. B. Gerhardsson, *Tradition and Transmission in Early Christianity,* Coniectanea neotestamentica 20 (Lund: Gleerup, 1964); idem, *Die Anfänge der Evangelientradition* (Wuppertal: R. Brockhaus, 1977), English trans.: *The Origins of the Gospel Traditions* (Philadelphia: Fortress Press, 1979).

75. M. Murko, "Bericht über eine Bereisung von Nordwestbosnien . . . behufs Erforschung der Volksepik der bosnischen Mohammedaner," in Sitzungsberichte der Kaiserlichen Akademie der Wissenschaften in Wien, Philosophisch-historische Klasse 173 (Vienna, 1913); other reports in Sitzungsberichte 176 (1915), and 179 (1915); furthermore, see idem, "Neues über südslawische Volksepik," *Neue Jahrbücher für das klassische Altertum* 43 (Leipzig, 1919): 273–96.

76. M. Parry, "Studies in the Epic Technique of Oral Verse-Making," *Harvard Studies in Classical Philology* 41 (1930): 73–149; 43 (1932): 1–50. On the application of Parry's ideas to Plato, see J. A. Notopoulos, "Mnemosyne in Oral Literature," *TAPA* 69 (1938): 465–95.

Albert Bates Lord[77] of Harvard. Village reciters studied by these scholars proved to have the capacity for memorizing an immense amount of traditional material, and in one case a minstrel was able to quote around 80,000 verses by heart.[78] Most interesting was this observation: Whereas the structure of the story told in the epic was preserved without changes by different traditionists from generation to generation, the expressions used by them were varied with considerable freedom.

Confrontation with the flexibility of such oral traditions has also impressed historians of ancient Greek literature.[79] Although most New Testament scholars are used to thinking in terms of fixed sources, some have also been willing to learn from experiences made by students of folklore and oral traditions. This is evident from the interdisciplinary dialogue arranged in 1977 by William O. Walker at Trinity University of San Antonio, Texas. Here the above-mentioned folklore specialist, A. B. Lord of Harvard, gave the first main lecture and illustrated possibilities to explain the similarities and differences between the Gospels by paying attention to such unity of stability and flexibility as is found in oral traditional literature.[80]

At the same colloquium a professor of Judaic studies, Lou H. Silberman of Vanderbilt University, illustrated the remarkable wandering of fixed themes in Jewish literature and found similar cases in the Gospels.[81] He explained this wandering of text units as evidence for their earlier participation in oral traditions, of which flexibility was characteristic.

Silberman's instructive conclusion may be rendered here:[82]

> A century ago, scholars assumed unquestioningly that a literary work had its sources in literary works (for, after all, were not these scholars themselves ransacking literary works to fabricate new literary works?). And even now, when we have come to affirm that behind some or many of the literary works we deal with there is an oral tradition, we still manipulate such traditions as though they too were "literary" works.

This is reminiscent of a passage quoted above from Gieseler's support of

77. A. B. Lord, "Homer and Huso," *TAPA* 67 (1936): 106–13; 69 (1938): 439–45; and numerous later studies on ancient Greek and southern Slav literature.

78. Murko, "Bericht über eine Bereisung," 284–85.

79. H. Fränkel, *Dichtung und Philosophie des frühen Griechentums,* 2d ed. (Munich: Beck, 1962), 9–27; A. Lesky, *Geschichte der griechischen Literatur,* 2d ed. (Bern: Franke, 1963), 32–58; C. A. Trypanis, *Greek Poetry from Homer to Sefiris* (London: Faber & Faber, 1981), 32. Further titles in E. R. Haynes, *A Bibliography of Studies Relating to Parry's and Lord's Oral Theory,* Documentation and Planning Series 1 (Cambridge: Harvard Univ. Press, 1973).

80. A. B. Lord, "The Gospels as Oral Traditional Literature," in *The Relationships Among the Gospels: An Interdisciplinary Dialogue,* ed. W. O. Walker (San Antonio: Trinity Univ. Press, 1978), 33–91.

81. L. H. Silberman, "Habent sua fata libelli. The Role of Wandering Themes in Some Hellenistic Jewish and Rabbinic Literature," in *Relationships Among the Gospels,* 195–218.

82. Ibid., 215.

Herder's theory (above, p. 11). It was as early as 1818 that Gieseler made these reservations against the anachronistic view of the evangelists as working in their studies with manuscripts, which they sometimes copied and sometimes changed.

In recent years the synoptic problem has thus been taken up again by several open-minded theologians and historians. Many scholars not mentioned here have also taken part in the discussion. Unfortunately no agreement can be observed. In fact, the four leading theories that German Protestants, such as Storr and Griesbach, Lessing, Koppe, and Herder, elaborated shortly before 1800 are still competing with each other in the modernized forms which are found in the contemporary discussion. As far as the synoptic question is concerned, scholars are still divided into the four camps at issue. Each group seeks illumination from a different span of the horizon.

Whichever of the four options is preferred, the present author wants to emphasize that it ought to be supplemented by considerations about the empirical circumstances under which the oral traditions were developed in the early church and then adopted by the evangelists. It is a question of the concrete historical relationships between tradition and redaction as well as between the oral and the written gospel.

Representatives of redaction criticism have been occupied with this problem. But their dependence on the two-source theory implies that reflections of the oral traditions are seen only in Mark and Q, not in what Matthew, Mark, and Luke show together or when they are compared with each other.

Similar limitations are found in recent attempts to reconstruct the development from Jesus to the oral traditions and the written documents. Werner H. Kelber's book *The Oral and the Written Gospel* of 1983 takes the Mark and Q hypothesis for an established truth and uses hermeneutical rules for a categorical separation of the oral traditions and the written documents.[83] Two impressive volumes of papers delivered at Cambridge in 1979 and Tübingen in 1982, both published in 1983, certainly open more possibilities to follow the lines from Jesus to the apostles and the evangelists.[84] But several of the articles still reduce such possibilities by not taking sufficiently into account that oral traditions must have been a link between Jesus and the written material in all of its parts, and not only with regard to one Gospel or some other document elected to be a source.[85]

83. W. H. Kelber, *The Oral and the Written Gospel: The Hermeneutics of Speaking and Writing in the Synoptic Tradition, Mark, Paul, and Q* (Philadelphia: Fortress Press, 1983).

84. Farmer, ed., *New Synoptic Studies;* P. Stuhlmacher, ed. *Das Evangelium und die Evangelien. Vorträge vom Tübinger Symposium 1982* (Tübingen: Mohr/Siebeck, 1983).

85. B. Reicke, "A Test of Synoptic Relationships: Matthew 10:17–23 and 24:9–14 with Parallels," in *New Synoptic Studies*, 209–29.

Chapter Two

The Distribution of the Material

Each of the four New Testament Gospels may be divided into sections called pericopes, of which a considerable number represent thematic and structural analogies in one or more of the other Gospels. A division of the material into such units is found, for instance, in the synopsis of Kurt Aland or that of Heinrich Greeven.[1] Aland counts 367 pericopes in all four Gospels, and Greeven gives a number of 275 to the Synoptic Gospels. In both cases the boundary remains inevitably subjective and, above all, is uncertain among short sections. But the divisions at least give an approximate idea of the circumference and distribution of the material.

Starting from Aland's 367 pericopes of all four Gospels, Joseph B. Tyson has counted 178 in Matthew, 115 in Mark, and 186 in Luke.[2] In order to perceive the extent of the relationship between the Synoptic Gospels, he sorted out pericopes that occur commonly or represent analogies in two or three Gospels, so that in any case their theme, and eventually their structure and language, point to considerable similarities. In contrast to other statistics of the Synoptics, none of the competing source critical hypotheses were taken as a basis for this one, but each Gospel was considered by itself. Tyson wanted to discover the circumference of "sequential parallelism" in the texts, that is, the number of corresponding sections of two or three Gospels that occupy the same position in bordering contexts. In other words, he was not only interested in how many pericopes are common to two or three Gospels but also as to how many of these analogies occur

1. K. Aland, *Synopsis quattuor evangeliorum* (Stuttgart: Württembergische Bibelanstalt, 1964, and later editions). A. Huck, *Synopse der drei ersten Evangelien mit Beigabe der johanneischen Parallelstellen,* 13th rev. ed. by H. Greeven (Tübingen: Mohr/Siebeck, 1981).

2. J. B. Tyson, "Sequential Parallelism in the Synoptic Gospels," *New Testament Studies* 22 (1976): 276–308. More detailed statistics are found in J. B. Tyson and T. R. W. Longstaff, eds., *The Computer Bible,* Synoptic Abstract 15 (Wooster, Ohio: The College of Wooster, 1978). The former study, however, offers an easier survey and is sufficient to give an idea of the approximate proportions.

as parallels in the same context. Sometimes two differing sets of numbers then emerge (noted in the table below with "or"), because text elements occasionally appear unified in one Gospel and separated in another.

On the basis of Tyson's numbering, but including supplemental calculation of special units, there arises the following arithmetic of the pericopes that appear in one, two, or three of the Synoptic Gospels. It is a question (1) of units common to two or three Gospels and the extent to which they appear in contextual parallelism and (2) of comparable units that belong to different contexts. Such noncontextual analogies may be called *"alibi analogies,"* and their frequency will be studied together with that of pericopes found in only one Gospel.

Common Units and Contextual Parallels

The 178 pericopes of Matthew, the 115 of Mark, and 186 of Luke are the starting point. It is to be illustrated how many pericopes are common units in two or three Gospels and how many of these represent contextual parallelism. Where the last criterion is applicable to three Gospels, "context-parallel triple traditions" can be spoken of.

Number of pericopes: 178 in Matthew, 115 in Mark, and 186 in Luke.

105 or 110, respectively, are common to Matthew and Mark;
 90 or 91 of these (84%) are contextual parallels;
 57 of them also find contextual parallels in Luke.

95 or 96, respectively, are common to Mark and Luke;
 73 or 72 of these (76%) are contextual parallels;
 57 or 56 of them also find contextual parallels in Matthew.

126 or 131, respectively, are common to Matthew and Luke;
 61 or 60 of these (49%) are contextual parallels;
 57 or 56 of them also find contextual parallels in Mark.

The numbers 57–56 in this table indicate pericopes that appear in a similar context within three Gospels. Considered together, these pericopes represent a contextual parallelism between triple traditions which is to be viewed as a fundamental structure of the synoptic material. It is a question of a purely structural and not a genetic perspective. The triple traditions can just as well be considered either as a cause for similarity or as a result of assimilation. In any event, context-parallel triple traditions comprise 32 percent of the material in Matthew, 49 percent in Mark, and 30 percent in Luke, judging from an unbiased enumeration of the pericopes. This corresponds to a scant third of the two longer Gospels and nearly a half of Mark.

The numbers 90–91, 73–72, and 61–60 in the table designate pericopes that

appear in contextual parallelism when two Gospels are compared, though 57–56 of these cases are identical with the contextual parallels already counted among the triple traditions. Here the convergence of Matthew and Mark comprises no less than 84 percent of the common material, and the comparison of Mark and Luke results in 76 percent, while the contextual parallelism between Matthew and Luke is only 49 percent.

Furthermore, whereas the 49 percent that represent the amount of contextual parallelism between Matthew and Luke are based on 61–60 pericopes, 57–56 of these actually belong to the context-parallel triple traditions. There are only 4 contextual parallels in Matthew and Luke without support in Mark, and they pertain to two separated accounts which are both linked with the Baptist and Christ's baptism (Matt. 3:7–11a; 4:2–10; 11:2–6, 7–19; Luke 3:7–9; 4:2b–13; 7:18–23, 24–35). In a wider context, however, only the first two of these pericopes occupy the same location (Matt. 3:7–10 // Luke 3:7–9; Matt. 4:2–11a // Luke 4:2b–13). They are intimately connected with the context-parallel baptism account which is also supported by Mark (Matt. 3:13–17 with par.), and therefore must be considered as reduced triple traditions (below, pp. 81–82). Other double traditions of Matthew and Luke without support in Mark, representing that frequency type which may be named Q, are never found in contextual parallelism.

Alibi Analogies and Special Units

Beyond the two context-parallel double pericopes just mentioned (Matt. 3:7–10; 4:2–11a and par.), the correspondence between Matthew and Luke in contrast to Mark is comprised of many *alibi* analogies or comparable entities that do not occur in parallel contexts. A further individuality is represented by the special units, pericopes found in only one Gospel. The numbers produced in the table below convey an idea of the frequency of these *alibi* analogies and special units. Inevitably the degree of frequency is a question of approximation, because sometimes even fragments of pericopes can be considered as synoptic units. Tyson, for instance, calculated smaller units and therefore obtained higher numbers, which appear in brackets below.

There are 75 [82] units in Matthew without any contextual parallels;
- 6 of these have *alibi* analogies in Mark without contextual parallels or any counterparts in Luke,
- and 35 have *alibi* analogies in Luke without counterparts in Mark (a frequency type which may here be called Q), while 34 are special units.

Then there are 15 [12] units in Mark without any contextual parallels;
- 6 of these have *alibi* analogies in Matthew without contextual parallels or any counterparts in Luke,

and 4 have *alibi* analogies in Luke without contextual parallels or any counterparts in Matthew,
while 5 are special units.

Concerning these Markan *alibi* units, their topics and the spread of their analogies may be illustrated as follows:

Topics	Matt.	Mark	Luke
unclean spirits	—	3:11	4:41
measure	7:2	4:24	6:38
sheep	9:36	6:34	—
fresh water	10:42	9:41	—
salt	5:13	9:50	14:34
forgiveness	6:14–15	11:25–26	—
watchfulness	24:42–44; 25:13–14	13:33–37	12:35–40

Special units of Mark are found in 1:1 (title); 3:20–21 (anxiety of the relatives); 4:26–29 (seed); 7:31–37 (*ephphatha*); 8:22–26 (blind man).

Finally, there are 88 [108] units in Luke without any contextual parallels;
31 of these have *alibi* analogies in Matthew without counterparts in Mark (the frequency type here called Q), and 4 have *alibi* analogies in Mark without contextual parallels or any counterparts in Matthew,
while 53 are special units.

Thus 35 *alibi* analogies emerge when Matthew is compared with Luke, and 31 when Luke is compared with Matthew. In both cases they have no counterparts in Mark, and together with the 4 above-mentioned contextual parallels of Matthew and Luke they form Matthean and Lukan double traditions which correspond to the material ascribed by proponents of the two-source hypothesis to a Logia source or Q. As mentioned above, however, only 2 of these 4 units are parallel in a wider context (Matt. 3:7–10; 4:2–10 // Luke 3:7–9; 4:2–12), and they belong to a sequence of context-parallel triple traditions dealing with Christ's baptism which Mark has abbreviated. Otherwise all double traditions peculiar to Matthew and Luke are characterized by a complete lack of contextual parallelism.

In fact, these specific Matthean and Lukan traditions have in no way proven themselves as deriving from a document or text collection. Mainly comprised of sayings, or logia, they oftentimes contain narratives too. The peculiar dispersion of the relevant 35 or 31 plus 4 units, among which there are only 2 really contextual parallels, shows that any supposition of a written source behind the Matthean-Lukan double traditions, such as the Logia source or the presumed document Q, is an illusion. In spite of the popularity of the hypothesis, this cornerstone of modern synoptic research has no substantial foundation. As a

neutral symbol for a category of analogies, Q may be used, and this is done in the present exposition, but with reference only to statistics, not to genealogy. If, on the other hand, the units common to Matthew and Luke are explained through any form of the utilization theories, whether it is Matthew → Luke or Luke → Matthew, the difficulty in understanding the dispersal of the Q material is reduced in half but not eliminated.

Only on the assumption of independent, freely circulating, not ordered traditions from which Matthew and Luke took over greater and smaller units of material as occasion demanded, can the constitutive flexibility of the double traditions in Matthew and Luke be explained. As is the case with regard to the special units of each Gospel, it has to be assumed that Matthew and Luke received their double units from available traditions and inserted them where a topic was to be illustrated. Even though sporadic records of these traditional units are not inconceivable, their notorious flexibility appears explainable only on the basis of living oral traditions. Besides, the Gospel of Mark also represents a few such double traditions, for, as the above table shows (p. 27), there are also 6 *alibi* analogies between Matthew and Mark and 4 between Mark and Luke which are not supported by Luke in the first case and Matthew in the second. With the exception of Mark 3:11 (unclean spirits), they all contain didactic sayings. Mark thus sometimes used circulating traditions of a similar kind as those which Matthew and Luke took up for their units. In the table above (pp. 26–27), the latter are designated as Q in the sense of a category, not of a document. With this layer of tradition the evangelist Mark had fewer contacts, but occasionally he touched upon it.

There are no general distinctions between the triple and double traditions of the Synoptic Gospels beyond the fact that triple traditions present a relative parallelism, while double traditions of Matthew and Luke are characterized by complete flexibility.

Both categories of Gospel traditions are comprised of narratives as well as of sayings. The double traditions of Matthew and Luke do not only contain logia and were by no means proven to have been a written source, and so the conventional expression "Logia source" is false. In fact, there is a frequent oscillation between different types. The context-parallel accounts concerning the temptation of Jesus offer an example of this. At the beginning they consist of a context-parallel triple tradition (Matt. 4:1 with parallels); in the middle section, by far the greatest part, there is a Matthean-Lukan double tradition (Matt. 4:2–11a // Luke 4:2b–13); at the end one detects a Matthean-Markan double tradition (Matt. 4:11b // Mark 1:13b). Here the double traditions of Matthew and Luke or Matthew and Mark are not limited to logia but are based upon an organic relationship between narrative and dialogue. On the other hand, the synoptic chapter that contains the parable of the sower and other parables (Matt. 13:1–52 with par.), is substantially built on triple traditions, but they have been complemented with double and special traditions. Here the theme is not narrative,

although this is often the case in triple traditions, but just that sort of teaching which is generally more characteristic of double traditions belonging to the Q category.

Beyond statistics, no general differences of the triple and double traditions can be established, neither theologically nor stylistically. Each evangelist—including Mark—has taken over and worked over similar traditions in a personal fashion, and the latter are available only in the existing redaction. Reconstruction of the inputs will always be a vain enterprise, for lack of older documents. Of course this is often attempted, for instance with regard to some particular theology of Q, but it has only been possible to produce fragments taken out from the actual texts by vivisection. The extant triple, double, and special traditions of Matthew, Mark, and Luke always possess a Matthean, Markan, or Lukan peculiarity of theology and language. In each category of traditions, particularities independent of the evangelists cannot be demonstrated without involving a vicious circle. What remains possible is a purely quantitative or statistic definition of the categories implying that triple, double, and special traditions are distinguished by their distribution on three, two, or merely one Gospel.

This distribution is explained by the reciprocal effect of "supply and demand." Certain traditions were more accessible or meaningful to one evangelist and less to another. It cannot be proved empirically to what extent original triple traditions may have been curtailed into double and special traditions, or primitive special and double traditions may have been expanded into triple traditions. This alternative can perhaps be decided in special cases. But general schemes concerning a literary development, such as the two-source hypothesis, inevitably work like a Procrustean bed. On the one hand, with regard to context-parallel triple units the dependence of the Gospels on each other can always be considered in an opposite direction, as the competitive utilization theories show (chap. 1). On the other hand, the constitutive flexibility of the large *alibi* material is not explainable through any literary manipulations, as was already emphasized by Johann Gottfried von Herder and Johann Carl Ludwig Gieseler on psychological grounds. Instead, the explanation lies in the principle of supply and demand, that is, each synoptic writer had a certain material at his disposal, which had been transmitted and formulated in various ways among the Christians and which he took up, eventually rearranged, broadened, or limited according to his interests.

Everywhere in the Synoptic Gospels the triple, double, and special units are so distributed that all categories are completely mixed and intimately connected. The mosaic pattern of this distribution cannot be the result of a detailed editing. It must, rather, depend upon psychological factors within the development of tradition units. No fixed written sources are distinguishable among the persistently changing and merging frequency types.

Even within the context-parallel triple traditions, analogies in the vocabulary never lie on the same line, as should be the case on the basis of the utilization and

proto-gospel theories. Most texts in one verse or clause show a certain similarity between Matthew and Mark, but in the next one a correspondence between Matthew and Luke or Mark and Luke, so that a striking zigzag structure emerges. Examples are given below (pp. 109, 123–30, 141–43).

In the double traditions of Matthew and Luke, the counterparts are always scattered in various contexts. As mentioned before, one apparent exception is the context-parallel double traditions in Matt. 3:7–12 // Luke 3:17–18 and Matt. 4:2–11a // Luke 4:2b–13 which form a framework of the context-parallel triple tradition concerning the baptism of Jesus (Matt. 3:13–17 with par.). But a textual analysis (below, pp. 81–82) discloses them as partially reduced triple traditions. Mark presented the person of the Baptist shortly before dealing with Christ's baptism, and then quite briefly sketched the temptation of Jesus in the wilderness, while Matthew and Luke in both cases presented more details. In all other double traditions of Matthew and Luke such contextual parallelism is missing, for their subsequent double traditions—what may be called the actual Q traditions—appear with unrestrained flexibility.

A literary editorial work cannot explain either that curious zigzag pattern of the context-parallel triple units or this notorious flexibility of the Q traditions. Topographic and thematic, acoustic and psychological factors must have acted upon the development and formation of the material, before the tradition was laid down literarily.

Division According to Topographic and Thematic Aspects

The 178 pericopes of Matthew, the 115 of Mark, and the 186 of Luke's Gospel portray Jesus' life in a predominantly similar manner. Not seldom individual points differ, but the main characteristics develop similarly and are held together by 56 or 57 context-parallel triple traditions. This synoptic perspective on the life of Jesus is, with the exception of the passion story, different from the Johannine view. But neither the synoptic nor the Johannine outline can a priori claim a greater truthfulness than its respective partner; rather, both perspectives must complement each other.

In any case the synoptic writers represent a common topographic and thematic division of the story into three main parts:

Part I: Birth and childhood accounts of Matthew and Luke, which are based upon special units and oriented to Bethlehem, form an introduction to the baptism account. The latter essentially consists of context-parallel double and triple traditions; it is topographically linked to the area of the Jordan.

Part II: Here follows the portrayal of an intensive and contingent activity of the Master in Galilee. At the beginning, however, the differences between the Gospels are striking: Matthew has Jesus start with a sermon on a mountain somewhere in Galilee, Mark with healings in Capernaum, and Luke with a sermon in Nazareth.

The conformity between the Synoptics, which dominates the preceding baptism account, has suddenly been given up here. Contextual parallelism is found only in a short triple tradition, which Matthew has linked to the Sermon on the Mount (chapters 5—7), while Mark and Luke have linked it to miracles in Capernaum (Matt. 7:28–29 with par.). First in the middle and then at the end of the Galilean sector one will find context-parallel triple traditions playing a role and becoming somewhat more numerous, yet they are not significant to such an extent as later when Jesus approaches Jerusalem and Golgotha. In the middle part of the Galilean section the synoptic writers present the picture of a further activity in Capernaum and the western shore of the Galilean Lake, but still with several variations. Jesus then visits countries around this lake, expanding his activities each time from the shore of the lake in various directions; here it is Mark who has presented the most detailed picture. In the last part of the Galilean section, Jesus returns to Capernaum in order to instruct the apostles in the house of Peter's mother-in-law; and the richest material was presented by Matthew.

Part III: After the Galilean section the story is abruptly shifted to Perea in Matthew and Mark, whereas Luke has filled the gap with his "travel narrative," which represents teaching in Transjordan. For this report he used special units and Q material, and several of the traditions available to him may already have been connected with Decapolis and Perea across the Jordan. The didactic concern of the travel account is directly continued in the following section, where Luke runs parallel with Matthew and Mark in their Perean section. Here context-parallel triple traditions begin to form dominant elements of the presentation.

In the following accounts concerning the experiences and activity of the Master in Jerusalem, the contextual parallelism rises significantly. Within the reports on the last supper, the crucifixion, the burial, and the visitation of the tomb, context-parallel triple traditions are constitutive throughout, and because they are supported even by John's Gospel, they extend themselves into a context-parallel quadruple tradition.

Concerning the concluding reports on the appearances of the risen Lord, differences in detail are observable again. Nevertheless, the synoptic writers still remain in mutual agreement on the topic, and there is support from John in this context.

Hence, there are three main parts of the synoptic portrayal of Jesus' life that allow themselves to be differentiated. The first is linked with Bethlehem and the Jordan River, the second with Galilee and Capernaum especially, and the third with Transjordan, Judea, and Jerusalem. With regard to this basic structure the Synoptic Gospels deviate from John, except in the passion narrative. The fourth evangelist has not portrayed any such contingent and successive activity of Jesus in Galilee, Transjordan, and Judea. He has recorded several visits of Christ in Judea and Jerusalem, and even a mission to Samaria (John 2:1, 13; 3:22; 4:3–42; 5:1; 7:10; 10:22), before reporting on the final entry of Jesus into the capital (12:12). It cannot be proved whether the synoptic distribution of the events on Bethlehem and the Jordan River, on Galilee and Capernaum, on Transjordan, Judea, and Jerusalem, or the presentation found in the Fourth Gospel is more in accordance with historical circumstances. In any case, that division into three main parts characterizes the synoptic presentation, in spite of individual devia-

tions. An inherent tendency to such a localization of the episodes and quotations was possibly connected with several of the traditions before they were recorded by Matthew, Mark, and Luke.

While the main parts of the synoptic presentation are thus concentrated on these areas: (I) Bethlehem and the Jordan, (II) Galilee, and (III) Transjordan, Judea, and Jerusalem, the pericopes found in each of the main parts group themselves, according to topography and theme, into subdivisions which may be called "blocks." This designates a cluster of pericopes in the synoptic material, which, in spite of variations and dislocations, represents a certain degree of convergence in regard to topography and theme. Although the blocks are discovered through a study of parallels and nonparallels in a synopsis, every text unit found in a block is to be treated as existing only for itself within each of the Gospels. The units involved may be compared with the "monads" of Gottfried Wilhelm Leibnitz which have no windows. Furthermore, the blocks must not be misunderstood as sources of texts; they are only schemes for a closer grouping of the synoptic pericopes.

A topographic and thematic distribution of the entire synoptic material on such blocks will contribute to understanding the formation of the synoptic traditions. The exact demarcation of the blocks is certainly discussable, but in view of the topographic framework and the thematic context it seems feasible to let the pericopes of the synoptic Gospels divide themselves within the parts (I—III) upon the following 12 blocks (the number 12 is coincidental and does not have any symbolic meaning):

Part I comprises two blocks topographically and thematically different, and with the following contents: (1) birth and childhood of Jesus; (2) appearance of John the Baptist and events at the baptism of Jesus.

Part II presents various episodes and logia without a systematic order, but Galilee and some neighboring regions serve as a common general framework. Paying attention to the shift of scenes and themes, one may divide the material into the following blocks: (3) introductory sermons and healings in Capernaum; (4) different events before and after the calling of the tax collector in Gennesaret; (5) instruction, discussion, and parables; (6) wanderings to regions around the Lake of Galilee; (7) teaching in Capernaum.

Part III comprises the following blocks, while the scenes and themes change in systematic progression: (8) a travel account found only in Luke, which illustrates Christ's teaching in Transjordan; (9) a travel report common to the Synoptic Gospels, which presents his subsequent teaching in Perea; (10) discussions in the temple area; (11) a farewell speech given on the Mount of Olives; (12) the passion narrative, in which the institution of the Last Supper, the trial of Jesus, his crucifixion, and the resurrection form the main themes.

The table below presents further details. With regard to each block, it shows the theme and the extent of the pericopes as well as their eventual parallelism. The context-parallel triple traditions are framed, pointing out that in such cases

the Synoptic Gospels feature extraordinarily large convergence. Some context-parallel double traditions are framed in dots, and this is also the case with some context-parallel special traditions that, in spite of formal differences, show a certain thematic similarity. Arrows pointed upward or downward indicate *alibi* analogies in an earlier or later context of the Gospel under consideration. In the right margin are notes about the frequency types that appear in each pericope. Not every iota has been included, for our purpose is to illustrate the characteristic fluctuation of convergence and deviation in the material as a totality.

Synoptic Tables

T = Triple tradition
framed = context-parallel T
D = Double tradition in Matthew and Mark, or in Mark and Luke
Q = Double tradition in Matthew and Luke
framed with dots = context-parallel double tradition in Matthew and Luke
S^{Mt}, S^{Mk}, S^{Lk} = Single tradition
framed with dots = S standing in contextual parallelism
with an S which represents a somewhat related topic
↑↓ = *Alibi* analogy to be found in an earlier or later context

Block 1
Christ's Birth and Childhood

	Matt.	Mark	Luke	
Title resp. prologue	—	1:1	1:1–4	$S^{Mk}S^{Lk}$
Genealogy	1:1–17	—	↓	$S^{Mt}S^{Lk}$
Annunciation of John	—	—	1:5–25	S^{Lk}
Annunciation of Jesus	1:18–25	—	1:26–38	$S^{Mt}S^{Lk}$
Magnificat	—	—	1:39–56	S^{Lk}
Birth of the Baptist, Benedictus	—	—	1:57–80	S^{Lk}
Birth of Jesus, salutation by shepherds or wise men	2:1–12	—	2:1–20	$S^{Mt}S^{Lk}$
Jesus as child in the temple, Nunc dimittis	—	—	2:21–38	S^{Lk}
Flight to Egypt	2:13–21	—	—	S^{Mt}
Migration to Nazareth	2:22–23	—	2:39–40	$S^{Mt}S^{Lk}$
Jesus as boy in the temple	—	—	2:41–52	S^{Lk}

Block 2
Christ's Baptism and Related Events

	Matt.	Mark	Luke	
John the Baptist	3:1–6	1:2–6	3:1–6	TS^{Lk}
Preaching of John	3:7–10	—	3:7–9 +10–14	$D^{MtLk}S^{Lk}$
Baptism with water, Spirit, and (Matt. and Luke) fire	3:11–12	1:7–8	3:15–18	TD^{MtLk}
Baptist imprisoned	—	—	3:19–20	S^{Lk}
Baptism of Jesus	3:13–17	1:9–11	3:21–22	TS^{Mt}
Genealogy of Jesus	↑	—	3:23–38	$S^{Mt}S^{Lk}$
Temptation of Jesus	4:1–11	1:12–13	4:1–13	$TD^{MtLk}S^{Mt}$
Passing to Galilee	4:12–17	1:14–15	4:14–15	T

Block 3
Activity in and near Capernaum

	Matt.	Mark	Luke	
Opposition in Nazareth	(4:13a)↓	↓	4:16–30	$(T)S^{Lk}$
Calling of Peter and three disciples	4:18–22	1:16–20	↓	$T(S^{Lk})$
Jesus with great crowds and the disciples on a mountain	4:23—5:1	↓	↓	T
Sermon on the Mount	5:2—7:27	—	↓	QS^{Mt}
Jesus in Capernaum	↑(4:13b)	1:21	4:31	(T)D
Enthusiasm of the crowd	7:28–29	1:22	4:32	T
Unclean spirit	—	1:23–28	4:33–37	D
Mother-in-law, healings in the evening	↓	1:29–34	4:38–41	T
Desert (cf. below)	—	1:35–38	4:42–43	D
Preaching tour	—	1:39	4:44	D
Calling of Peter	↑	↑	5:1–11	$(T)S^{Lk}$

Block 4
Events Before and
After the Call of Levi/Matthew

	Matt.	Mark	Luke	
Leper	8:1–4	1:40–44	5:12–14	T
Desert (cf. above)	—	1:45	5:15–16	D
Centurion's servant, healings in Capernaum, candidates for discipleship, storm, Gadara	8:5–34	—↑—↓↓	↓↑↓↓↓	TQ
Paralytic in Capernaum	9:1–8	2:1–12	5:17–26	T
Levi/Matthew in Gennesaret, fasting	9:9–17	2:13–22	5:27–39	T
Jairus	9:18–26	↓	↓	T
More healings	9:27–34	—	—	S[Mt]
Sending of the Twelve	9:35—10:42	↓—	↓—	TQS[Mt]

Block 5
Instruction,
Discussion, and Parables

	Matt.	Mark	Luke	
Instruction about the Baptist	11:1–19	—	↓	Q
Woes on Chorazin, etc., rejoicing	11:20–30	—	↓	QS[Mt]
Discussion on picking of corn	12:1–8	2:23–28	6:1–5	T
Discussion on a Sabbath healing	12:9–14	3:1–6	6:6–11	T
Return to the lake, great crowds (cf. below)	12:15–21	3:7–12	↓	T
Jesus with the Twelve on a mountain	↑	3:13–19	6:12–16	T
Jesus on a plain, great crowds (cf. above)	↑	↑	6:17–19	T

Sermon on the Plain	↑	—	6:20–49	QS^{Lk}
Centurion's servant	↑	—	7:1–10	Q
Widow at Nain	—	—	7:11–17	S^{Lk}
Instruction about the Baptist	↑	—	7:18–35	Q
Discussion on anointment through a woman	↓	↓	7:36–50	TS^{Lk}
Women following Jesus	—	—	8:1–3	S^{Lk}
Anxiety of the relatives (cf. below)	—	3:20–21	—	S^{Mk}
Beelzebul accusation, defense	12:22–37	3:22–30	↓(↑)	TQ
More than Jonah and Solomon	12:38–42	—	↓	Q
Danger of backsliding	12:43–45	—	↓	Q
True relatives of Jesus (cf. above and below)	12:46–50	3:31–35	↓	T
Instruction through parables	13:1–52	4:1–34	8:4–18	TQDS^{MtMk}
True relatives of Jesus (cf. above)	↑	↑	8:19–21	T

Block 6
Excursions in Various Directions

	Matt.	Mark	Luke	
Storm	↑	4:35–41	8:22–25	T
Gadara	↑	5:1–20	8:26–39	T
Jairus	↑	5:21–43	8:40–56	T
Critics in Nazareth	13:53–58	6:1–6a	↑	T
Sending of the Twelve	↑	6:6b–13	9:1–6	T
Reaction of Antipas	14:1–2	6:14–16	9:7–9	T
Execution of John	14:3–12	6:17–29	↑	(T)D
Feeding of five thousand	14:13–21	6:30–44	9:10–17	T
Walking on the sea	14:22–33	6:45–52	—	D

Healings in Gennesaret	14:34–36	6:53–56	—	D
Discussion on washing of hands	15:1–20	7:1–23	—	D
Phoenician woman	15:21–28	7:24–30	—	D
Many healings, a deaf man	15:29–31	7:31–37	—	DS^{MtMk}
Feeding of four thousand	15:32–38	8:1–9a	—	D
Discussion on signs at Magdala and Dalmanutha	15:39—16:4	8:9b–12	—	D
Leaven of the Pharisees	16:5–12	8:13–21	↓—	D
Blind man at Bethsaida	—	8:22–26	—	S^{Mk}
Confession near Caesarea Philippi (Luke: Bethsaida)	16:13–20	8:27–30	9:18–21	T
First prediction of suffering	16:21–23	8:31–33	9:22	T
Conditions of discipleship	16:24–28	8:34—9:1	9:23–27	T
Transfiguration	17:1–8	9:2–8	9:28–36a	T
Elijah redivivus	17:9–13	9:9–13	9:36b–37a	(T)D
Epileptic boy	17:14–21	9:14–29	9:37b–43a	T

Block 7
Teaching in Capernaum

	Matt.	Mark	Luke	
Second prediction of suffering	17:22–23	9:30–32	9:43b–45	T
Temple tax	17:24–27	—	—	S^{Mt}
Children as model	18:1–5	9:33–37	9:46–48	T
Foreign exorcist	—	9:38–41	9:49–50	D
Excommunication of a seducer	18:6–9	9:42–48	↓—	T
Salt	↑	9:49–50	↓	T
Lost sheep	18:10–14	—	↓	Q
Reproving a brother	18:15–20	—	↓—	QS^{Mt}
Remission 77 times	18:21–22	—	↓	Q
Unmerciful servant	18:23–35	—	—	S^{Mt}

Block 8
Teaching in Transjordan

	Matt.	Mark	Luke	
Disappointment in Samaria	—	—	9:51–56	S[Lk]
Candidates for discipleship	↑	—	9:57–62	Q
Sending of the Seventy	↑	—	10:1–12	(T)QS[Lk]
Woes over Chorazin, etc.	↑	—	10:13–16	Q
Return of the Seventy	—	—	10:17–20	S[Lk]
Rejoicing	↑	—	10:21–22	Q
Blessed eyewitnesses	↑	—	10:23–24	Q
Law question of a scribe	↓	↓	10:25–28	T
Good Samaritan	—	—	10:29–37	S[Lk]
Mary and Martha	—	—	10:38–42	S[Lk]
Our Father	↑	—	11:1–4	Q
Prayer for bread	—	—	11:5–8	S[Lk]
Prayer for fish and egg	↑	—	11:9–13	Q
Beelzebul accusation, defense	↑	↑	11:14–23	T
Danger of backsliding	↑	—	11:24–26	Q
Blessing of Mary	—	—	11:27–28	S[Lk]
More than Jonah and Solomon	↑	—	11:29–32	Q
Lamp on a stand, light in the eye	↑	—	11:33–36	Q
Speech against Pharisees	↓	—	11:37–54	Q
Confession, providence	↑	—	12:1–34	QS[Lk]
Preparedness	↓↑	—	12:35–59	QS[Lk]
Catastrophes in Jerusalem, patience with a fig tree	— (↓)	— (↓)	13:1–9	S[Lk](D)
Crippled woman	—	—	13:10–17	S[Lk]
Mustard seed, leaven	↑	↑	13:18–21	T

Narrow gate	↑↓	—	13:22–30	Q
Three more days in Perea	—	—	13:31–33	S^Lk
Lamentation over Jerusalem	↓	—	13:34–35	Q
Dropsical man	—	—	14:1–6	S^Lk
Order at the tables	—	—	14:7–14	S^Lk
Invitation of outsiders	↓	—	14:15–24	Q
Conditions of discipleship	↑	—	14:25–35	QS^Lk
Recovering the lost	↑—	—	15:1–32	QS^Lk
Renouncing material goods: steward, Pharisees, Lazarus	—	—	16:1–32	S^Lk
Excommunication of a seducer	↑	↑	17:1–2	T
Remission 7 times a day	↑	—	17:3–4	Q
Faith as a mustard seed	↑	—	17:5–6	Q
Service on the field, at the table	—	—	17:7–10	S^Lk
Grateful Samaritan	—	—	17:11–19	S^Lk
Kingdom of God invisible	—	—	17:20–21	S^Lk
Surprising as the Flood	↓	—	17:22–37	Q
Judge and widow, Pharisee and publican	—	—	18:1–14	S^Lk

Block 9
Teaching in Perea
and Activity at Jericho

	Matt.	Mark	Luke	
Divorce	19:1–12	10:1–12	—	D
Admitting children	19:13–15	10:13–16	18:15–17	T
Rich young man	19:16–30	10:17–31	18:18–30	T
Laborers in the vineyard	20:1–16	—	—	S^Mt
Third prediction of suffering	20:17–19	10:32–34	18:31–34	T

Sons of Zebedee followers in suffering	20:20–28	10:35–45	—(↓)	D(T)
Bartimaeus	20:29–34	10:46–52	18:35–43	T
Zacchaeus	—	—	19:1–10	S[Lk]
Administration in the master's absence, using the pounds well	↓	—	19:11–27	Q

Block 10
Entry Into Jerusalem,
Temple Cleansing, Discussions

	Matt.	Mark	Luke	
Jesus with crowd on Mount of Olives	21:1–9	11:1–10	19:28–38	T
"Dominus flevit"	—	—	19:39–44	S[Lk]
Entering the city	21:10–11	11:11	—	D
Cleansing the temple	21:12–17	↓	19:45–46	T
Barren fig tree	21:18–19	11:12–14	(↑)	D(T)
Cleansing the temple (as above)	↑	11:15–19	↑	T
Punishing the fig tree, prayers granted (thus Mark)	21:20–22↑	11:20–26	—	D
Legitimation question of high priests	21:23–27	11:27–33	20:1–8	T
The two sons	21:28–32	—	—	S[Mt]
The wicked tenants	21:33–46	12:1–12	20:9–19	T
Invitation of outsiders	22:1–14	—	↑	Q
Tax question of Pharisees (Luke: high priests)	22:15–22	12:13–17	20:20–26	T
Levirate question of Sadducees	22:23–33	12:18–27	20:27–40	T
Law question of a scribe	22:34–40	12:28–34	↑	T
David on the Messiah	22:41–46	12:35–37a	20:41–44	T

Speech against Pharisees (Matt.) or scribes (Mark, Luke)	23:1–36	12:37b–40	20:45–47↑	TQS^Mt
The widow's mite	—	12:41–44	21:1–4	D
Lamentation over Jerusalem	23:37–39	—	↑	Q

Block 11
Farewell Speech
on the Mount of Olives

	Matt.	Mark	Luke	
No stone on another	24:1–3	13:1–4	21:5–7	T
False messiahs, war rumors	24:4–8	13:5–8	21:8–11	T
Persecution of the early church	24:9–14↑	13:9–13	21:12–19	T
Abomination, flight to the mountains	24:15–22	13:14–20	21:20–24	T
Messiah not here, not there	24:23–26	13:21–23	↑—	(T)D
Surprising as lightning	24:27–28	—	↑	Q
Destruction of the world, Son of Man on a cloud	24:29–31	13:24–27	21:25–28	T
Fig tree showing leaves	24:32–33	13:28–29	21:29–31	T
Preservation of "this people," permanence of Christ's words	24:34–35	13:30–31	21:32–33	T
Time of judgment unknown	24:36	13:32	(Acts 1:7)	D
Surprising as the flood	24:37–41	—	↑	Q
Surprising like a snare	—	—	21:34–36	S^Lk
Administration in the master's absence (cf. below)	↓	13:33–34	↑	T
Watchfulness	24:42–44	13:35–37	↑	T
Maintaining the household	24:45–51	—	↑	Q
Virgins with lamps	25:1–12	—	—	S^Mt

Administration in the master's absence, using the talents well (cf. above)	25:13–30	↑—	↑	TQ
Sheep and goats	25:31–46	—	—	S[Mt]
Jesus in the temple and on the Mount of Olives	—	—	21:37–38	S[Lk]

Block 12
Trial, Eucharist,
Crucifixion, and Resurrection

	Matt.	Mark	Luke	
Conspiracy of high priests	26:1–5	14:1–2	22:1–2	T
Anointment in Bethany	26:6–13	14:3–9	(↑)	T(S[Lk])
Judas' betrayal	26:14–16	14:10–11	22:3–6	T
The last supper	26:17–29	14:12–25	22:7–23	T
Discipleship as table service	↑	↑	22:24–30	TQ
Peter's denial (cf. below)	↓	↓	22:31–34	T
Purse, bag, sword	—	—	22:35–38	S[Lk]
To the Mount of Olives, Peter's denial (cf. above)	26:30–35	14:26–31	22:39↑	T
Gethsemane	26:36–46	14:32–42	22:40–46	T
Jesus arrested	26:47–56	14:43–52	22:47–53	T
Jesus examined by the high priest (Luke: by Sanhedrin)	26:57–75	14:53–72	22:54–71	T
Delivered to Pilate	27:1–2	15:1	23:1	T
Judas' suicide	27:3–10	—	—	S[Mt]
Jesus before Pilate	27:11–14	15:2–5	23:2–5	T
Jesus before Antipas	—	—	23:6–16	S[Lk]
Barabbas released, Jesus convicted	27:15–26	15:6–15	23:17–25	T
Mocking in praetorium	27:27–31	15:16–20	—	D

	Matt.	Mark	Luke	
Simon of Cyrene	27:32	15:21	23:26	T
Women lamenting	—	—	23:27–31	S[Lk]
The two criminals	↓	↓	23:32	T
Crucifixion	27:33–54	15:22–39	23:33–48	T
Women at the cross	27:55–56	15:40–41	23:49	T
Burial	27:57–61	15:42–47	23:50–56	T
Guards at the tomb	27:62–66	—	—	S[Mt]
The empty tomb	28:1–10	16:1–8 (+9–11)	24:1–12	T
Bribing the guards	28:11–15	—	—	S[Mt]
Epiphany on the way to Emmaus, interpretation of Scripture, meal	—	(16:12–13)	24:13–35	S[Lk]
Epiphany in Jerusalem, meal, interpretation of Scripture, instruction to spread the gospel (cf. below)	—	(16:14–18)	24:36–49 (cf. John 20:19–29)	S[Lk]
Epiphany on a mountain (in Matt. on a mountain in Galilee, in Luke on the Mount of Olives), instruction to spread the gospel	28:16–20 (cf. John 21:1–23)	(16:19–20)	24:50–53 (+ Acts 1:6–12)	S[Mt]S[Lk]

Chapter Three

The Origin of the Synoptic Material

This chapter deals with the principal factors that occasioned the formation of the preliterary traditions, afterward written down by the synoptic evangelists. Chapters 4—6 will apply these principles to the material, using the scheme of three parts and twelve blocks to facilitate the survey. The activity of the evangelists as redactors of the material will be studied in chapter 7.

Living Traditions Attested by Luke, Papias, and Ignatius

First of all, the very earliest witness concerning the origin of synoptic traditions is to be consulted, and this is the prologue of Luke. Although it will also be discussed in chapters 4 and 7, some aspects of it may be pointed out here.

In his dedication to Theophilus, the author began with a reference to contemporary evangelists (Luke 1:1): "Many have undertaken (*ἐπεχείρησαν*, "taken in their hand") to draw up an account of the events which have taken place among us." By these words Luke did not assert that other Gospels had already been produced and published, but informed Theophilus and other readers that some contemporaries were preparing records of reminiscences concerning Jesus. Knowing that collections of relevant traditions had been started by other evangelists, among whom one can very well presuppose the editors of Matthew and Mark, Luke had decided to write on the subject from his points of view for the benefit of Theophilus and other readers with similar interests. He did not say that he used books as sources, but explicitly referred to oral traditions by adding these words (1:2): "as have transmitted (*παρέδοσαν*, "orally communicated") to us those persons who, from the beginning, had become eyewitnesses and servants of the word." This means that Luke exclusively referred to an oral Jesus tradition (*παράδοσις*) that was personally represented by witnesses to the life and death of Christ and by other servants of the word, known to have been active from the very beginning of Christian preaching and teaching. Luke claimed ability to base his account on such members of the oldest community and their living memory,

whereas he did not hint at written sources with a single word. Moreover, when speaking of what the early witnesses and ministers "have transmitted to *us*" (1:2), he included those other authors who, at the same time, were occupied with a composition of Gospel accounts. Thus the *vox viva,* the living tradition, was seen as the common basis for the records planned by the other editors as well as by Luke himself. It was exactly because of his personal contacts with traditionists representing the earliest community that Luke expected Theophilus and other readers to be convinced about the reliability of Christian teaching (1:4).

Matthew and Mark have made no corresponding statements regarding their sources, but valuable information on them has been afforded by Bishop Papias of Hierapolis in Phrygia, who collected traditions on the evangelists around A.D. 110. His declarations will be studied more closely in chapter 7, and here it will only be a question of the importance he ascribed to living traditions.

Papias felt obliged to defend the Gospel of Mark against critics, and for this purpose emphasized that Peter's **διδασκαλίαι,** that is, units of his oral preaching and teaching, were the material that Mark had written down as Peter's interpreter (Eusebius, *EH* III.39.15). He stressed that Peter never composed a book on the life of Jesus, but that Mark had remembered and reproduced the apostle's teaching units which Peter used to present "according to the occasional needs," and this means when a certain topic had to be illustrated. The topical communications transmitted by Peter were also called **λόγια κυριακά,** "reports about the Lord," and defined as dealing with "what had been either said or done by Christ." In this way Papias already characterized the pericopes which modern scholars discern in Mark as well as in the other Gospels and which are dominated either by quotations of Christ's words or by narratives on his works.

Among the fragments of Papias preserved is a short remark on Matthew too, and it corresponds to his declaration on Mark insofar as the evangelist Matthew is also said to have compiled the **λόγια** (Eusebius, *EH* III.39.16). The word **λόγια** is here a breviloquence for **λόγια κυριακά,** and Papias wanted to say that Matthew also collected quotations and narratives, available to him in the form of living oral units. But whereas Papias mentioned that Mark was the interpreter of Peter, so that Mark must be supposed to have presented in Greek what Peter may preferably have reported in Hebrew or Aramaic, Matthew was said to have produced his collection in Hebrew, which expression Papias may have used for Aramaic, as is the case in the New Testament. After this, Papias stated that everyone translated Matthew's reports as well as possible, evidently having the Greek Gospel of Matthew in mind. Papias did not explain from whom Matthew had taken over the **λόγια** in question, but in any case he thought of traditions circulating in the community. The breviloquence **λόγια** may also imply that Matthew was, like Mark, supposed to have collected reports about the Lord especially used in the preaching and teaching activity of Peter, and in any case this corresponds to the interest Matthew has taken in Peter by placing this apostle regularly in front of those who hear the words of Jesus (Matt. 4:18 e.p.).

Independently of that eventually common allusion to Peter in the statements on Matthew and Mark, however, Papias saw nothing but oral reports on words and works of Jesus in the **λόγια** collected by the two evangelists, and to him these were reports that had circulated in the apostolic community. The general principle Papias followed was also that living traditions, called the *vox viva,* were always more reliable than written documents (Eusebius, *EH* III.39.4).

Other witnesses from the beginning of the second century, to be analyzed more closely in chapter 7, attest the same attitude toward oral traditions as Papias in the fragments here quoted. In A.D. 114, the bishop of Syrian Antioch, Ignatius, declared the church's living traditions on Christ to be the only reliable basis for belief, whereas documents could be falsified (Ignatius, *Philadelphians* VIII.2). By this author and his contemporaries, the word **εὐαγγέλιον** was always used in the singular, as in the New Testament, and designated the good message commonly preached among the believers. The same meaning is found in the Greek headings given around A.D. 100 to the four Gospels: **εὐαγγέλιον κατὰ Μαθθαῖον**, and so on, to be studied more closely in chapter 7. In translation, this formula means: "The Good Message in the Version of Matthew," or "Mark," and so on, which implies that each of the evangelists has presented the common oral message in his own way. Only after the middle of the second century, Christianity began to speak of Gospels in the plural and to think of them as literary products. Until then attention was focused on the oral Jesus traditions that were still living in the church, and everyone was convinced that the evangelists had used a common material as the basis of their books. This conviction was not due to anachronistic thinking, for oral traditions must have been even more fundamental when the evangelists compiled their pericopes than later when the witnesses of the early second century attested the permanence of the *vox viva* in the church. Further details are considered below in chapter 7.

Self-Contained Pericopes and Comprehensive Sequences

It is exactly the predominance of the *vox viva* in the early church, confirmed by the witnesses quoted above, which explains why the material found in the Synoptic Gospels does not appear in the form of coherent firsthand accounts but mainly in the form of separate traditional pericopes. The units collected by the evangelists were generally not available to them as spontaneous and informal reminiscences, but as pieces of tradition frequently told and molded into distinctive forms.

In each of the Synoptic Gospels most of the material is dispersed on pericopes which consist of self-contained, freestanding units revealing typical structures and representing definite categories. One may, for instance, consider the narrative tradition about Christ's baptism, which appears in contextual parallelism within all Synoptic Gospels (Matt. 3:13–17 with par.). In concentrated form it tells that

Jesus came to the Jordan and was baptized, that he received the Spirit, and that a heavenly Voice proclaimed him as the Son of God. These items are sufficient to make the report a self-contained, independent unit. A connection with the preceding and subsequent pericopes has only been established by an insignificant "then" or the like. The report had evidently received its concentrated and rounded-off shape before it was adapted to its present context. As an example of didactic traditions with a similar concentration on essential items and with an independent position in the context, one may pay attention to the Lord's prayer (quoted in Matt. 6:9–13 and Luke 11:2–4; its continuation in Matt. 6:14–15 has a counterpart in Mark 11:25–26). The prayer had no doubt been formed and used in the church before it was taken up in different contexts by the evangelists. Most narrative and didactic traditions in the Synoptic Gospels retain such traces of having circulated as independent units on a preredactional level.

On the other hand, some comprehensive sequences may also be observed in the synoptic texts.

With regard to narrative elements, a substantial exception to the predominance of independent pericopes is found in the coherent passion story (Matt. 21:1—28:20 with par.). It consists of several units, but the overall structure of the drama is essential. Concerning didactic units, a shorter example of a comprehensive structure is found in Christ's topically coherent preaching on the law in the Sermon on the Mount (Matt. 5:17–46). Such an inclination to present the material in a comprehensive sequence is also characteristic of two mainly context-parallel complexes, one of which contains parables (Matt. 13:1–52 with par.) and the other prophecies (Matt. 24:1—25:46 with par.).

On a larger scale, traces of a general structure common to the Synoptic Gospels are found in the 56 or 57 pericopes that represent context-parallel triple traditions. For the following reasons these cohesive elements must also be ascribed to a living oral tradition and cannot be derived from a written document: (1) As the tables in chapter 2 show, the frequency of context-parallel triple pericopes is extraordinarily different within the individual sections of the material. In some blocks they dominate and in others they are rare and surrounded by text units without any contextual parallelism. No literary manipulations can explain this notorious variation. (2) Kept together in contextual parallelism, the pericopes in question nevertheless comprise internal differences with regard to their vocabulary, and these differences shift between the Gospels in such a haphazard way that a pattern issues which is too wobbly to be the result of any literary redaction. The greatly varying distribution of the 56 or 57 context-parallel triple pericopes and their oscillating vocabulary rather indicate that preliterary textures formed a common background and were gradually agglomerated to a traditional structure which allowed thematic concord and linguistic discord at the same time.

The fundament of this comprehensive structure, represented by 56 or 57 triple pericopes in contextual parallelism, may be sought in apostolic preaching and teaching, especially in recollections of Peter. However, as is evident from the

considerable differences between the synoptic and the Johannine approaches to the life of Jesus, the contextual parallelism of the 56 or 57 synoptic pericopes does not imply any more or less adequate reproduction of the historical sequence of events. Rather, it indicates that some fundamental recollections, presented in apostolic preaching and teaching, were apt to be kept in a certain order during the development of the tradition. Why were these items of the tradition more respected than others? It must have been because they went back to authoritative traditionists, and in this perspective there is reason to assume that it was Peter and his group who gave the context-parallel triple units their special weight in the development of the synoptic material.

Impulses from Jerusalem

As was pointed out, Luke declared in his prologue that he intended to edit traditions communicated to him orally by persons "who, from the beginning (ἀπ' ἀρχῆς), had become eyewitnesses and servants of the word" (Luke 1:2). By this reference to the beginning of Christian preaching and teaching, Luke meant the Jerusalem church (cf. ἀπ' ἀρχῆς in John 15:27, ἐν ἀρχῇ in Acts 11:15). When thus assuring Theophilus and other readers that he was going to present traditions personally communicated to him by members of the earliest Jerusalem congregation, he also granted such a contact with traditions to those other evangelists he said were occupied at the time with similar projects (Luke 1:1). For he obviously included them when he appealed to traditions that the original eyewitnesses and servants of the word "have delivered to us" (1:2).

Chapter 7 will demonstrate the possibilities Luke had of collecting information from Jerusalem through contacts with Silvanus, Philip, and others. For the moment it is to be observed that Luke's reference to Jerusalem traditions is confirmed by the fact that all the Synoptic Gospels contain material that reflects a Jerusalem perspective.

This becomes especially obvious in the last part of the synoptic books, where the experiences of the Lord during the passion week in Jerusalem are described and where context-parallel triple units are completely dominant. As is unanimously acknowledged by New Testament students, it must be supposed that the formation of gospel traditions began with these coherent reports on Christ's works and words in Jerusalem. But the passion story has also become concentrated on such episodes and quotations as were especially relevant for the church in Jerusalem when dealing with common problems and concerns—for instance, regarding the temple (Matt. 21:13 with par.), the discussions with various representatives of Judaism (21:23; 22:15, 23, 35; 23:2 with par.), the destiny of the Jerusalem congregation (24:4, etc., with par.), and the celebration of the eucharist (26:26–27 with par.).

Even in the preceding sections of the synoptic texts, such Jerusalem aspects have influenced the material. One may think of the following peculiarities: the

priority repeatedly ascribed to Peter, James, and John (Matt. 4:18, 21 // Mark 1:16, 19 e.p.), three of the apostles who became the first leaders of the Jerusalem church (Acts 1:13, etc.); the references in Galilean speeches of Jesus to a persecution of the church to be expected from the Jews (Matt. 5:10–12; 10:17–25), corresponding to what happened in Jerusalem after the death of Christ (Acts 4:1, etc.); the definition of a correct altar sacrifice (5:23–24); or the joy expressed by Mary and others (Luke 1:46, etc.) in analogy to the jubilation of the first Christians (Acts 2:46).

These circumstances enforce the reference of Luke to traditionists representing the beginning of Christian preaching and teaching in Jerusalem. And there are other reasons as well to seek the first roots of the synoptic traditions in the Jerusalem church.

Language factors do not at all impede this principal derivation of the synoptic traditions from Jerusalem. It became obvious in later years that Aramaic and Greek, and in general Judaism and Hellenism, were not so isolated from each other as scholars were earlier inclined to believe. Many inhabitants of Palestine were bilingual, as proved by the Qumran library and the Bar Kochba letters. Aramaic was certainly preferred by people in Jerusalem (Acts 22:2), but there were indeed many Greek-speaking Jews in the city (John 12:20; Acts 2:9–10; 6:9; 7:58; 9:29; synagogue inscription of Theodotus found on Mount Ophel, referred to below on p. 120), and since the first years after Christ's death the Jerusalem church included outstanding Greek-speaking believers and a group called Hellenists (Acts 4:36, Barnabas; 6:1, Hellenistic widows; 6:5, Stephen, Philip, and other Hellenists; 12:12, Mark; 15:22, Silvanus).

Under these circumstances it becomes evident that even if Peter and other apostles generally presented their reports in Aramaic, as is to be supposed on account of Papias's declaration on the *λόγια* collected by Matthew in "Hebrew," a translation of the preaching and teaching material into Greek may very well have taken place in their next environment and in the earliest years. The references of Papias to several translators of Matthew's collection and to Mark as Peter's interpreter (above, p. 46) can be directly applied to the bilingual environment in which the good news was preached by Peter and other early disciples. Furthermore, the vocabulary of comparable pericopes in the Greek texts of Matthew and Mark, and partly of Luke, comprises such remarkable similarities besides variations that some common dependence on circles of early believers, among whom the Aramaic units had been transposed into Greek, must be assumed. The most reasonable explanation for the partial concordance, which emerges when the Greek diction of individual synoptic pericopes in one Gospel is compared with that of parallels or analogies in another, is found in the public activity of preachers and teachers in the Jerusalem church, where Aramaic and Greek were used in alternation.

After all, though a philological analysis of the synoptic texts discloses many similarities in the Greek vocabulary of comparable pericopes, Papias was not

incorrect when he stated, on the one hand, that Matthew's collection of the reports circulating in Hebrew or rather Aramaic was translated by several collaborators and, on the other hand, that Mark served as the interpreter of Peter, so that his Gospel was based on Greek translations of the apostle's reports. The similarities in the formulation can be understood as the result of a relative harmony already preestablished owing to historical factors. In other words, the material in question was based on similar Aramaic units, in both cases known from the preaching and teaching activity of Peter and other apostles. These units had been given a certain Greek shape in the church before the redactors of Matthew and the evangelist Mark began to edit their texts. When the redaction of the two Gospels took place, the diction of their individual pericopes was influenced by rudimental Greek translation units which circulated orally in the Jerusalem church.

To some extent this may also be suggested with regard to Luke. Although its Greek style is often more elaborate, the formulation of several pericopes in Luke is also reminiscent of that in the other Synoptic Gospels. It is especially true of the context-parallel triple traditions in Luke, and they confirm the claim of the evangelist to have collected traditions of eyewitnesses active from the beginning.

However, with regard to material in Luke outside the context-parallel triple units, there are indications of a particular background, yet also with a center in Jerusalem. Already in his prologue Luke has alluded to a certain dualism among the Jerusalem traditionists from whom the material was derived, and then has explained this dualism in the Book of Acts. He characterized the competence of his authorities under two aspects, when he wrote about persons "who, from the beginning, had become (1) eyewitnesses and (2) servants of the word" (Luke 1:2). In the view of Luke, it was a prerogative of the Twelve to have been "eyewitnesses" from the beginning (Acts 1:21–23, about the election of Matthias; cf. Acts 11:15; John 15:27), although Luke was able to think of some women as important eyewitnesses, too (Luke 8:23; 23:49; 24:10). Besides the eyewitnesses, however, Luke mentioned traditionists whose merit it was to have been "servants of the word" from the very beginning. In this connection, it must be supposed that Luke indicated disciples who did not belong to the apostolic group of eyewitnesses but had also preached and worked in Jerusalem from the beginning of the church. Luke did, in fact, know such experienced Christians from his journeys with Paul, and these had formerly been leading among the Greek-speaking disciples in Jerusalem and the so-called Hellenists (Acts 6:1). One of them was Silvanus, the Jerusalem delegate to Antioch (Acts 15:22) whom Luke, according to the first "we" report of Acts, knew from Paul's second journey (16:11, 19). Another one was Philip, who had been among those responsible for the charity meals in Jerusalem (6:5), then preached and taught in Samaria and on the west coast (8:5–40), and finally, according to another "we" report, served as the host of Paul and Luke in Caesarea (21:8). During the captivity of Paul in Caesarea from A.D. 58 to 60, to which the Philemon letter alludes (since Paul, in v. 9, emphasizes

that he is "now also" a prisoner), Luke even had opportunities to share experiences with Mark (Philemon 24), who had been a Greek-speaking hearer of Peter in Jerusalem (Acts 12:12) and then followed Barnabas and Paul to Cyprus (13:5) as their assistant (ὑπηρέτης, "servant"; cf. the reference to original "servants of the word" in Luke 1:2). The contacts of Mark and Luke in Caesarea, attested by Philemon, are a convenient explanation for the similarities between the Gospels which they were going to write, and preferable to any theory of literary utilization.

On the whole, Luke's acquaintance with these former members of Greek-speaking groups in the Jerusalem church accounts for the provenance of the traditions which he submitted to Theophilus and other Hellenistic readers. This is true of his Gospel both as to (1) its parallelism with Mark and (2) its Q traditions and special material.

1. In the first instance, the Third Gospel is characterized by several context-parallel triple traditions and other elements that represent a particular similarity with the Second Gospel. The personal confrontation of the evangelists can best explain why Luke was able to present analogies to many pericopes of Mark that had a background in the preaching and teaching activity of Peter and other members of the apostolic circle in Jerusalem. In this context it was generally Mark who inspired Luke, but in some passages Luke has preserved more of the apostolic tradition than Mark, which is especially obvious in connection with the Sermon on the Plain (see pp. 90–91, 103–4).

2. Beyond the Markan parallels, Luke has retained numerous Q units and special traditions, which he compiled in the birth and childhood stories, in the Sermon on the Plain and the travel narrative (Luke 1:5—2:52; 6:20–49; 9:51—18:14). As will be demonstrated in the analysis of the relevant blocks, the particular interests here displayed—for example, in the joy of the pious, the poor widows, the common meals, and the foreign mission—show that Luke took over traditions from Philip and other representatives of the Hellenistic circle in Jerusalem occupied with charity meals as well as with preaching and teaching.

Other Local Aspects

In several cases the events described and the sayings quoted had originally been attached to the places mentioned or presupposed in the texts (below, 1); in other cases this was not so. Some narratives or quotations were only based on a theme and circulated to begin with as separate units without any topographical information (2); some may earlier have included local reminiscences that were changed or abandoned in the process of transmission (3). The two latter types of units received a new localization when they were embodied in different sections of the synoptic material, whether this happened on the level of tradition or redaction.

1. Examples of a localization that is probably historical are offered by the

reports on the baptism at the Jordan (Matt. 3:13 with par.), a healing in Capernaum (Mark 1:29 with par.), a conversion at the Gennesaret customs station (Matt. 9:9 with par.), a conversion in Jericho (Luke 19:9), the anointment in Bethany (Matt. 26:6 // Mark 14:3), and the fundamental elements of the drama in Jerusalem (Matt. 21:1—28:10 with par.). In such cases the apostles and other persons involved may have contributed to the preservation of topographical reminiscences.

2. Numerous examples of tradition units without any primary local aspects are given by the Q material, which has been inserted by Matthew and Luke in quite different contexts. Thus several quotations found in the Matthean Sermon on the Mount (Matt. 5:1—7:27) and the Lukan Sermon on the Plain (Luke 6:20–49) correspond to each other, but the two speeches have different textual places and different geographical frames. Furthermore, a considerable number of *alibi* analogies to parts of the Matthean sermon emerge later in the Lukan travel narrative—for instance, the Lord's prayer (Matt. 6:9–13; Luke 11:1–4). On the whole, a tendency of Matthew can be observed to let instructive double traditions of the Q type and in addition didactic single traditions illustrate a teaching activity of Jesus in Galilee, whereas Luke was inclined to let his didactic Q units and single traditions illustrate a teaching of the Master during his journey through Transjordan to Judea. In some cases Jesus may actually have used the same words in different parts of the country. But the notorious topographical differences between Matthew and Luke with regard to didactic units of the Q type were mainly due to the nontopographical nature of this material, which allowed the traditionists and the evangelists to use it where it suited their interests best.

3. Occasionally it can be noticed that a narrative or a quotation has been attracted by a certain text complex, so that its original localization was altered.

Thus the first public activity of Jesus was probably not so exclusively related to Capernaum and its neighborhood as Mark has indicated (1:16—4:34). A reason for the concentration of the narratives on east Galilee may rather have been that several Markan traditions were transmitted by disciples coming from this region. Especially it seems likely that Peter, consciously or unconsciously, presented his recollections in the perspective of the house-church in Capernaum of which his mother-in-law was the hostess (Mark 1:31), and several hearers, including Mark, can also have associated the traditions of Peter with the apostle's background there. In this context the recollections of some Galilean women may also be considered (Matt. 27:56 with par., about Mary Magdalene and others).

Another example showing that a tradition may have been given a local framework based on interests of the traditionists is the second half of the Matthean commission speech, which foretells a Jewish persecution of the Twelve in Galilee (Matt. 10:17–24). Its *alibi* analogies in Mark and Luke are parts of Christ's farewell speech in Jerusalem and deal with the church there in view of a persecution by Jewish authorities (Mark 13:9–13 // Luke 21:12–19). Matthew

or his redactors wanted to show that Jesus had already foreseen such a persecution in Galilee, from where several of the apostles, including Matthew, had come, and therefore used the pericope in question for the great commission speech.

A further example of local shifting is offered by Luke in connection with the question of a scribe about the foremost command of the law (Luke 10:25–28). Matthew and Mark referred the question to Christ's sojourn in Jerusalem (Matt. 22:34–40 // Mark 12:28–34), but Luke to his wandering through Transjordan. In both cases the story was told in Jerusalem, yet a difference came up because Matthew and Mark had gotten it from the apostolic circle, while Luke had received it from Hellenistic believers, several of whom had come with Jesus from Transjordan and were inclined to recall this landscape, and even to support the positive view of the Samaritans which is expressed in the context of the story (Luke 9:51–56; 10:29–37).

Such wanderings of traditions and their anchoring in another surrounding with special interests supply an explanation for some of the local and temporal deviations that emerge from a comparative study of the Synoptic Gospels. Whether the local shift of a tradition occurred in connection with its transmission or editing cannot be determined on principle.

As it turns out from the observations made in the last two sections, the general topographical picture offered by the Synoptic Gospels was based on personal factors affecting the development of traditions in the early church. In anticipation of details pointed out in the subsequent analysis of the relevant blocks, the development can be reconstructed in the following way.

In principle, all synoptic traditions were formed on the basis of the passion story, which is relatively coherent and similar in block 12 of the Synoptic Gospels as well as in John. The oldest apostolic circle and other Christian circles in Jerusalem, which still bore in mind the events of the last supper and the crucifixion, developed the passion story in varying but substantially identical forms. At the meal, celebrated in the house-churches (Acts 2:46, κλῶντες κατ' οἶκον ἄρτον), a report about the institution of holy communion was developed and repeated, and this is the one which the synoptic evangelists took over and which Paul imparted to the believers in Corinth (1 Cor. 11:23, παρέλαβον . . . ὃ καὶ παρέδωκα ὑμῖν). *Mutatis mutandis,* the practice implied a Christian analogy to the Jewish Passah Haggadah, in which the exodus from Egypt was recalled in order to explain the origin and meaning of the ceremony (Mishnah, *Pesachim* X.4). In addition to the retrospect on the institution, those responsible for the Christian meals recalled other events of the Easter week, and so the passion section of the Gospels developed in the house circles.

Since the members of the house circles had also to be strengthened concerning Christian faith and the church's mission in general, information was further needed about what Jesus had done and said before his suffering began, and the

material of blocks 3 to 11 was thus formed out in retrospect. In this connection, Galilean disciples such as Peter and other apostles played decisive roles as eyewitnesses, and their communications about the life of Jesus, their occupation with liturgy and teaching have been designated by Luke as characteristic activities (Acts 1:22; 2:42; 6:4). Thus when the leader of the Hebrew apostles, Peter, preached before the multitude in the temple (Acts 2:46; 3:11; 4:1; 5:12) or taught at the breaking of bread in house-churches (2:46), especially in the community led by Mark's mother (12:12), his reports on the life and teaching of Jesus received a Galilean orientation because of his background. Women from Galilee who, like Mary Magdalene, served as eyewitnesses of the cross and the tomb of Jesus (Matt. 27:55–56 with par.) contributed to such Galilean traditions. Moreover, numerous pilgrims from Galilee, and especially from Transjordan according to Luke, had accompanied the Master to Jerusalem (Matt. 19:2 // Mark 10:1; Luke 12:1, *μυριάδες*). For such reasons many Jesus traditions of Matthew and Mark became concentrated on Galilee, those of Luke also connected with Transjordan.

Certainly the regional traditions were accessible to the evangelists in various ways, and several of them were selected and revalued for personal reasons. Matthew represented a special concern for the learning and teaching of the apostles in Jerusalem and therefore pointed out that Jesus had already imparted fundamental instruction to them in Galilee (Matt. 5:1—7:29; 9:35—10:42; 13:51–52). Mark mainly paid attention to the activity of Jesus in Capernaum and east Galilee (Mark 1:16—4:34; 9:30–50), and this was due to Peter's family association with Capernaum (1:29), especially actualized in the house-church of Mark's mother in Jerusalem (Acts 12:12). Luke used less material connected with this region and instead adapted several traditions about west Galilee (Luke 4:16–30), Samaria (9:51–56; 10:29–37; 17:11–19), and especially Transjordan (9:57—18:30), which indicates that he did not rely upon Peter and the apostles so much as Matthew and Mark, but that he also listened to other early "servants of the word" (Luke 1:2).

Under these circumstances a simplified picture of Jesus' life, implying one activity in Galilee, one in Transjordan, and one in Judea, emerged in blocks 3 to 11 of the Synoptic Gospels. The reason was that primarily Galilean, and partly Transjordanian, disciples and pilgrims contributed to the development of the traditions in Jerusalem, supplementing the passion story with episodes and quotations connected with their home countries. As is understood through a comparison with the Gospel of John and its reports on repeated pilgrim journeys of Christ to Jerusalem, the biographical pictures found in the Gospels of Matthew, Mark, and Luke merely correspond to selected epochs in the life of Jesus.

As will be demonstrated below in connection with block 2, which deals with the baptism of Jesus, the starting point for blocks 1 and 2 was another kind of activity in the early church. This was the instruction of candidates for baptism, who had

to be informed on the baptism of Jesus and his divine origin in order to understand in whose name they were baptized.

Further remarks on the life setting of synoptic traditions in baptism and eucharist will be found in the next section.

Evidence of Three and Two Synoptic Witnesses

With regard to frequency, a difference between three categories of pericopes was pointed out and illustrated by the tables in chapter 2: triple traditions, double traditions, and single traditions. Owing to their specific distribution, two special kinds of triple and double units play dialectic roles in the material, and these are (*a*) the context-parallel triple traditions, which represent a fundamental stratum of the synoptic texts, and (*b*) the *alibi*-analogous double traditions of the Q category, by which Matthew and Luke augment the triple pericopes in places that always shift.

Between subdivisions a and b, a certain difference of the function involved may also be observed, insofar as most context-parallel triple units contain narratives, and most Q traditions contain sayings of Jesus. The difference corresponds to a twofold activity of the early church in Jerusalem, as it has been characterized by the Book of Acts in a quite unsophisticated way: (*a*) a meal service called the breaking of bread, first celebrated by local groups in private homes (Acts 2:42, 46; 4:35; 6:2, 4; cf. 20:7, 11), and (*b*) a word service implying proclamation and instruction about Christ and his message, first offered by the apostles in the temple (2:42, 46; 3:11; 5:12; 6:2). At the esoteric meals, the believers may especially have been reminded of the passion and other events in the life of Jesus; at the open meetings, the public may especially have been confronted with the sayings of Jesus concerning discipleship.

Religious meals were also practiced in Judaism by Pharisees (Luke 14:1, a Sabbat Qiddush) and Essenes (1QS VI.2); a public word service was characteristic of the synagogues. A division of the interest on narrative and didactic traditions is even found in the Jewish Talmud, where the elements are distributed on Haggada, or "narrative" topics, and Halacha, or "behavior" themes.

However, the dualism found in the synoptic material was only a tendency due to different settings in life: on the one hand liturgical meditation and on the other proclamation and instruction. In later centuries the two activities were separated by the church and distributed on the *missa fidelium* and the foregoing *missa catechumenorum*. Within the New Testament, narrative and didactic elements are still mingled with each other in a dialectic manner.

Parallel Triple Traditions, Mainly Narrative

As pointed out in chapter 2, there are 56 or 57 context-parallel triple pericopes in the Synoptic Gospels. In principle they consist of narratives, and they are

remarkably concentrated in the reports on the baptism of Christ, the holy communion, the crucifixion, and the resurrection.

Being represented by Mark in a most distinct way, the context-parallel triple units comprise 49 percent, or nearly half of all pericopes in his Gospel (above, p. 25). This implies a preference for narrative material, and the Second Gospel is actually stamped by endeavors to recount the "beginning of the good news" (Mark 1:1) with many vivid details, whereas didactic interests are less often represented than in Matthew and Luke.

Consideration of Peter's importance for Mark explains why the evangelist has mainly presented narrative material. Papias referred to this dependence, although he did not localize the contacts (below, p. 167). It is otherwise known about Mark that his mother possessed a house in Jerusalem where Peter and several members of the early church used to meet (Acts 12:12). Very likely it was essentially on the basis of traditions imparted by Peter to this community that Mark compiled the material of his Gospel. Confirmation of the assumption is offered by the concentration of Mark's narrative on Capernaum, where Peter was at home (above, p. 53).

In such a circle of Christian fellow boarders interest was not so much concentrated upon the conversion of outsiders and their preparation for baptism, but rather upon edification of the initiated concerning the beneficial activities of Jesus from the time of the calling of Peter and the other earliest apostles (Mark 1:16–20). That is why Mark contains less kerygmatic and didactic material than Matthew and Luke. Its edifying purpose is perceptible in the accumulation of narratives, which the redactor has given a more popular and colorful form than what is found in the other synoptic texts. The life setting of Mark is comparable to the reading of edifying and entertaining stories during the common meals of a religious order. Certainly the triple traditions dominant in Mark also offer examples of teaching. This is so in the parable chapter, in the discussion about ritual purity, in the instruction about ecclesiastic problems, and in the admonitions of the early church to steadfastness in future trials (Mark 4:1–34; 7:1–23; 9:33—10:31; 13:1–37). Nevertheless the triple traditions in Mark are predominantly of narrative kind and deal especially with the miracles of Jesus in Capernaum, Gennesaret, and in the regions around the Lake of Galilee. Peter and other apostles reported about such miracles at religious meetings of believers already baptized. The relatively esoteric character of Mark's narrative is also confirmed by two opposite tendencies of his miracle accounts: on the one hand, there are endeavors toward visualization and popularization, and on the other, there is emphasis upon the messianic secret. Examples of these principles of concretization and discretion are found already in the story of the demoniac in Capernaum (Mark 1:25–26, convulsion, silence) and frequently thereafter.

Though the Gospels of Matthew and Luke contain many elements not found in Mark, a fundamental stratum is also represented in them by the 56 or 57 context-parallel triple units which are mainly of narrative kind.

As a retrospective study of the table in chapter 2 shows, the accordance cannot be derived from Mark. The frequency of the contextual parallels is great in the passion section but diminishes gradually in the preceding blocks and is close to zero at the beginning of the Galilean section, while another inclination toward parallelism is discovered in connection with the baptism report. No editor would have changed his attachment to a written document in this amazing way. Another difficulty in using Mark for a literary derivation of Matthew and Luke is caused by the arbitrary manner in which verbal similarities and differences alternate within comparable pericopes.

When compared with parallels in Matthew or Luke, several passages of Mark instead make it necessary to presuppose different traditions in the background. An example of this is the abrupt conclusion of the short reference to Christ's temptation in Mark 1:13b: "and he was with the animals and the angels served him," which is quite incomprehensible without a comparison with the more complete tradition found in Matthew's parallel. In 1:32, *ὀψίας γενομένης, ὅτε ἔδυσεν ὁ ἥλιος* represents an auditory contamination of two phrases, of which one appears in Matthew and one in Luke, and there are many such cases where Mark couples two different expressions found in Matthew and Luke. Mark 3:7–8 presents a list of hearers coming from similar regions as those mentioned by the context-parallel in Luke 6:17, but no instruction of the multitude corresponding to the Sermon on the Plain which follows in Luke appears in Mark, and the reference to the audience remains pointless after this Markan abbreviation. Nevertheless, feeling that a speech was needed for the audience, Mark constructed a bridge to the parable speech in 4:1–34 by inserting a boat in 3:9 which he mentioned again in 4:1. In 4:12, the clauses *ἵνα βλέποντες βλέπωσιν*, and so forth, as well as *μήποτε ἐπιστρέψωσιν*, are based upon the verbal quotation of Isa. 6:9–10 which is found only in Matthew, so that Mark has abbreviated some material that was earlier more complete. As the study of details will also show in chapters 4 and 5, Mark cannot be regarded as the literary source of Matthew and Luke in such cases.

For this reason and with regard to the aforementioned peculiarities of the context-parallel triple pericopes, the appearance of parallels to Mark in Matthew and Luke cannot be derived from the extant text of Mark.

In fact, the extensive harmony represented by the context-parallel triple pericopes must be traced back to common traditions. Since the reports on Christ's baptism and passion represent the highest degree of harmony within the synoptic material, it becomes evident that oral traditions concerning these cycles in the life of the Lord were fundamental. That such bulks of tradition units were kept in triple contextual parallelism within the synoptic texts indicates their dependence on preachers and teachers with a special authority, and in this context one may think of Peter and the apostles.

As in Mark, the authoritative position of Peter is also discernible in Matthew, only under somewhat different aspects. In the First Gospel, attention has not

been drawn so much as in the Second to early events in Capernaum (Matt. 8:14–17, for instance, represents later and shorter counterparts to Mark 1:21–38). Instead, the first concern of Matthew or his redactors was to report on the instruction of the apostles on a mount in Galilee just after the call of Peter, James, and John (Matt. 5:1—7:29). In spite of his occasional weakness, Peter is also regularly mentioned as the representative of the apostles when they receive instructions from their Master (10:2; 14:28; 16:16–23; 17:1, 4, 24–26; 18:21; 19:27; 26:33, 35, 37, 40). These passages betray a close connection between Matthew or his redactors with Peter and the apostolic circle, and their preparation for authoritative preaching and teaching is here especially brought into focus. Such concerns for apostolic instruction have brought about that several narrative pericopes of Matthew are found in other contexts than in Mark and Luke—for instance, with regard to six of the ten miracle stories that appear between the Sermon on the Mount and the commission speech (Matt. 8:14–17, 23–34; 9:18–26). Here the particular order depended upon subordination of narrative elements to didactic material and was also meant to accentuate the call of Matthew by Jesus, seen as the great physician (9:12). Just the coordination of the narrative triple units in question with two surrounding didactic sections, which deal with the instruction of Peter and the other apostles (5:1—7:29; 9:35—10:42), confirms that the redactors considered the inserted narrative material as being especially based on apostolic traditions. Further observations will be found in chapter 5.

Notwithstanding these particularities, there are narrative outlines in Matthew that are similar to those in Mark. The essential concord is explained by the assumption of a parallel dependence on the kerygmatic activity of Peter and the apostles in Jerusalem. At the same time, the relative agreement of the Greek vocabulary within comparable pericopes of both Gospels is conveniently understandable if the relevant tradition units are supposed to have been translated and recited in Jerusalem before Mark and the redactors of Matthew began to collect them.

Luke is closer to Mark than to Matthew concerning the narrative outlines, but differences in relation to Mark may also be noticed. In his parallels to the Galilean part of Mark, Luke has not placed the call of Peter at the beginning, and the whole section in question contains only a few vague references to Galilee (Luke 4:31, a town in Galilee; 4:44, Judea in the main text instead of Galilee; 5:17, Galilee and Judea; 8:26, the country of Gadara opposite Galilee). Above all, the fourth and fifth of the six excursions described by Mark in 4:35—9:29 are missing in Luke (the so-called great lacuna between 9:17 and 18). In relation to Matthew, a remarkable particularity of Luke is found in the fact that its Q traditions, unlike the Matthean ones, are mostly not connected with Christ's activity in Galilee. With the exception of the Sermon on the Plain, the Q traditions of Luke are instead, together with single traditions, found in the travel narrative which is referred to Transjordan and contains an entire third of the

book (9:51—18:14). Luke has also refrained from mentioning any revelation of the risen Lord in Galilee. This relative disinterest in Galilee, counterbalanced by a preference for Transjordan, indicates that Luke not only took into account Galilean disciples like Peter and the Hebrew apostles but also listened to other "servants of the word" who conveyed to Luke reminiscences of Christ's visit to Transjordan, where the inhabitants often were Hellenists. In other parts of the present study, Luke's personal connection with Hellenists from Jerusalem and especially with Philip in Caesarea are pointed out (p. 121). His confrontation with Mark in Caesarea during the years 58 to 60 is also to be considered (p. 168).

Yet the convergence of narrative pericopes is quite considerable in Mark and Luke, for it includes not only the 56 or 57 context-parallel triple units but also some pericopes that form contextual parallels exclusively in Mark and Luke (Mark 1:21–38 // Luke 4:31–43; Mark 4:35—5:43 // Luke 8:22–56; Mark 6:6–13 // Luke 9:1–6), while in Matthew they are either found in other contexts or missing (above, pp. 35–37). In all of his context-parallel pericopes, however, the evangelist Luke represents a vocabulary that is so different from that of Mark that no copying of a manuscript appears probable. Another dissimilarity to be observed is that Luke, in comparison with Mark, has contracted the Galilean perspective and instead paid attention to Transjordan, as mentioned above. No literary manipulation with Mark as model can explain this disarrangement.

More reasonable is the conclusion that Mark's and Luke's relative convergence in the narrative structure of their Gospels, along with remarkable differences and transpositions found in the Third Gospel in comparison with the Second, was due to personal contacts of Luke with Mark and in addition with some representative of Transjordanian traditions. Occasions for a confrontation of Mark and Luke were given while both evangelists stayed in Caesarea (according to Philemon 24, as demonstrated below, p. 168). Luke had also opportunities there to hear from Philip about Transjordanian traditions of the Hellenists in Jerusalem, which he used for his travel narrative (below, p. 121).

Every approach to the synoptic problem must focus the alternating similarity of Mark with Matthew and Luke. Outside the triple stratum, Mark is either more related to Matthew or to Luke. As will be argued in chapter 7, this enigma is explained on realistic terms by the assumption that Matthew and Mark collected traditions from Peter and the apostles in Jerusalem and that Mark and Luke shared experiences in Caesarea.

Ambulant Double Traditions, Mainly Didactic

Quite other historical factors led to the nonsystematic distribution of double traditions on Matthew and Luke without support in Mark. Such pericopes are here called Q traditions in the sense of a statistic category without any presupposition of a document. A few Q traditions are narrative, such as the report on the centurion's servant (Matt. 8:5–13; Luke 7:1–10), but most of them are didactic and represent either proclamation or teaching. There are, for instance, the

expressly didactic elements of Matthew's Sermon on the Mount (Matt. 5:1—7:27): to some of them, analogies may be found in Luke's non-context-parallel Sermon on the Plain (Luke 6:20–49) and to others in very scattered contexts, such as the analogies to Matt. 5:13–16 in Luke 14:24–25 and 11:33.

As illustrated by the table in chapter 2, 35 pericopes of Matthew and 31 of Luke are double traditions without analogies in Mark—the difference of the numbers is due to occasional variations in the cohesion of pericope elements. In addition, there are 34 single units in Matthew and 53 in Luke, many of which have also to do with teaching (e.g., Matt. 5:17–37 about the law of Moses; Luke 10:29–37 about the Good Samaritan).

The hotchpot-like distribution of the Q traditions in Matthew and Luke speaks against the widespread opinion that Q was a document and likewise against the alternative derivation of the Q material from either Matthew or Luke.

It will be demonstrated in chapter 4 that some context-parallel elements of Matthew and Luke, which appear in connection with the Baptist, the baptism, and the temptation—namely, in parts of Matt. 3:7—4:11 and Luke 3:7—4:13—do not belong to those double traditions which may be called Q in the sense of being absent in Mark. Adjacent and substantial elements of these texts are triple traditions with short analogies in Mark 1:7–13, and the latter presuppose knowledge of the more detailed traditions found in Matthew and Luke (see below, pp. 81–82). In the background was a common tradition complex, of which Mark has only preserved the central report on Christ's baptism and some concentrated notes on surrounding circumstances, because he did not find it necessary to recall so many items connected with the institution of the baptism which his readers had already received. The context-parallel non-Markan elements of Matthew's and Luke's reports on the Baptist and so on are not Q traditions but parts of traditions abbreviated by Mark.

Reserving the symbol Q for double units exclusively found in Matthew and Luke without support in Mark, it must be observed that all of them are scattered in the texts without the least order. The whole group of traditions here called Q consists of *alibi* analogies. It is not conceivable that any editor would have cut out just these traditions from a manuscript and inserted them here and there in his presentation, consistently avoiding preserving the extant order, though he gladly observed the order when dealing with items found in the context–parallel triple traditions.

One had rather think of Q as separate didactic tradition units which circulated in the Christian community and were quoted ad hoc when a specific topic was to be illustrated.

Actually the didactic Q traditions do not represent any specific category within the material, for their contents are essentially comparable to those of didactic triple or single traditions. There are no material, but only statistic, differences between didactic units that function in the texts as triple, as double, or as single traditions. According to the principle of supply and demand, some elements were

used by three or two evangelists and some by one. Moreover, several didactic Q traditions are combined with didactic triple or single traditions in all the Synoptic Gospels. This implies that a didactic unit was sometimes enforced by the addition of another didactic unit, available to or interesting for the traditionists or the evangelists independently of the frequency types involved.

First it may be observed that some didactic pericopes are found among the context-parallel triple traditions, so that Mark also supports them. This applies to the question of fasting (Matt. 9:14 with par.); two discussions about breaking the Sabbath (12:1–14 with par.); the parable chapter (13:1–52 with par.); significant parts of Christ's teaching in Capernaum (18:1–22 with par.), and his revelations about the fate of Jerusalem and the patience of the early church (24:1–44 with par.). In such cases Mark contains didactic units in the same context, and sometimes to the same extent, as Matthew and Luke. Occasionally the narrative context-parallel triple traditions, which refer to important episodes of Jesus' life, were thus supplemented by examples of his teaching. It did not occur through insertion of material borrowed from another written collection but was the result of contacts between recollections of events in the life of Jesus and of sayings quoted from his teaching.

Since the interest of Mark's hearers and readers was concentrated on stories to be told (already evident from Mark 1:1, *ἀρχὴ τοῦ εὐαγγελίου ᾿Ιησοῦ Χριστοῦ*, "Rise of the Good News About Jesus Christ"), didactic traditions were only inserted here and there in Mark, and this was especially done when ethical problems of the believers needed to have light shed upon them, as concerning the question of fasting (Mark 2:18–22).

But if material for teaching was the most important concern, as in Matthew and Luke (e.g., Matt. 5:2, *ἐδίδασκεν αὐτοὺς λέγων*; Luke 1:4, *περὶ ὧν κατηχήθης λόγων*), then narrative traditions would incidentally be adapted to the instructive elements. This priority of didactic complexes is found in Matthew, above all in the sequence of ten miracles (Matt. 8:1—9:34) which have been clustered between the Sermon on the Mount (5:1—7:29) and the commission speech (9:35—10:42). A similar tendency is represented by Luke in the proleptic report on the sermon of Jesus in Nazareth (Luke 4:16–30) and especially in the travel narrative which is absolutely dominated by material for instruction and discussion (9:51—18:14).

Because of their interest in the teaching of Jesus, the evangelists Matthew and Luke have also included a multitude of teaching units beyond the above-mentioned triple traditions of the didactic kind, and this extra material appears either as double or special traditions. In comparison with Mark, there are supplements here, but the difference is purely quantitative and should not be interpreted as evidence for any genetic priority of the shorter Gospel, because abridgment of the subject matter in Mark is just as conceivable as enlargement in Matthew and Luke. The surplus of didactic elements in Matthew and Luke is partly found in association with some of the above-mentioned didactic pieces of context-parallel

triple traditions, partly without such connections, and they alternate between double traditions of the Q category and special traditions.

Companions to didactic triple traditions, consisting of double or single units, appear in the following places of Matthew: just before two context-parallel triple units containing discussion about breaking the Sabbath (Matt. 11:2–30) and just after one unit of this kind dealing with the Beelzebul controversy (12:38–42); in the parable chapter as thematic supplements of context-parallel triple parables (13:24–30, 33, 36-52); before and after context-parallel triple traditions about instruction of the apostles in Capernaum (17:24–27; 18:10–35); and after context-parallel triple prophecies on the fate of Jerusalem and the patience of the early church (24:37—25:46).

Luke has preserved many counterparts to these logia of Jesus, which Matthew has presented as companions to context-parallel triple traditions, and these double traditions of the category Q always form *alibi* analogies. Most of them are found together with single traditions in Luke's travel account, which occupies a third of his Gospel (Luke 9:51—18:14). With regard to its purpose, this middle section of Luke is clearly didactic, for here the evangelist has inserted a large number of examples for instruction of the disciples and discussion with opponents (e.g., Luke 11:1–4, the Lord's prayer; 11:14–23, the Beelzebul controversy). Its closest environment is also didactic, seeing that in Luke the travel narrative appears between two didactic sequences, of which the one refers to Christ's conclusive teaching in Galilee (Luke 9:43–50) and the other to his continued teaching in Perea (18:15–34). Both surrounding contexts include didactic triple units that are contextual parallels to parts of didactic sequences in Matthew and Mark (Matt. 17:22—18:35 // Mark 9:30–50, and Matt. 19:1—20:19 // Mark 10:1–34). Whereas the other evangelists indicated the change of scene from Galilee to Perea by only a short remark (Matt. 19:1 // Mark 10:1), Luke filled out the interval between the context-parallel triple sequences connected with Galilee and Perea, respectively, by double and single traditions illustrating Christ's teaching on his way from north to south. There are only vague references here to a peregrination from Galilee to Jerusalem (Luke 9:51; 13:29), but Luke must have thought of Transjordan, for after the disappointment in a village of Samaria (9:52–53) Jesus was obviously understood to have passed on through Perea (a gentile environment suggested by 10:7–8; Antipas as tetrarch of Perea mentioned in 13:31 [the reference to Samaria in 17:11 being a mere retrospect caused by the catchword "gratitude" in 17:9]; an explicit parallelism with Matthean and Markan reports on Perea in 18:15ff.).

Why do so many didactic traditions of the type Q appear in the Galilean section of Matthew and in the Transjordanian section of Luke? It cannot have depended on manipulations with a literary document, for there would have been no sensible reason for any of the evangelists to detach and scatter all double traditions of the category Q, while he was keen on preserving the established order when dealing with triple traditions. Only the historical circumstances

under which the formation and transmission of the didactic units took place on the oral level can provide the answer to this question. In the early church both the apostles and the Hellenists were occupied with teaching and discussion (indications of this in Acts 2:42—5:42 passim, and 6:10—7:53, respectively), and there is reason to assume they used quotations of the Lord's sayings to illustrate their speech (Acts 1:1, 5). In principle, the quotations circulated as separate units centered on a special topic, and they could therefore be used in any context to illustrate the problem in question, as was done by Paul on different occasions (1 Thess. 4:15 e.p.). Since Matthew belonged to the circle of apostles from Galilee, while Luke had connection with some of the Hellenists from Transjordan, the didactic traditions available to each of them received an orientation either toward Galilee or toward Transjordan, although it did not much affect the internal structure of the units.

This is especially noticeable with regard to didactic elements of rhetorical sequences found both in the First and the Third Gospel. Several elements of Matthew's Sermon on the Mount (Matt. 5:1—7:27) and commission speech (10:1–42) are Q traditions with *alibi* analogies in Luke; but while in Matthew these speeches are directed to the twelve apostles in Galilee, some of Luke's corresponding pericopes figure as parts of a sermon given to the multitude on a plain (Luke 6:17–49) or to the seventy disciples in Transjordan (10:1–12), and some appear later in scattered parts of Luke's travel account (11:1–4, 9–13, 33–36; 12:2–12, 22–34; 14:25–27). It was because separate reminiscences of the Lord's words served as illustration of practical questions in different circles of believers that such Q traditions were referred either to Galilee or to Transjordan.

Consequently the starting point of the synoptic didactic traditions has to be seen in the apostolic and Hellenistic teaching activity in Jerusalem. In this context, reminiscences of Christ's sayings were used to illustrate relevant topics. Apostles and other disciples quoted words of Jesus ad hoc, because of their actual meaning for the Christians and independently of their original setting in the life of Jesus. Some of the quotations were formed out in pericopes, and others were preserved in the form of short phrases.

Parts of this didactic material were taken over by all the three synoptic evangelists in combination with the narrative pericopes occurring as context-parallel triple units (above, p. 62). Other parts of the didactic material were used only by Matthew and Luke, and therefore form those double traditions here symbolized by the letter Q. The relative agreement of such double units leads to the understanding that some common formation had taken place on a preliterary stage, but the total absence of contextual parallelism excludes any possibility of a literary source as the basis for the agreements. Connections with different circles of traditionists offer the only explanation why corresponding Q units are often found in the Galilean sector of Matthew and the Transjordanian sector of Luke.

The absence of actual Q units in Mark, on the other hand, is only a symptom of the evangelist's less concern for didactic material. All that can be said is that while

some didactic traditions, accessible to Matthew and Luke, were also used by Mark, others were not. Mark concentrated his interest on narrative edification, and the reason why he did not refer so much to didactic exhortations as Matthew and Luke was that he collected a material that was meant for believers already informed about the faith and life of a disciple.

Particular interests of the traditionists or the evangelists also led to the inclusion of such didactic traditions as one Gospel represents alone. Single traditions of this kind occur several times in Matthew's Sermon on the Mount (e.g., Matt. 5:17–37) and in Luke's travel account (e.g., Luke 10:29–37; 15:11—16:15); in Mark there is only a short example in the parable chapter (Mark 4:26–29).

Some didactic units are thus found in three Gospels, several in two, and some in one Gospel. The difference is sufficiently explained by the principle of supply and demand. Individual traditions were more or less available to the evangelists, and they also interested them more or less.

Life Setting in Baptism and the Eucharist

As the tables in chapter 2 indicate, there is heavy concentration of context-parallel triple traditions upon or around the text units that deal with Christ's baptism and passion. This offers an opportunity to explain under which practical circumstances the synoptic traditions began to be developed: on the one hand, in connection with Christian baptism when the Lord's own baptism had to be recalled and, on the other hand, in connection with the eucharist when Christ's passion had to be retold. A closer examination of the relevant texts will confirm this in chapters 4 to 6, but a few general observations may be inserted here.

The three Synoptic Gospels unfold a picture of Christ's activity which is common in the general outlines, but on account of its topographical simplicity distinguishes itself from the presentation found in the Fourth Gospel. After his baptism, Jesus is said to announce the kingdom in Galilee and in the north, and his pursuit there is not interrupted by those repeated visits to Jerusalem which John has testified. Only after the completion of his activity in Galilee is Jesus found moving through Transjordan and especially Perea to Judea, in order to fulfill his fate in Jerusalem. Whether these synoptic outlines exactly follow the historical course of the Master's life cannot be established with certainty, for John has drawn other contours. One has merely to ask why the synoptic writers, after dealing with the birth and baptism of Jesus, registered a continuous activity in Galilee and in the north, and in addition a single wandering through Transjordan or at least Perea to Judea, before the final drama in Jerusalem was reported. The answer is found as soon as the order in which the Christian traditions developed is taken into consideration.

Despite the simplicity of the synoptic itinerary, as compared with the Johannine account, it was not chiefly based upon a preordained diagram portraying the life of Jesus. Only the pericopes dealing with the Lord's baptism and passion

show traces of preformed structures taken over by the synoptic writers in relative concordance. The other textual units consist of pericopes that are much less coherent. A few of them appear with primary references to chronological and topographical circumstances, but originally they were also independent and received their places in the present texts during the transmission and redaction of the material. The synoptic itinerary must in fact be understood in the light of tradition history. It mainly depends upon the order in which traditions of Christ's life and teaching were developed and collected.

First of all, it was no coincidence that context-parallel pericopes of three synoptic texts reached a maximum in the magnetic fields of the Lord's baptism and last supper. The early Christian church expressed its communion through baptism and holy meals (Acts 2:38, 42 e.p.), and even if these ceremonies were practiced in a certain analogy to baptisms and banquets of the Essene movement (1QS III.9; V.2, 4), the Christians exclusively celebrated their baptism and eucharist with reference to the Messiah Jesus, who had received baptism and instituted the eucharist. On liturgical grounds the Christian baptism and eucharist became a framework for information concerning relevant moments in the life and teaching of Jesus. Christian candidates for baptism were to be informed about the Lord's baptism and of important facts connected with it, and the partakers of the eucharist had to be reminded of the institution of this meal and the circumstances associated with it. So the Christian sacraments formed motives for the development of the relevant traditions and in addition offered guarantees for the remarkable continuity of these traditions when spread to various circles of believers. This is how the culmination of context-parallel triple traditions in the circumference of Jesus' baptism and last supper are to be explained.

In addition, there was a need to inform the candidates and those baptized about experiences, achievements, miracles, and utterances of Jesus Christ known from his life before the baptism and the passion, respectively. This information could be offered only in a retrospective manner. With regard to Christ's birth and childhood, there were rather few remote and vague traditions available. Concerning the public ministry pursued between his baptism and passion, separate reminiscences and traditions could be formulated and circulated, but most of them were originally connected with ethical and practical questions without any fundamental relationships to biographical circumstances. Galilean and Transjordanian witnesses, however, were inclined to pay special attention to what Jesus was known to have said and done either in Galilee or in Transjordan before he approached Jerusalem and Golgotha, and so a number of topical units received a secondary topographical orientation.

Consequently the main parts of the synoptic material resulted from a retrospect expansion of the liturgical accounts on Christ's baptism and last supper. Around these cores, three larger text complexes were gradually developed, which are here called parts I and II–III. Which of these complexes was developed first cannot be established. Normally the baptism of the believers took place before

their invitation to the meal (Acts 2:38, 42), but this does not give the baptismal complex of traditions a higher age in relation to the eucharistic one. Within the perspective of tradition history, the accounts of the Lord's baptism and last supper can be regarded as chronologically parallel issues, based on two liturgical acts of the primitive church. At the end of the baptismal complex, which is treated below as part I, there is a context-parallel triple unit containing an outlook toward the activity of Jesus in Galilee according to part II, and this shows that traditions about the Galilean ministry existed when the complex regarding Christ's baptism and related circumstances was formulated.

The provenance of the synoptic traditions may thus be reconstructed in the following way. (1) Christian baptism and holy communion served as life settings of traditions that deal with the Lord's baptism and last supper and that represent a great amount of verbal agreement between the synoptic texts. (2) Since the candidates for baptism and the participants of the eucharist had also to be informed about circumstances preceding and following Christ's baptism and last supper, context-parallel triple units which surround these fundamental reports were developed. These are found in the textual sections that are treated below as blocks 2 and 10 to 12 which also tell about the preconditions and consequences of Christ's baptism and the events during the passion week. (3) In connection with Christian preaching and teaching on the one hand and with sacramental communion on the other, there was a further need to develop and impart retrospective information about experiences and utterances of Jesus which preceded his baptism and passion, respectively. Individual reminiscences and traditions were presented in this context, generally based on particular subjects that had to be explained because of questions emerging in the community, or according to occasional needs, as Papias said about the communications of Peter (above, p. 46). Originally these units circulated separately, and mostly without chronological and topographical attributes. (4) Gradually the pericopes became parts of more comprehensive sections, here treated as blocks 1 and 3 to 9. The latter, which deal with Christ's public ministry, became referred either to Galilee or to Transjordan owing to the provenance of the informants. Matthew and Mark were especially connected with Peter and the Galilean apostles, and Luke more with Hellenists among whom several had been with Jesus in Transjordan.

In this manner the Synoptic Gospels received their main structure, implying that Jesus went to Galilee after his baptism; that he worked there and in the north without interruption, which has been described by Matthew and Mark with more details than by Luke; that Jesus afterward walked through Transjordan according to Luke; and that eventually he came to Perea and Judea according to all synoptic writers.

Chapters 4 to 6 will illustrate this development with regard to the pericopes found in the main parts and blocks, on which the whole material is distributed here in order to simplify the orientation.

Chapter Four

Part I: Christ's Birth, Childhood, and Baptism

Matt. 1:1—4:17 with Parallels

The first major part of the Synoptic Gospels tells of events preceding the public ministry of the Master from Nazareth (Matt. 1:1—4:17; Mark 1:1—15; Luke 1:1—4:15). In the tables in chapter 2, the items are distributed on blocks 1 and 2. Block 1 is represented by the Gospels of Matthew and Luke, in the form of an ingress and various narratives on the Savior's birth and childhood, which took place in Bethlehem and Jerusalem (Matt. 1:1—2:23; Luke 1:1—2:52). Mark has only an ingress here (Mark 1:1). Block 2 describes, in all Synoptic Gospels, the baptism of the Son of God in the Jordan and related circumstances (Matt. 3:1—4:17 with par.). In block 1, Matthew and Luke have a few points in common but essentially deviate from each other and find no counterparts in Mark. Block 2 is characterized by a considerable harmony of all Synoptic Gospels, for concerning John the Baptist and the baptism of Jesus, context-parallel triple traditions and equivalent double traditions prevail. As the analysis of blocks 1 and 2 will show, the reason for this change from divergence to convergence was that a rather established report on the baptism attracted more or less homogeneous traditions about related circumstances.

In the following exposition, the names of Matthew, Mark, and Luke are provisionally used to indicate the redactors of the relevant Gospels. The historical identity of their authors will be discussed in chapter 7.

Block 1
Christ's Birth and Childhood
Matt. 1:1—2:23; Mark 1:1; Luke 1:1—2:52

The picturesque narratives in block 1 about the birth of the Savior in Bethlehem, the escape to Egypt, and the visits of the child to Jerusalem are found only in Matthew and Luke. The presentation of details is largely individualistic (Matt. 1:1—2:23; Luke 1:1—2:52), and Mark has no counterparts to those episodes.

Preambles

An ingress of various kinds is found at the beginning of the synoptic texts, that is, a short phrase introducing each Gospel (Matt. 1:1; Mark 1:1; Luke 1:1–4). This does not refer to the titles found above the texts ("The Good News According to Matthew," and so forth, to be discussed in chapter 7) but to introductory elements of the first chapters. Here the evangelists have given their information different functions.

Matthew has introduced the first chapter by the following heading: "Genealogy of Jesus Christ, son of David, son of Abraham" (Matt. 1:1). This heading forms the ingress of the subsequent family tree (1:2–17), which contains 3 times 14 names from Abraham to Jesus in correspondence with Chronicles, and the expression "genealogy" or "family tree" (*βίβλος γενέσεως*) was derived from the creation story (Gen. 5:1, *sēpher tōledōt,* about Adam). In postexilic Judaism, levitic genealogies attracted great interest (Esd. 2:6–63 e.p.), and in the same way Matthew has inserted a Davidic family tree. The numerical tally of the Hebrew letters Dwd was 14, and so the 3 times 14 generations were meant to represent the kingdom of David under the aspects of preparation, evolution, and visitation.

A characteristic tendency of Matthew emerges in this ingress and family tree: the concern for scriptural learning, by which Jesus should be confirmed as the Messiah and Davidic king. It represents a religious particularism, implying concentration on Israel and prophecy (cf. Matt. 1:21–23, etc.), which Matthew has later expanded into a religious universalism (28:18–20). Luke has later inserted a family tree, but here the universalism is the point, since Jesus is traced back to Adam as the representative of all humankind (Luke 3:23–38).

Mark has introduced his text with a rubric that has a wider meaning than Matthew's ingress. It runs: "Rise of the Good News About Jesus Christ, Son of God" (Mark 1:1). The christological title "Son of God" is not supported by all manuscripts but is found in most of them and is generally characteristic of Mark; in any case, this text-critical question has no weight here. It is important to observe what the "Good News," or "Message" (*εὐαγγέλιον*), means in the present context. Neither in this rubric nor in the inscriptio read above the text, "The Good News According to Mark," does the word *εὐαγγέλιον* denote a document. As will be demonstrated in chapter 7, the New Testament exclusively understood *εὐαγγέλιον* as the oral message of Christ spread in the church. With the rubric, "Rise of the Good News About Jesus Christ," Mark announced his intention of illustrating the historical background of Christian preaching and teaching. This use of the word "rise" or "beginning" (*ἀρχή*) with reference to the life of Jesus also finds analogies in Luke and John (Luke 1:2–3, *ἀπ᾽ ἀρχῆς, ἄνωθεν*; John 1:1, *ἐν ἀρχῇ*; John 15:27, the disciples who had followed Jesus as his witnesses from the beginning; 1 John 1:1–3, "what was from the beginning . . . we impart to you").

In spite of his allusion to the "beginning," however, the second evangelist did

not treat the birth and childhood of Jesus, but started with the baptism of John (studied below as part of block 2). The explanation often suggested, that Mark did not know any traditions of Christ's birth and childhood, implies a *petitio principii*. It is only legitimate to start from positive historical evidence. According to the witness of Papias, Mark had written down and compiled διδασκαλίαι, or teaching units, presented orally by Peter (Eusebius, *EH* III.39.15). Luke has also indicated in Acts that Mark's mother was the leader of a house-church in Jerusalem, with which Peter had special contacts (Acts 12:12). Circumstances further treated in chapters 6 and 7 justify the assertion that Mark collected teaching units presented by Peter in connection with common meals of such house-churches (Acts 2:46). This implies that Mark had an audience in mind that had already received baptismal instruction, so that no detailed information about the prehistory was required for them. Such practical factors explain why Mark was content with a few reminiscences of John the Baptist (Mark 1:2–8) and, after the report on the baptism of Jesus (1:9–11), inserted only a short allusion to his temptation (1:12–13).

Luke introduced his Gospel with a prologue, including a personal dedication, and gave the text an official Hellenistic style (Luke 1:1–4); later he also introduced the Book of Acts with such a prologue and dedication (Acts 1:1). With regard to the division of the work on two books, both introduced with a prologue and a dedication, Hellenistic analogies such as Josephus's two books *Against Apion* can be referred to.

The dedication was given to a person by the name of Theophilus (Luke 1:3; Acts 1:1). He is not known from other documents, but whether he existed or not, his name was meant to represent the readers Luke had in mind. Theophilus was addressed in a polite way as κράτιστος, which means "very honorable" (Acts 23:26; 24:3; 26:25; Josephus, *Against Apion* 1.1). Luke intended to submit to him a διήγησις (1:1), which is to be translated as "official report," and to do this "accurately" and "in order." Theophilus evidently was regarded by Luke as a magistrate or another member of the upper class in Greco-Roman society, and the evangelist thought of readers in this environment.

As a representative of gentile Christianity, Theophilus was said to have been instructed about elements of the life of Jesus (1:4). Luke intended to increase and substantiate his knowledge so that Theophilus should realize the certitude (ἀσφάλεια) of the gospel when preaching and teaching it himself. The reference to those who had been "servants of the word from the very beginning" (1:2) also indicates that Theophilus was supposed to become a competent preacher and teacher and was not regarded only as a common member of a house-church as were the readers of Mark. For this reason, Luke endeavored to describe the very first beginnings of the gospel proclamation, and has also treated events prior to Christ's baptism at length (1:5—3:30). Luke then assured that original eyewitnesses and preachers had transmitted the material to him (παρέδοσαν ἡμῖν). By appealing to eyewitnesses and servants of the word active from the very

beginning, Luke indicated preachers who had belonged to the early church. In some of them Luke saw the apostles, but also referred to other prominent authorities, for in comparison with Matthew and Mark he paid less attention to such traditions as were connected with Peter, Galilee, and Capernaum (in his Gospel there are, for instance, no parallels to Matt. 14:22–16:12 // Mark 6:45—8:26, and only short counterparts to Matt. 17:27—18:35 // Mark 9:33-50, without references to Galilee and Capernaum). As will be demonstrated below in different connections and conclusively in chapter 7, Luke was especially supported on the one hand by Mark (Philemon 24) and on the other by the Hellenists in Jerusalem and particularly by Philip in Caesarea (Acts 21:8). Luke indicated such traditionists by saying he relied upon "servants of the word active from the beginning." It is also to be observed that Luke exclusively referred to oral traditions, when he adduced these original eyewitnesses and servants of the word (1:2, **καθῶς παρέδοσαν ἡμῖν**, "as they have reported orally to us"; cf. **παράδοσις**, "tradition").

When he alluded to several contemporaries occupied with similar works (1:1), Luke literally remarked they had "undertaken" (**ἐπεχείρησαν**) to compose a "report" (**ἀνατάξασθαι διήγησιν**), and this means he knew of similar projects not yet completed. Above all, Luke probably had Mark in mind, since there is reason to assume that both evangelists had personal contacts with each other and since there are particular similarities between their Gospels. Luke, however, did not claim to have read any book of another evangelist, but only indicated the use of individual traditions. He felt it was time now to collect such traditions in written form.

Narratives

After the Matthean heading to which a family tree is attached, and equally after the Lukan prologue which includes a dedication, Matthew and Luke have presented various narratives that deal with Christ's birth and childhood and form the corpus of block 1, whereas Mark offers no counterpart here.

In this first part of the prehistory there are neither triple traditions nor double traditions of the Q type, but two series of Matthean and Lukan units which mostly diverge, although in central points they also converge.

The table above (p. 34) offers a survey of the pericopes in the sequence of each Gospel. An arrow found in the Lukan column indicates that an *alibi* analogy to the Matthean family tree appears later in Luke. On the right hand the distribution of the special material in the relevant section is noted. Three pericopes of each Gospel are framed in dots to indicate that in spite of their different vocabulary they form slight analogies with regard to their topic and clear parallels with regard to their context.

At the beginning and at the end of the sequences compared, the elements of each Gospel differ from those of the other. In the middle section, however, a parallelism of the topics is observable, although the wording is different. The

annunciation of Christ's birth, conveyed by an angel in one case to Joseph and in the other to Mary (Matt. 1:18–25; Luke 1:26–28), as well as the reverence paid to the child by wise men and pious shepherds (Matt. 2:1–12; Luke 2:1–20), constitute topical counterparts which are also contextual parallels. The same is true of the notice about the move to Nazareth (Matt. 2:22–23; Luke 2:39–40).

Certainly those who receive the revelations are different persons: in one case Joseph and in the other Mary; in one case "wise men" and in the other shepherds. But three of the events are really analogous in both traditions: (1) An angel, sent by the Lord to Joseph or Mary and quoting Isa. 7:14, announced the action of the Holy Spirit upon the virgin engaged to Joseph and the birth of a Davidic child whom they should call Jesus (Matt. 1:20–23; Luke 1:31–35). (2) A few pious men, longing for the arrival of the Davidic king or the savior of Israel, experienced the appearance of a brilliant celestial body or of radiant heavenly angels, and thus were made aware of his birth (Matt. 2:2; Luke 2:9–11). (3) They were led to the city of David, Bethlehem, there paid reverence to the newborn descendant of David, and then returned home (Matt. 2:9–12; Luke 2:12–20). In these points there is a substantial analogy of the topics and a significant parallelism in the order. Furthermore, the announcement of Christ's birth and the salutation of the newborn child is the logical center of the relevant sequence in both Gospels.

An influence of Asiatic or Hellenistic myths has often been assumed by modern scholars but imposes even greater problems upon the texts. How could the mythologies of the Gentiles, presently known to students of comparative religion through critical editions, have been available to the narrators of early Christianity? Admittedly the virgin birth and the presence of angels transcend the current view of the world. Both motifs, however, correspond to expectations familiar to the environment of Joseph and Mary, and the birth stories of Matthew and Luke do not indicate any complicated mythology but just contain artless reports on the experiences of a man and a woman graced by God.

The reason why the two versions of the birth stories partly converge and partly diverge is found in the fact that Joseph and Mary had different importance for Matthew and Luke, although the course of events retold in the two Gospels is essentially the same. Matthew has consistently described experiences of Joseph (Matt. 1:16, 19–25; 2:13–15; 19:23), whereas Luke has suggested recollections of Mary (Luke 1:26–38, 39–56; 2:19, 33, 48, 51) and directly emphasized this in two cases (2:19, 51). It is possible that Matthew received some information about Joseph from the Lord's brothers in Jerusalem (Matt. 13:55; Acts 1:14) and that Luke got his stories from some women in Jerusalem who knew Mary (Acts 1:14), and such recollections of eyewitnesses do quite often bear a personal stamp. During the later formation of the traditions, special interests of the evangelists have also contributed to some differences.

1. Matthew reflects a special concern for the fulfillment of holy prophecy. At each moment of the action, scriptural passages are quoted and applied to the

messianic child (Matt. 1:22–23; 2:5–6, 11, 15, 17–18, 23). These didactic remarks form a structural element of the Matthean birth stories. In other contexts too, the intention of the Matthean circle was the promotion of Christian scriptural learning, and the training of scribes for the kingdom of heaven was explicitly said to be a chief task of the apostles (13:52).

This apostolic occupation with Old Testament prophecies explains why the experiences of Joseph are described in terms of scriptural fulfillment. Christ's descendance from David (Matt. 1:1) is delineated up to Joseph on the basis of Chronicles (1:2–17). As a son of David, Joseph himself represents a special sensibility for the prophecies of the Old Testament (1:23; 2:23).

Occupation with scriptural prophecy was also what Matthew meant when he called the visitors of the child "wise men" coming from east (2:1, *μάγοι ἀπὸ ἀνατολῶν*, without article). Here the Greek expression *μάγοι* is not to be explained by peripheral examples of Persian "magi" and the like. Rather, one has to consider biblical traditions. In a characteristic way the word *μάγος* and related expressions are used in the Septuagint version of Daniel, where they denote the hero as an expert of scriptural learning and prophecy, who surpasses the other scholars of the royal court (Dan. 1:20—5:15: Hebr. *'aššāph,* "soothsayer"; Aram. *ḥakkīm,* "wise man"; Greek *μάγος*, "learned man," in the context alternating with *σοφός*, "wise man," and *σοφιστής*, "wisdom expert"). On account of these biblical analogies there is reason to understand the "wise men" in Matthew as experts of Scripture and apocalypticism.

It must also be observed what the evangelist verbally stated about the motive of the wise men (Matt. 2:2): They came to Jerusalem, because they had observed the star of the Messiah at its rise (*εἴδομεν αὐτοῦ τὸν ἀστέρα ἐν τῇ ἀνατολῇ*). By noticing the specific terminology, one will also discover which prophecy was meant to have been studied by them. It was the well-known prophecy of Balaam (Num. 24:17) about the royal "star of Jacob," which God would let rise (*ἀνατελεῖ ἄστρον*). In the New Testament era, the Balaam prophecy was studied intensely by the scholars of the Essenes in the Jordan valley east of Jerusalem (1QM XI. 6f.; *Damascus Document* VII. 18–21; 4 Q Testimonia 9–13). These scholars were also occupied with the secrets of the celestial phenomena (1 Enoch 72:1—82:20; cf. 2 Enoch 11:1—16:8). Accordingly, the homeland of the "wise men coming from east" (*sic,* because in Matt. 2:2 *ἀνατολαί* has no article) should not be sought in some remote parts of Asia but in the Jordan valley where Essene baptists scrutinized the holy prophecies in order "to prepare the way of the Lord" (Isa. 40:3, quoted in 1QS VII.14 with the same intention as in the Gospels). By their precious gifts (Matt. 2:11), the wise men were also meant to pursue fulfillment of prophecy (Isa. 60:6).

The endeavors of Matthew's redactors to promote a Christian scriptural learning were also behind the incorporation of a few particular traditions, which surround the reports common to Matthew and Luke on the annunciation of the birth and the salutation of the child. (1) At the beginning of Matthew, the

genealogy of Jesus (1:1–17) is a piece of scriptural information for which Chronicles was the main source. By tracing the ancestry of Jesus back to Abraham and David (1:1), Matthew demonstrated the accomplishment of salvation history in Christ. (2) In the last part of the prehistory, the occupation with scriptural learning finds an expression in several biblical quotations meant to illustrate the dispensations of God when the child was protected at the flight to Egypt and the move to Nazareth (2:13–23). These special traditions of Matthew were added in order to show that Old Testament oracles were fulfilled before and after the birth of the messianic child. Here the interest was not in the description of the events, since these were supposed to be known to the readers, but rather in prophetic sayings apt to explain why the events in question took place: (*a*) why the family stayed rather shortly in Egypt (2:15); (*b*) why the population around Bethlehem was not willing to accept the message of consolation (2:18); (*c*) why the child Jesus grew up in Nazareth (2:23).

Another characteristic element of the Matthean prehistory is the so-called formula quotations of the following type: "This took place in order to fulfill what had been spoken . . ." (Matt. 1:23; 2:5, 15, 18). They are even found in the main part of the Gospel (3:3; 4:14; 8:17; 12:17–21; 13:14–15; 21:14) and confirm Matthew's didactic concerns. It is also significant that Peter is always seen as standing in front of the disciples when Jesus imparts his instructions to them (4:18; 8:14; 10:2; 16:18; 17:1, 25; 18:21; 19:27; 26:34, 37, 40, 75). For just this reason, the instructions of Jesus which are given first in Galilee and later in Jerusalem, have a transparent reference to problems approaching the early church in Jerusalem (e.g., Matt. 5:10–11, 21, 23; 6:19–20, 25; 7:15, 21; 10:17–25; 24:4–26). Peter and other apostles are said to have taught in Jerusalem, especially in the area of the temple (Acts 2:42, 46; 3:11; 5:42), and to have concentrated their activity on this service of the word (6:2). In doing so, they may have used formula quotations to enforce their arguments, and the redactors of Matthew seem to owe their predilection for such quotations to the apostles.

In the Matthean birth and childhood stories, however, the central elements are the experiences of Joseph and the salutation of the child by wise men coming from east. Joseph manifested an ideal response to the biblical directives and the heavenly dispensations regarding the messianic child, and of all people versed in Scripture, these wise men, who eagerly awaited the appearance of the messianic star, were the first to be confronted with the newborn one. The concern of Matthew or his redactors for scriptural learning was the reason for the concentration of interest on these persons.

2. In the prehistory of Luke, as in that of Matthew, the center is represented by the two pericopes that deal with the annunciation of the birth and the salutation of the child (Luke 1:26–38; 2:1–20). Their orientation, however, is somewhat different. Luke and his traditionists were concerned with the joy of the elect, now greeting the era of salvation, and in a transparent manner referred the events of the past to this present situation. Whereas reflections on salvation history are

dominant in Matthew, eschatological anticipations represent the substantial elements in Luke.

Mary first received the characteristic greeting of the angel (Luke 1:28, 30): "Rejoice (χαῖρε, here in a literal sense), you favored one, because the Lord is with you. . . . For you have found grace with God." This corresponds to the joy of the apostles (Luke 6:23; 10:20; 19:37) and the jubilation of the early church (Acts 2:46; 5:41), to which Mary belonged (1:14). Mary was also reported to have sung in the name of the elect and favored community (Luke 1:47–48): "And my spirit rejoices in God my Savior. . . . From now on all generations will bless me." The joy, which is going to reign in the holy people at the birth of the child, is also the point of the angel's message to the shepherds (Luke 2:10), and the eulogy heard from the celestial host is addressed to those elect who are to receive God's benevolence (2:14). Everything is seen in the perspective of the newborn Christian community and reported in order to confirm its triumphant jubilation. Luke was especially conscious of two circumstances: that Mary had later belonged to the early church (Acts 1:14) and that exultation and jubilation characterized the life of her Christian fellows in Jerusalem (Luke 24:52–53; Acts 2:11, 46–47; 3:8–9, 25; 4:24, 30; 5:41). Moved by the same enthusiasm, the traditionists of Luke told that Mary, seeing before her the child and its community, was overwhelmed by the joy of the dawning salvation era.

Luke's emphasis on the experiences of Mary (2:19, 51) is also to be understood in the light of his general fidelity to recollections about women of importance behind or within the early church. In the prehistory there are the Baptist's mother Elizabeth, the virgin Mary, and the widow Anna in the temple (1:5–23, 39–45; 2:36–38), and in the main parts of the Gospels the sisters Mary and Martha (10:38–42) and some female disciples who followed the apostles to Jerusalem (8:3; 23:49; 24:10). In the Book of Acts, Luke has especially mentioned the widows supported by the Jerusalem church (Acts 6:1), the mother of Mark in Jerusalem (12:12), and the daughters of Philip in Caesarea (21:9). Even if Luke had not met Elizabeth and Mary, he probably received his knowledge about them when he was together with Mark and Philip in Caesarea (according to Philemon 9 and 24, cf. p. 68; Acts 21:8, in a "we" report). These men were among the so-called servants of the word active from the beginning (Luke 1:2), and in Jerusalem there were possibilities for Mark because of his mother (Acts 12:12) and for Philip because of the widows (6:5) to hear what believers and especially the women in Jerusalem told about the mother of the Baptist and the Savior. Luke's reports on Elizabeth and Mary can therefore be supposed to depend on local traditions. The explicit references to personal recollections of Mary (Luke 2:19, 51) even indicate that she had communicated some of her experiences to those believers who elaborated the stories taken over by the evangelist. His concentration of the birth and childhood narratives on the mothers of John and Jesus had to do with his access to such Jerusalem traditions.

In the Lukan birth story, the visitors of the newborn child are not wise men

arriving from east, as in Matthew, but shepherds coming from a field (Luke 2:8). The reason why Luke's traditionists preferred such witnesses is found in the biblical conception of a shepherd as guarantor for protection and welfare (Isa. 40:11; Ps. 23:1, 5; Matt. 9:36; Mark 6:34; Luke 17:7; John 10:9; 21:15–17; Acts 20:28; Eph. 4:11; 1 Peter 5:2). Luke's numerous allusions to distribution of food and to common meals (Luke 4:25; 5:29; etc.) depended on his contacts with Hellenists occupied with the charity meals in Jerusalem (see pp. 120, 124). By denoting the first visitors of the child as shepherds, Luke's traditionists were able to indicate pioneers of their own social activity.

The reports of the annunciation of the birth and the salutation of the child are the fundamental elements of the Lukan prehistory, and in spite of the variations caused by the concentration on Mary, they find essential counterparts in the Matthean prehistory. What precedes and succeeds these basic traditions consists of narrative and poetic elements, peculiar to Luke but intimately connected with the central stories. As an introduction to and a continuation of the central narratives, Luke has added this special material to enrich the fundamental information. First there are three pericopes dealing with the parents and the birth of the Baptist (Luke 1:5–25, 39–56, 57–80), then two dealing with the experiences of Jesus as a child and a boy in the temple (2:21–40, 41–52). Whereas the Baptist stories point toward the birth of the Messiah, expected with enthusiastic joy, the childhood stories proceed from this joyful event. The eschatological jubilation of the early church living in the shadow of the temple (Acts 2:46) has found an expression in both contexts, and a central role is played by the mother of the messianic child seen in the perspective of the early church. Some further comments will verify the connections on both sides with the central topics of block 1 in Luke.

1. Christian proselytes had to be taught about the relationship between John and Jesus, because the environment had sometimes identified the Baptist with the Messiah (Luke 3:15) and because people in Jerusalem still remembered the activity of John (Acts 1:22; 10:37). To this purpose the confrontation of the mother of the Baptist with the mother of the Savior was recalled, and it was portrayed in such a way as to actualize the transition from the old to the new covenant (Luke 1:39–45). Programmatic utterances of Jesus, later quoted by Luke, confirm this function of John in salvation history (7:26–28; 16:16).

Elizabeth was said to have understood the Virgin's pregnancy as introducing the era of salvation, and then Mary was allowed to sing that hymn called "Magnificat" (Luke 1:46–55), in which she personifies the church and welcomes the new era. Concerns of the Jerusalem community are revealed here in connection with the exaltation of the humble (*ταπεινοί* = *ʿanāwīm,* 1:48–52) and the feeding of the hungry (1:53).

The importance of the Baptist as the precursor of the Savior further gave an impulse to the insertion of the preceding stories about the birth of John (1:5–35, 57–66), and in this connection his father was represented as singing a hymn

called "Benedictus" (1:67–79), which is also colored by the enthusiasm of the early Christian believers, as Luke saw them. Characteristic motifs are here: the salvation offered by the son of David (v. 69), the holiness of his adorers (vv. 74–75), the mission of his forerunner (v. 76), the grant of forgiveness and salvation (vv. 77–79a), and the promulgation of the gospel of peace (v. 79b). Zechariah's hymn is a prolepsis of what the apostolic community felt, according to Luke, when it rejoiced over the son of David and the approach of salvation (Acts 2:30, 46–47).

2. Following upon the Christmas gospel, there are two pericopes according to which Jesus as a little child and as a young boy was brought to Jerusalem (Luke 2:21–40, 41–52). Here too, attention is concentrated on Mary and the temple in such a characteristic way that concerns of the primitive Christian community living in the shadow of the temple come to a clear expression.

Simeon's thanksgiving in the temple, known as "Nunc dimittis" (2:29–32), was quoted in order to announce that messianic prophecy had now been replaced by divine reality (v. 30: "for my eyes have seen your salvation"). In this connection, pre-Lukan traditionists in Jerusalem reminded their audience of the Essene prophet Simon, who had worked in Jerusalem with a great success around A.D. 1 (Josephus, *Antiquities* XVII.346; *War* II.113). The two forms of the name, Simeon and Simon, were at the time equivalent (1 Macc. 2, 3, 65, etc.). As proved by the Hymns of Thanksgiving found at Qumran (1QH), such improvised songs based on the biblical vocabulary were cultivated by the Essenes. Thus early Christians in Jerusalem presented Simeon's eulogy, "Nunc dimittis," to make evident that Essene baptists had realized they were to be replaced by Christian confessors.

The influence of the primitive community upon the Lukan prehistory is also confirmed by the subsequent recollection of the widow Anna, who is said to have worshiped in the temple night and day (2:36–38). As the Hebrew widows formed an important group within the primitive community (Acts 6:1), it was encouraging for them to hear about the encounter of a Hebrew widow with the holy child in the temple.

Finally there is the visit of the young boy Jesus to the temple (2:41–52). When he was going to be twelve years old (*ὅτε ἐγένετο*, an inchoative imperfect), that is, before the normal beginning of biblical studies at the age of twelve, the boy impressed the rabbis by his knowledge of divine revelation. Jesus then told his parents that he should be at home in the house of his heavenly Father. By recalling this Jerusalem episode, Luke desired to demonstrate that Jesus, before the usual school age, interpreted Holy Scripture better than Jewish scholars and that he should dispose of the temple, the center of Jewish learning. Once again, Luke ascribed the story to a personal reminiscence of Mary (2:51). Such communications were relevant for the early Christians who, like Jesus in his last days, discussed with the Jewish scribes in the temple area and especially in the portico of Solomon (John 10:23; Acts 4:1; 5:17).

On the whole, the Lukan prehistory represents a remarkable consideration of persons in contact with the temple, such as the father of John, a prophet connected with the Essenes, a widow, and rabbis in the temple area (Luke 1:9, 2:27, 37, 46). The parents of Jesus were also said to sustain contacts with the temple (Luke 2:21, 41). Mary later belonged to the apostolic circle (Acts 1:14), which prayed in the temple (2:42, 46). Thus the personal details of the Lukan prehistory correspond to interests represented by the early church in Jerusalem.

Purpose

Whereas block 2 is characterized by context-parallel triple traditions with the report on the baptism of Jesus as the central topic (below, p. 79), block 1 only contains fragmentary analogies between Matthew and Luke in connection with the annunciation and salutation narratives, to which Mark does not represent any counterparts. The reason for this difference was that relatively uniform recollections of Christ's baptism and related circumstances were still available, while there were only vague traditions about the prehistory.

However, there was a specific need for information about the circumstances under which the child Jesus was born. It was important to inform candidates for baptism about that descendant of David and spiritual Messiah in whom they were to be embodied by their baptism. Within the perspective of tradition history the central elements of block 1—the reports on the annunciation of Christ's spiritual birth and his salutation by pious visitors—are thus to be understood as informative supplements to baptismal teaching. Such teaching is represented by the report on Christ's baptism in block 2, which describes experiences made by Jesus at his baptism with particular regard to experiences to be made by the believers at their baptism—for instance, the reception of the Spirit and the birth to a new life (below, p. 80). In addition, the candidates for baptism had to learn that Jesus was the one who fulfilled the promises given to David, that his birth was caused by the Spirit as was their new birth in baptism, and that he was adored by proselytes when still a newborn child. These are characteristic themes of Matthew's and Luke's central narratives in block 1. A certain analogy is found in a sermon, by which Peter is said to have exhorted proselytes to a baptism in the name of Jesus (Acts 2:38). He prepared this invitation by appealing to the Lord's connection with David (2:25) and possession of the Spirit (2:33). Matthew and Luke were generally led by catechetical ambitions, particularly in view of baptism (Matt. 28:20, as conclusion; Luke 1:4, as introduction), and in their prehistories therefore included such retrospective traditions about the conception of the Davidic child and its first confessors, whereas Mark left out corresponding traditions because he wrote for readers who had already received elementary instruction.

In order to give their reports on the annunciation of the birth and the salutation of the child a wider framework, Matthew and Luke then added special units, on

the one hand confirming the child's descent from David (Matt. 1:1–17) and describing his protection in persecution (2:1–23), and on the other hand defining his relationship to the Baptist (Luke 1:5–25, 39–80). These single traditions were also intended to satisfy interests of proselytes and candidates for baptism.

Block 1 thus forms a background to block 2, in which the report on Christ's baptism is the substantial element.

Block 2
Christ's Baptism and Related Events
Matt. 3:1—4:17 with Parallels

The traditions gathered in block 2 make hearers and readers familiar with John the Baptist, and then especially tell about the baptism of Jesus in the river Jordan, about his temptation in the desert and his departure for Galilee (Matt. 3:1—4:17 with par.).

While there are no context-parallel triple traditions in block 1 and merely a fragmentary specimen of the kind in block 3 (Matt. 7:28–29 with par.), triple contextual parallels are throughout dominant in block 2. They are found in five pericopes of the block (Matt. 3:1–6, 11–12, 13–17; 4:1–11, 12–17, all with contextual parallels in Mark and Luke). As organic extensions of these context-parallel units, also supported by Mark, there are three Matthean-Lukan double traditions which, in distinction to the regular Q traditions, appear in contextual parallelism. One of them forms a separate pericope (Matt. 3:7–10 // Luke 3:7–9, about the preaching of John), the others are surplus elements within two of the five parallel units mentioned above (Matt. 3:12 // Luke 3:17, on the approaching Judge; Matt. 4:2–11a // Luke 4:2b–13, on the temptation of the Messiah). These elements, which lack support in Mark, logically supplement the information given by the triple traditions and cannot be regarded as heterogeneous ingredients. In addition, there are some verses peculiar either to Matthew or to Luke which, in an equally pertinent way, supplement the contextual material (Matt. 3:14–15, a discussion about Christ's baptism; 4:13–16, a scriptural testimony; Luke 3:10–14, 19–20, further information about John).

Consequently, block 2 cannot be traced back to different sources, for here triple, double, and single traditions are nestling in each other. Within this complex there is merely a quantitative difference between the Gospels, either implying that Mark has sometimes presented a shorter version or that Matthew and Luke have included more of the relevant material. On practical accounts the extant traditions were occasionally abbreviated by Mark or supplemented by Matthew and Luke. Yet the common structure is obviously essential, seeing that context-parallel triple traditions serve as the indispensable fundament of the narrative complex and receive support from double and single traditions which are consistently related to the matters treated in the common traditions. Every-

thing forms a triple accord, in which given themes have been followed through in a harmonious way. Owing to this coherence, block 2 is unique within the synoptic material.

Christ's Baptism

The consistent dependence of block 2 upon established traditions is due to the central function of the report on the baptism of Jesus (Matt. 3:13–17 with par.). Plainly the other units of the block are connected with this topic, since the particulars concerning John form a preparation and the narrative on the temptation deals with a sequel to the baptismal event.

However, the story of Christ's baptism was not told as a contribution to his biography but in order to promote the understanding of Christian baptism. The general importance of baptismal instruction was underlined by Matthew in his conclusion and by Luke in his introduction (Matt. 28:19–20, "baptizing them and teaching them"; Luke 1:4, "things of which you have been catechized"). One has to consider this interest when reading the synoptic texts on Christ's baptism.

Indeed the historical baptism of Jesus was portrayed as a sublime prototype of Christian baptism and recorded for the instruction of proselytes. To this purpose, items were emphasized which, *mutatis mutandis,* could be understood to be common experiences of Christ and the Christians.

At the Savior's baptism three moments were significant: (1) Jesus saw the heavens open and the Spirit coming upon him. (2) He heard the voice of God proclaiming him as the Son. (3) Then the heavenly Voice, according to Matthew and Mark, conveyed to Jesus the benevolence of the Father, and according to Luke, confirmed his new birth. Although the experiences of Jesus were unique, the election of the details was connected with a desire to apply them to experiences going to be made by Christian neophytes on a human level.

From the New Testament, numerous passages can be quoted to show that candidates for baptism were also to participate in (1) the distribution of the Spirit, (2) the granting of sonship, and (3) the experience of a new birth:

1. Concerning the Spirit: Matt. 3:11 with par.; John 1:33; 3:5–8; Acts 1:5; 8:15, 17; 9:17; 10:44–48; 11:15–16; 19:6; 1 Cor. 6:11; 12:13; 2 Cor. 1:22; Gal. 3:2; Eph. 1:13; 4:4; Titus 3:5; Heb. 6:4; 1 Peter 1:2; 1 John 5:6–8
2. The sonship: Matt. 5:9; 8:12; 13:38; 17:26; Luke 16:8; 20:36; John 1:12; 11:52; 12:36; Rom. 8:14–21; 2 Cor. 6:18; Gal. 3:26; 4:6; Phil. 2:15; 1 Thess. 5:5; 1 John 3:1, 2, 10; 5:2
3. The new birth: John 3:5–6; Rom. 6:4; Titus 3:5; James 1:18; 1 Peter 2:2

Because the account of Christ's baptism involves emphasis upon experiences which, duly modified, would be imparted to Christians by means of their baptism in the name of Jesus, the synoptic baptismal report is understandable as a text accompanying the baptismal act. In a corresponding way the eucharistic report accompanied the eucharistic ceremony, as will be demonstrated in the commentary on block 12.

Preliminaries and Consequences

From tradition-historical points of view, the liturgical function and life setting of the synoptic baptismal report explains why the other elements of block 2 have also been preserved by the synoptic evangelists in great uniformity. They were all occasioned by the baptismal narrative and placed around it as further illustrations. In catechism it was usual to repeat the story about Christ's baptism, and here a need was felt to include teaching about its direct preliminaries and consequences. As a result, the message of the precursor John was made the subject of an introduction, while the attacks of the tempter on the baptized Son of God were referred to as a sequel to his baptism.

The synoptic pericopes dealing with the Baptist and the tempter were thus also created to serve the information of candidates for baptism in the early church, and the circumstances implied that such information was needed. On the one hand, the proselytes of the community were still familiar with the baptismal movement of John (Acts 1:22; 10:37; 11:16) and had therefore to be informed about the relationship between the Baptist and the Savior, with regard both to their connection and to their difference (Matt. 3:11 with par.). On the other hand, the neophytes had to be warned against temptations meeting in this world, especially with regard to those which Jesus had resisted in an exemplary way (Matt. 4:3, 6 and 9 // Luke 4:3, 9 and 6): aspirations for material welfare ("not bread alone"), miraculous achievements ("throw yourself down"), and political influence ("all kingdoms of the world").

Thus the entire contents of block 2 were determined by subjects of baptismal teaching. As the oral traditions had received a rather fixed structure in this context, the pericopes of block 2 became dominated by context-parallel triple traditions in striking dissimilarity from those of blocks 1 and 3.

Here the consonance, based upon context-parallel triple traditions, is even intensified by context-parallel double traditions of Matthew and Luke, a phenomenon that does not appear otherwise (above, p. 26). Without complete parallels in Mark, Matthew and Luke have illustrated John's exhortation to conversion and his presentation of the Messiah, as well as the drama of temptation, by textual units that correspond to each other with regard to their contents and context (Matt. 3:7–10 // Luke 3:7–9; Matt. 3:12 // Luke 3:17; Matt. 4:2–11a // Luke 4:2b–13).

These context-parallel double traditions differ from the Q traditions, which always consist of *alibi* analogies. And they were not taken over from any particular layer of traditions, because they form absolutely consistent elements of the extant triple traditions, so that only their absence in Mark stamps them as double traditions.

It is especially obvious in the Markan treatment of the temptation story (Mark 1:12–13) that certain traditions contained in block 2 have been shortened by the second evangelist. Mark has only mentioned that Jesus fasted and was tempted,

but has not mentioned either to which temptation he was exposed or that he subdued the devil, as told by Matthew and Luke. After alluding to the desert, to the forty days, and to the satanic temptation, Mark abruptly intimated that Jesus was "among the wild beasts" and that "the angels served him" (v. 13b). The context-parallel double traditions of Matthew and Luke cannot have originated from these brief Markan notes. Rather, it must have been Mark who curtailed the story, presupposing that his readers were familiar with a more detailed tradition.

Without a certain knowledge of Christ's trial and triumph, Mark's reference to the animals and the angels remains senseless. A modern reader can reconstruct the process with the aid of Matthew's information about the angels (Matt. 4:11). Mark, however, could not ask the original readers to consult the written text of Matthew in order to make the story reasonable. Instead, the hearers and the readers, whom Mark had in mind, must have been generally informed about the baptism of Jesus and his temptation, so that he could expect them to understand the hints at the angels and the animals in the desert. As former candidates for baptism, Mark's readers had already been confronted with Christ's baptism and temptation. Mark therefore found it sufficient to remind hearers and readers first of John's person and preaching and then of Christ's baptism, after which he only hinted at the temptation in the desert.

By his reference to the animals and the angels Mark in fact recalled to memory Psalm 91, which Matthew and Luke have quoted in their parallel reports (Matt. 4:6 // Luke 4:10). According to this psalm, understood as messianic prophecy, the Messiah would be exposed to dangerous lions and serpents (Ps. 91:13), but protected by angels (91:11–12), and the verses in question are exactly what Matthew and Luke have cited. It becomes evident that Psalm 91 had been used in Christian catechism and that here the animals and the angels were interpreted as opponents and defenders, respectively, of Christ and the neophytes.

Mark's version of the temptation story thus proves to depend on a shortening of catechetical traditions which, in the versions of Matthew and Luke, appear in a more complete form because these evangelists had a great concern for kerygma and instruction. Seeing that Mark mainly addressed readers who had received elementary instruction, it becomes understandable that he left out several of the elements used for Christian catechism. From the traditions in question, Mark therefore adopted no material corresponding to what Matthew and Luke have gathered in block 1, and less material found within the complex here called block 2.

Transition to Galilee

All Synoptic Gospels agree in letting part I at the end of block 2 be concluded with a pericope in which it is stated that Jesus passed to Galilee just after his baptism (Matt. 4:12–17 with par.). This triple unit forms a bridge between parts I and II, but it remains in the perspective of the Judean baptismal story and does

not belong to the subsequent Galilean section. Here the activity of Jesus in Galilee is only touched upon in the form of a summary, whereas the details imply a retrospect on the Baptist and Christ's baptism in Judea.

Matthew and Mark have begun this Judean retrospect with a reference to John the Baptist (Matt. 4:12 // Mark 1:14), and Luke with one to Christ's reception of the Spirit (Luke 4:14). By all evangelists Galilee is here mentioned only by name, without any further details. Matthew has a reference to Capernaum, but in the traditions that he preserved, the city was vaguely seen at a distance as a place on the shore of the lake in the region of two northern tribes (Matt. 4:13). What also confirms the Judean perspective of the pericope is the Scripture quotation that follows, since Matthew has presented Galilee here as an object of foreign mission, in which the light of the gospel would be spread from the sea to across the Jordan (4:15–16). Matthew and Mark have then formulated the Lord's admonition to conversion (Matt. 4:17 // Mark 1:15) in literal analogy to John's earlier preaching (Matt. 3:2; Mark 1:14; Luke 3:3). Luke has only concluded the block by a summary reference to a successful teaching of Jesus in Galilee (Luke 4:15).

In a significant way the synoptic evangelists thus let the Galilean outlook here analyzed culminate in Christ's missionary activity. Matthew and Mark did it by saying he began preaching (*κηρύσσειν*), Luke that he was teaching (*ἐδίδασκεν*). Both expressions were meant to illustrate the result of the impulse given at his baptism. On the whole, the context-parallel triple tradition in question recalls baptismal topics, for it refers back to the person of John, the Spirit empowering Jesus since his baptism, and his admonition to conversion in continuation of John's preaching. Originally this piece of tradition was seen in the perspective of Judean neophytes, who had been taught about John the Baptist and the baptism of Jesus and had also heard in general terms of Christ's subsequent activity in Galilee. Just as the whole sequence found in block 2 includes material based on baptismal teaching, so also does the concluding reference to Christ's fruitful proclamation of the kingdom and the conversion especially apply to candidates for baptism.

Chapter Five

Part II: Jesus in Galilee and Adjacent Countries

Matt. 4:18—18:35 with Parallels

After the short outlook upon the activity of the Master in Galilee found at the end of part I in block 2, the major part II (Matt. 4:18—18:35 with parallels) begins with block 3 (Matt. 4:18—7:29 with par.). Here variations between the Gospels dominate. Matthew and Mark start with the calling of Peter's group on the west coast of the Lake of Galilee (Matt. 4:18–22 // Mark 1:16–20), Luke with a sermon of Jesus in Nazareth (Luke 4:16–30). Then in blocks 4 and 5 various examples of a healing and teaching activity in Capernaum and the next surroundings are cited (Matt. 8:1—13:52 with par.), followed in block 6 by an extent of the action to other regions in the north (Matt. 13:53—17:11 with par.). Part II ends in block 7 with Christ's return to Galilee and his instruction of the apostles in Peter's house at Capernaum (Matt. 17:22—18:35 with par.).

Block 3
Activity in and near Capernaum
Matt. 4:18—7:29 with Parallels

In the following presentation, block 3 designates various texts that are specific to each synoptic writer, although their common task is to describe Christ's first activity in Galilee. According to Matthew and Mark, the beginning took place in Capernaum (Matt. 4:13, 18 // Mark 1:16, 21), according to Luke in Nazareth (Luke 4:16). As the above tables show (pp. 35–44), the deviation is not accidental. In each block from 3 up to 12 the frequency of context-parallel triple traditions decreases with their distance from the passion story in block 12, and in this perspective block 3 represents a minimum of contextual agreement. From the very beginning, part II is marked by these deviations in block 3, and here the disjointedness of the three Gospels represents an extremity of the fluctuation between blocks 3 to 12, which is illustrated by the tables.

The only context-parallel triple tradition found in block 3 is a short note about the enthusiasm of those who listened to the preaching of Jesus ("like one with

authority, not like the scribes," Matt. 7:28–29 // Mark 1:22 // Luke 4:32). Although most synoptic commentaries have missed the point, this note does in fact occupy the same place in the general flow of the reports.[1] On the other hand, it does not accomplish the same function in each Gospel. Matthew has let the note about the reaction of the public conclude the Sermon on the Mount, while Mark and Luke have used it to introduce a series of healings in Capernaum. For the rest, block 3 consists of quite disparate elements.

Obviously the deviations with regard to the Galilean beginnings were connected with various interests of the evangelists. Matthew was especially concerned with the instruction of the apostles given in the Sermon on the Mount (Matt. 5:1—7:27), and for that reason he only afterward treated the healings in Capernaum to which Mark and Luke paid more attention. Mark did not refer to anything like the Sermon on the Mount, but at once concentrated on several events in Capernaum (Mark 1:21–38). Luke also reported about the healings there, but started with a discussion in Nazareth concerning Christ's mission to Israel and the Gentiles (Luke 4:16–30). He stood less close to the apostle Peter than Matthew and Mark, and was also somewhat less interested in the primary mission to Israel. While later he emphasized the transition of Peter to the gentile mission (Acts 10:28), he mentioned the calling of Peter and his group (Matt. 4:18–22 // Mark 1:16–20) only at the end of the pericopes comprised in block 3 (Luke 5:1–11), and here made the expansion of the mission to all people the point (Luke 5:10).

The three synoptic writers thus heavily deviate from one another in the paragraphs here designated as block 3. A certain tendency of Mark and Luke toward the same order is found in their reports on the healings in Capernaum (Mark 1:21–39 // Luke 4:31–44), but since Matthew differs from them in this context, the only example of a triple parallel is the above-mentioned note on the reaction of the audience (Matt. 7:28–29 with par.). All other parts of block 3 are surprisingly irregular.

Because of this complete disunity regarding the very first activity of the Master, every hypothesis implying a literary dependence of the Gospels upon one another is unnatural. The same verdict must be passed upon derivations from a common document such as a proto-gospel or a logia source. Both the various utilization theories and the proto-gospel hypothesis as well as the two-source theory lead to the impossible outcome that each redactor or editor would stubbornly and radically have changed his source in block 3, just to be original when dealing with the very beginning of Christ's public ministry. Everyone would then, independently of the others but in rhythmic progression, have felt this lust for changes less and less in the further presentation, and finally yielded to contextual parallelism in block 12. Whether the synoptic evangelists, in the light of the aforesaid theories,

1. F. Neirynck, "The Sermon on the Mount in the Gospel Synopsis," *Ephemerides Theologicae Lovanienses* 52/4 (1976): 350–57.

are depicted as literary editors of an existing gospel or another document, two of them or all three must in these cases be supposed to have taken an extraordinarily peculiar attitude to the material. Analogies to such writers are known nowhere. What cannot even be regarded as being in the least possible is that two or three editors would have first avoided and then enlarged the parallelism, accurately marching in step with one another. All literary source theories are burdened with such absurdities.

The synoptic traditionists and editors will, rather, have received and ordered their units in block 3 from scattered reminiscences orally transmitted. In this block the strongly reduced parallelism was connected with the distance at which the events here to be told were lying in the retrospective of the Jerusalem church, whereas later blocks had to deal with closer reminiscences. With regard to the beginnings of the preaching activity of Jesus in Galilee, it was only vaguely outlined traditions that were at the disposal of the early church and the traditionists, while more established recollections were available concerning the final phase of his life in Jerusalem. Between these extremes the fluctuation of the context-parallel triple pericopes took place.

Independently of each other, the traditionists and the evangelists had to outline the beginnings in Galilee, as well as they could, on the basis of separate tradition elements. According to Papias (quoted below on p. 161), it was short expositions of Peter (*διδασκαλίαι*) that were used in the Gospel of Mark. Even if this information was given only with regard to Mark, such independent short units may also be supposed behind many pericopes of the other Gospels, especially those in the Galilean section. Since a fixed total structure, as the one found in the passion narrative, was lacking in regard to Galilee, the selection and order of the units were here, more than elsewhere, determined by the personal interests of the traditionists and the evangelists. In the pericopes here comprised as block 3, the following interests may be found to have been decisive.

Matthew—and the Greek translators of the First Gospel as well (Eusebius *EH* III.39.16)—especially wanted to portray Jesus in his role of teacher. For that reason, the Master's teaching in the Galilean synagogues was mentioned in the first place (Matt. 4:23). For the same reason, the whole material of the First Gospel was arranged on the basis of speeches given to instruct the apostles. Six characteristic speeches of this kind are found in Matthew 5—7; 10; 13; 18; 23; and 24—25, and they may be defined as (1) the Sermon on the Mount (5:1—7:27), (2) the commission speech (9:37—10:42), (3) the parable speech (13:1–52), (4) the discipline speech (17:24—18:35), (5) the anti-Pharisaic speech (23:1–39), and (6) the apocalyptic speech (24:1—25:46). Instruction of Christian scribes was explicitly mentioned as the point of the parable speech (13:52). Above all, the entire report culminates with the Lord's commandment to extend his teaching to all nations (28:20). Throughout this Gospel the apostles stand in the center, and they are thought of as the primary recipients and the further intermediaries of Christ's instruction concerning the kingdom of heaven.

It was because of this concentration upon the apostles as the objects and subjects of instruction that Matthew, in block 3, did not introduce Christ's activity in Galilee by a healing in Capernaum as did Mark, or by a discussion in Nazareth as did Luke. Right after the calling of the first apostles, Matthew instead mentioned a teaching activity in the whole of Galilee, by which great multitudes of people in Syria, Galilee, Decapolis, Judea, and Perea were attracted (4:23–25). These countries later became the mission fields of the early church (Acts 9:10, 31; 11:19), and so the first teaching of Jesus was supposed to have prepared the apostolic kerygma. Since the large crowds from the countries mentioned are then referred to at the beginning and the end of the Sermon on the Mount (Matt. 5:1; 7:28), they were, together with the apostles, presented as the first hearers of Christ's public teaching. As soon as possible, the Matthean circle has thus endeavored to offer a detailed instruction about participation in the new kingdom (Matt. 5:2—7:27).

It is also characteristic that elements meant to be helpful to solve problems of the early church were taken up in the Sermon on the Mount. This is illustrated by the topics of poverty and humility (Matt. 5:3–9), persecution (5:10–12), Mosaic laws (5:17–48), religious practice (6:1, etc.), material possessions (6:16–24), daily provision (6:25–34; 7:7–11), judgment about others (7:1–5, 15–20), and confession and obedience (7:21–27). The words quoted were probably based on reminiscences of Christ's teaching in Galilee and later in Jerusalem, but their presentation in the actual form corresponds to interests of the apostles and the early church. Because of this concern for instruction, the Matthean circle has moved the Sermon on the Mount to the beginning of the report on Jesus in Galilee.

A redactional movement of the material comprised in the Sermon on the Mount toward the beginning of the Galilean section is also reflected in *alibi* analogies between the introduction to the sermon in Matthew and elements found in later parts of Mark and Luke. It is confirmed by that unique context-parallel triple tradition which, in Matthew, serves as the conclusion of the sermon in question, and in Mark and Luke as the introduction to a series of healings in Capernaum. To illustrate the situation, a table is presented below, where the symbol)(is placed in front of the *alibi* analogies and the symbol // in front of the contextual parallels (see p. 88).

The first verse of Matthew's introduction to the Sermon on the Mount in block 3 (Matt. 4:23) contains information about the wandering of Jesus through Galilee, to which Mark and Luke present later counterparts, though still in block 3. Almost the same note is also found in later blocks, introducing the sending out of the Twelve according to Matthew in block 4, according to Mark and Luke in block 6 (Matt. 9:35; Mark 6:6; Luke 9:6). Obviously this note was a stereotyped formula, which Matthew used both for his Sermon on the Mount and for his commission speech, while Mark and Luke used it for the sending out of the Twelve on which they have reported in a much later context.

Frame Topics of Matthew's Sermon on the Mount
in Block 3 and Analogies in Blocks 4–6

// = contextual parallel,)(= *alibi* analogy

Topics	Block 3	Block 4	Block 5	Block 6
Preaching tour in Galilee	Mt 4:23)(Mk 1:38–39 //Lk 4:43–44	Mt 9:35 (Mt 9:36—10:42, sending of the Twelve)		Mk 6:6 cf. Lk 9:6 (Mk 6:7–13 //Lk 9:1–6, sending of the Twelve)
Crowd of people	Mt 4:24–25		Mt 12:15–16 //Mk 3:7–12 (Mk 3:9, a boat))(Lk 6:17–19	
Jesus on a mountain	Mt 5:1a		Mk 3:13a)(Lk 6:12 (Lk 6:17, a field)	
Disciples around him	Mt 5:1b		Mk 3:13b)(Lk 6:13a (Mk 3:14–19; Lk 6:13b–16, election of the Twelve)	
Ingress of speech	Mt 5:2		Lk 6:20a	
Contents of speech	Mt 5:3—7:27		Lk 6:20b–49	

Enthusiasm of the crowd	Mt 7:28
	//Mk 1:22a
	//Lk 4:32a			

Authority of the speaker	Mt 7:29
	//Mk 1:22b
	//Lk 4:32b			

The same is true of the following verses of the introduction to the Sermon on the Mount which defines the homelands of the listeners and presents Jesus with the apostles on a mountain (Matt. 4:24—5:1). It is later in block 5 that Mark and Luke, with similar words, have described the two circumstances and used them to introduce the election of the apostles (Mark 3:7–13; Luke 6:12–19). Remarkably enough, however, a contextual parallel to these parts of Mark and Luke is also found in Matthew's block 5 (Matt. 12:15–21), here implying a shortened duplicate of the introduction to the Sermon on the Mount in block 3. This short note of Matthew in block 5 is not followed up by any speech, nor is that true of its contextual parallel in Mark, although the reference to listeners anticipates some instruction. It is only Luke's parallel in block 5 (Luke 6:12–19) which serves a meaningful purpose, for it prepares the Sermon on the Plain (6:20–49). Because the Matthean contextual parallel fulfills no such function in block 5 (Matt. 12:15–21), it may be understood as the reminiscence of a tradition that is reflected in the contextual parallels of Mark and more fully in Luke. In the preliterary tradition, block 5 contained a protoplasm of the relevant introduction. Matthew has inserted this protoplasm in block 3 and used it to introduce the Sermon on the Mount, yet left behind a reminiscence of the protoplasm in block 5, its old position. For other reasons, Mark let the protoplasm remain a torso, and only Luke used it adequately in order to introduce his subsequent instruction speech, the Sermon on the Plain (below, p. 91).

The conclusion of the Sermon on the Mount ("the crowds were amazed at his teaching, because he taught as one with authority") is the only context-parallel triple tradition within block 3 (Matt. 7:28–29 // Mark 1:21–22 // Luke 4:31–32). In order to refer this traditional formula back to the Sermon on the Mount, the editors of Matthew introduced it by a redactional formula which occurs several times in Matthew: "when Jesus had finished saying these things" (Matt. 7:28, and later in 11:1; 13:53; 19:1; 26:1). Matthew was thus able to describe the enthusiasm of the people over the sermon with the same words as those used by Mark and Luke concerning the preaching of Jesus in Capernaum. However, while all the synoptic evangelists took up an obviously traditional formula about Christ's preaching success and while the formula now appears in contextual parallelism within the synoptic reports, it fulfills various functions in the framework. Matthew used the formula as a pivot for his insertion of the Sermon on the Mount into block 3, letting it serve as the conclusion of the sermon. Mark and Luke used the phrase about people's enthusiasm in block 3 as a bridge to their subsequent description of miracles in Capernaum.

Utilization theories cannot explain the remarkable flexibility of the synoptic texts here discussed and compared on the basis of the above table.

If one takes Matthew as the source of Mark and Luke, then Mark and Luke would have found Matthew's Sermon on the Mount too awkward within block 3, yet kept its conclusion and connected it with the subsequent healings. Luke would then have inserted a counterpart to the introduction of the Sermon on the Mount

and a shortened version of this sermon in block 5, but let it be held on a plain. Mark would have interpolated a counterpart to the same introduction in block 5 without letting it be followed by any sermon. If a priority of Matthew is assumed in this context, then Mark and Luke would have ruthlessly distorted a textual arrangement which already was consistent and meaningful, impressive and instructive.

Markan priority, as presupposed by the two-source theory, offers no better explanation of those *alibi* analogies between the frameworks of the Sermon on the Mount and the Sermon on the Plain which are found in blocks 3 and 5, respectively. In the Second Gospel there are but slight traces of analogies to the frameworks of the sermons quoted by the First and Third Gospels. Mark has first in block 3 information about the enthusiasm of the audience (Mark 1:22), and then in block 5 a description of the listeners and disciples on a mountain (3:7–19). These fragments of Mark could never have given rise to the Sermon on the Mount or the Sermon on the Plain.

Nor can the relevant text complex of Luke, as the two-source theory assumes, have resulted from a redactional combination of Mark's description of the listeners and disciples on a mountain (Mark 3:7–19; Luke 6:12–19) and a piece of Q containing the sermon on a plain (Luke 6:20–29). An obstacle for this derivation from Mark is the fact that Luke has not mentioned the multitude first and the apostles next, as Mark has done, but represents the opposite sequence (Luke 6:12–16 the apostles, 17–19 the multitude).

The only possible explanation of the peculiarity of the Second Gospel found in the present context is that Mark retained a tradition according to which the numerous listeners and the disciples were gathered to hear a speech, but left out details of the speech in question. Since his readers did not ask so much for elementary teaching, he refrained from bringing the instructive speech intended for the assembled crowd.

Yet the Markan text betrays a feeling that anyhow the crowd should hear a speech. To bring about a connection between the crowd and a later speech, Mark indicated that Jesus secured a boat on the shore (Mark 3:9, emphasized above in the table), and this is the boat he is said to have used later when giving the parable speech (4:1). By means of the boat, Mark let the later parable speech be a substitute for that instructive speech which the earlier reference to the audience makes the readers expect. Here he differs from Matthew and Luke, who have let their references to the audience directly anticipate instructive speeches given on a mount and on a plain. In this case Mark cannot have induced Matthew and Luke to their descriptions of the audience and their quotations of extensive speeches. On the contrary, Mark must be supposed to contain fragments of traditions which Matthew and Luke have displayed in their sermons on the mount and on the plain.

It is merely the Gospel of Luke that represents a neutral sequence with reference to the election of the apostles and Christ's teaching in block 5, while

Matthew and Mark have undergone editorial changes. (1) Matthew's way of presenting the multitude and the apostles as hearers of the Sermon on the Mount (Matt. 5:1, "his disciples came to him") is not in correspondence with the Gospel's other references to the apostles. In block 3, Matthew had thus far mentioned the calling of only four disciples (4:18–22), whereas the twelve apostles were introduced much later in block 5 (10:1–4). This confirms the observation that Matthew's Sermon on the Mount has been advanced to block 3 because of a special concern for apostolic teaching. Here the Matthean report cannot be regarded as primary. (2) Mark has, through its description of the audience in block 5 (Mark 3:7–12), let an instructional speech be anticipated without bringing it. Instead, a redactional connection between the multitude and the later parable speech was established by means of the boat mentioned above. This abridgment must also have been the result of an editorial activity and points to a reduced need for information about elementary teaching. (3) It is only Luke who has offered a logical sequence within the relevant parts of block 5. As the table shows (p. 88), Luke first presented the Master on a mountain where he called the twelve apostles (Luke 6:12–16), and then let him stand with them on a field (6:17a) where a multiethnic crowd had gathered (6:17b–19). There were representatives here from all over Palestine (called Judea by Luke), especially Jerusalem, and also from Phoenicia, to which the Hellenists of Jerusalem were later going to bring the gospel (Acts 11:19; 15:3). Whether the reference to the plain came from Luke or from his traditionists, the election of the apostles and the presence of the multitude appear in natural sequence as they are described by Luke. The references to the multitude (6:19) and the disciples (6:20a) form a logical introduction to the subsequent instruction (6:20b–49). It seems that in this case Luke has more faithfully than Matthew and Mark reflected the preliterary tradition. However, nothing beyond such a dependence on tradition can be asserted. The Hellenistic style of the Third Gospel and the localization of the sermon to a plain do not justify any suggestion that Luke's text influenced the corresponding passages of Matthew and Mark. Further remarks on Luke's Sermon on the Plain will be presented below when we are dealing with block 5.

Concluding this excursus on the frameworks of Matthew's Sermon on the Mount in block 3 and Luke's Sermon on the Plain in block 5, the following observations can be made concerning the relationships between tradition and redaction within block 3, in which context the Synoptic Gospels represent different pictures owing to the interests of the authors.

Matthew has inserted the Sermon on the Mount as early as possible in block 3, providing it with an introduction reminiscent of those used by Mark and Luke in block 5, and has also enriched the contents of the sermon to a considerable extent. A traditional formula about the enthusiasm of the hearers, which is the only context-parallel triple tradition found in block 3, served as the pivot for the sermon (Matt. 7:28–29 with par.). The insertion was due to Matthew's concern for an early presentation of apostolic teaching. However, in block 5 Matthew also

retained a reminiscence of traditions represented there by Mark and Luke (Matt. 12:15–21 // Mark 3:7–12 // Luke 6:17–19). In other regards, Matthew has shortened the material of block 3 in comparison with Mark and Luke.

On the other hand, Mark has made an effort in block 3 to reach Capernaum as soon as possible in the narrative and has given detailed reports of healings there. Right after the calling of Peter and three other apostles (Mark 1:16), a series of Capernaum reports sets in (1:21), and Capernaum then remains in the center of interest within block 3 and beyond. A few notes in block 3 vaguely hint at the environs of the city (1:35, 39), a few in block 4 also (1:40, 45), but later the story refers to Capernaum again (2:1). After the visit of Jesus to the customs station in Gennesaret (2:13–14), the narrative remains connected with the shore between Capernaum and Gennesaret up to the parable speech in block 5 (4:1–34). Block 6 then describes travels of Jesus from Capernaum and Gennesaret (6:35) in various directions, but in block 7 Jesus returns to a teaching in Capernaum (9:33). This strong concentration of Mark on Capernaum may be ascribed to the evangelist's special connection with Peter, whose mother-in-law owned a house in Capernaum and served as the hostess of Jesus and the disciples (1:29; the same house is meant in 2:1; 3:20, 32, and then mentioned in 9:33). It must further be observed that Mark's mother was the hostess of a house-church in Jerusalem which Peter was connected with (Acts 12:12), and here Peter may be supposed to have imparted reminiscences from Capernaum and Galilee to Mark. The Second Gospel's special orientation in blocks 3 to 7 is conveniently explained by these personal circumstances, on which more is to be said in chapter 7.

In the middle of block 3, Luke has told about the Capernaum healings in an order similar to that of Mark (Luke 4:31–44). Remarkably enough, however, Luke has even developed a more vivid style than Mark in this context (e.g., Luke 4:34, *ἔα!*; 4:35, *εἰς τὸ μέσον*; 4:39, *ἐπετίμησεν*; 4:41, *κραυγάζοντα*; 4:42, *ἦλθον ἕως αὐτοῦ, καὶ κατεῖχον αὐτόν*). Probably it was from Mark that Luke heard a report about the events in question, then he just popularized it further, and this explains the variations better than any theory of literary elaboration.

At the beginning of block 3, Luke has inserted a report on Christ's preaching in Nazareth (Luke 4:16–30). Because it presupposes a knowledge of earlier healings in Capernaum (4:23), this pericope must have been moved by Luke to the beginning of the Galilean section. The purpose was to satisfy the interest of Luke and his traditionists in the mission to the Gentiles, here confirmed by the words of Jesus about sending the first prophets of the old covenant to a Phoenician widow and a Syrian officer (4:25–27). Luke also knew of the later Hellenistic mission to Phoenicia and Syria (Acts 11:19). It was only at the end of block 3, after the healings in Capernaum dealt with in the middle of the block, that Luke inserted the calling of Peter and the sons of Zebedee (Luke 5:1–11). This calling took place in the presence of a great multitude (5:1, 3), and the overwhelming catch of fish in the deep water also points toward numerous conversions of people (5:9–10). In spite of his initial skepticism, Peter was thus made aware of the mission to

the nations, as he was later caused to replace particularism by universalism (Acts 10:15, 34–35). Because of Luke's concern for the mission to the Gentiles, the evangelist has not only prepared the central section of block 3 by reporting on that sermon in Nazareth but also concluded it by telling of Peter's calling to become a fisher of men.

In the arrangement of the pericopes found in block 3, the interest of the Matthean circle in the instruction of the apostles thus played a decisive role in the First Gospel, the association of Mark with Peter in the Second Gospel, and the occupation of Luke with the universal mission in the Third Gospel. The personal interests of the traditionists and the evangelists did here influence the reports more strongly than in later blocks. Because of the chronological and geographical distance of the Galilean events from the Jerusalem church any overall structures of the reminiscences were missing. It is true that Mark and Luke seem to have dealt with the pericopes concerning healings in Capernaum as a conglomerate, but concerning the same topic Matthew has only presented some *alibi* analogies later found in block 4. Except for this partial correspondence between Mark and Luke, the synoptic evangelists have always made personal choices in order to arrange their material in block 3.

Block 4
Events Before and After the Call of Levi/Matthew
Matt. 8:1—10:42 with Parallels

Most of the pericopes comprised in block 4 belong to the First Gospel (Matt. 8:1—10:42, partly with parallels). Here they form a systematic row of nineteen units distributed on two halves: first a series of ten miracles and a couple of other episodes surrounding the call of the publican (Matt. 8:1—9:34), then a circumstantial mission speech (9:35—10:42). On separate points in the first half of the block, Matthew contains four context-parallel triple traditions, the first one dealing with a leper (Matt. 8:1–4 with par.), the others with a paralytic, a publican, and the problem of fasting (9:1–17 with par.). While in Mark and Luke the publican appears under his pre-Christian name of Levi, in Matthew he is called by his Christian name of Matthew, but the obvious conformity of the context-parallel stories proves that it was a question of the same tax collector. All other pericopes occurring in the first half of Matthew's block 4 and even all belonging to the second half of the block consist of nonparallel triple or Q traditions and Matthean special units, which reflects a striving of the Matthean circle to fill the complex here designated as block 4 with rich material.

Mark and Luke present counterparts to the four contextual parallels found in the first half of block 4 in Matthew but let them follow directly upon each other: leper, paralytic, publican, fasting (Mark 1:40—2:22 // Luke 5:12–39). Otherwise the Gospels of Mark and Luke contain no units in block 4 with the exception

of a short note about Jesus in the wilderness (Mark 1:45b // Luke 5:12). Much later, in blocks 6 and 8, they also bring a few short *alibi* analogies to Matthew's detailed commission speech which fills the second half of block 4 (cf. below, pp. 98–99).

What is especially striking in the first half of block 4 according to Matthew is the systematic combination of the four context-parallel triple traditions (italicized in the table below) with several nonparallel triple and Q traditions, completed by two special traditions inserted at the end of the row in order to get a series of ten healings. Some elements of instruction on discipleship have also been added here. In its present arrangement, the Matthean aggregate thus forms a succession of reports on miracles and discipleship according to the following scheme, in which T symbolizes a triple tradition, while ↑ or ↓ indicates that parallels are found in earlier or later contexts:

Miracles as Topic	Discipleship as Topic
Matt. 8:1–4 *leper* (T, context-parallel)	
8:5–13 centurion (Q↓)	
8:14–15 mother-in-law (T↑)	
8:16–17 healings in the evening (T↑)	
	8:18–22 conditions of discipleship (Q↓)
8:23–27 stilling the storm (T↓)	
8:28–34 Gadara (T↓)	
9:1–8 *paralytic* (T, context-parallel)	
	9:9–13 calling of *Matthew* (T, context-parallel)
	9:14–17 no *fasting* required (T, context-parallel)
9:18–26 Jairus, hemorrhage (T↓)	
9:27–31 two blind men (S^{Mt})	
9:32–34 a mute (S^{Mt})	

In the list of miracle reports in the left-hand column, there are two italicized units representing context-parallel triple traditions and dealing with the healings of the leper and the paralytic. These have been combined with five *alibi*-analogous triple traditions, one Q tradition, and two Matthean special traditions. Consequently the entire complex implies ten miracle reports, but since the pericope dealing with the daughter of Jairus and the woman suffering from hemorrhage includes a twofold miracle and the report on stilling the storm

depicts a prodigy of nature, one may speak either of ten healings or of ten miracles.

Through this accumulation of miracles, the Matthean circle evidently wanted to illustrate the authority that the hearers of the Sermon on the Mount had discerned in Jesus (Matt. 7:29). In fact, the first half of block 4 in Matthew is to be understood as resulting from such editorial measures. No fewer than five of the miracle reports here at issue are triple traditions that do not form contextual parallels but *alibi* analogies, so that most likely they were inserted here to intensify the effect of the contextual parallels about the leper and the paralytic. Moreover, the two short and not very important particular traditions about two blind men and a mute were certainly added toward the end of the series for the purpose of maintaining the round number of ten miracles. Finally, each unit has been linked to its predecessor through a vague note on time and place. It begins with the formula, "when he came down from the mountain" (Matt. 8:1), and similar phrases introduce every pericope that follows. Accordingly, the sequence of ten miracles in Matthew 8 and 9 must be the result of careful editorial work.

In the right-hand column in the above list of pericopes that belong to the first half of block 4 in Matthew, three units having to do with discipleship are quoted. The first one is a Q tradition, to which Luke has a parallel at the beginning of the travel narrative, and the two others represent context-parallel triple pericopes.

In two places these references to discipleship interrupt the series of ten miracles, but in fact they are organic components of the present sequence. (1) The editors of Matthew have inserted the report on two persons wanting to follow Jesus in the very moment when the Lord had declared his intention to cross the lake from Capernaum (Matt. 8:18). In this way a logical succession of the pericopes was established through systematic redaction. (2) The conversion of the publican in Gennesaret and the subsequent discussion on fasting appear in direct succession to the story of the healing of the paralytic in Capernaum (9:1–8). Since all of these units are context-parallel triple reports, the sequence was here based upon a common synoptic tradition. The miracle and discipleship topics found in Matthew 8 and 9 are thus standing in logical relation to each other.

By means of the reports on the ten miracles the editors intended to confirm the authority of Jesus manifested in his Sermon on the Mount (7:29). Just as the general topic of the sermon in block 3 is that of conditions for discipleship, so the miracle stories in block 4 were used to emphasize the conditions and consequences of discipleship (8:22; 9:9, 15).

The reports on miracles and the references to discipleship are emphatically bound together in the central unit of the sequence in question, that is, the story about the calling of the publican Matthew (9:9–13). It is as the great physician that Jesus brings Matthew to conversion and discipleship (9:12), and both the preceding and the subsequent healings illustrate his capacity in this regard. Moreover, the replies given to the candidates for discipleship and the mastering of the tempest (8:18–22, 23–27) prepare the calling of the publican, which implied

that he left everything behind and followed the Lord, who had proved his power over storm and sea. Right after the publican's conversion, the question of fasting is treated with special reference to neophytes such as the publican (9:14–17). The three healing stories inserted after this pericope, one of which finds later analogies in Mark and Luke, while two are Matthean special traditions, continue to illustrate the power of the great physician who converted the publican Matthew.

In this way the accumulation of healing stories and references to discipleship in the first half of block 4 according to Matthew can be explained in the light of the narrative about the conversion of the publican Matthew, whom Jesus healed from sinfulness, made a disciple, and took into the group of the Twelve. Certainly it was not Matthew himself who made the pericope of his conversion such a magnetic field within the first half of block 4, but rather the editors of this Gospel who had a special interest in his person (cf. remarks on Matthew and Papias in chapters 3 and 7).

The second half of block 4 according to Matthew deals with that circle of the Twelve to which the tax collector Matthew was allowed to belong. It describes how Jesus sent out the twelve disciples to spread the gospel in Israel (Matt. 9:35—10:42). The detailed exposition consists of three parts. First there is an introduction (9:35—10:1); second, a list presenting the names of the twelve apostles (10:2–4); third, a speech dealing first with the activity and then with the destiny of Christ's messengers (10:5–16, 17–42). As will be pointed out in detail below, these instructions of the apostles were also meant to be applied to the activity and the experiences of the early church.

In the introduction and the first part of the commission speech according to Matthew (9:35—10:16), there are striking *alibi* analogies to Mark's and Luke's reports on the sending out of the Twelve belonging to block 6 (Mark 6:6b–13 // Luke 9:1–16), and to some extent also to Luke's similar report on the sending out of the Seventy within the travel narrative in block 8 (Luke 10:1–12). These analogies concern the theme as well as the vocabulary; for example: *περιῆγεν . . . τὰς κώμας διδάσκων* (Matt. 9:35; Mark 6:6); *προσκαλεσάμενος τοὺς δώδεκα . . . ἔδωκεν αὐτοῖς ἐξουσίαν πνευμάτων* (10:1; Mark 6:7; Luke 9:1); *μὴ κτήσεσθε χρυσόν*, etc. (10:9; Mark 6:8; Luke 9:3; 10:4); *εἰς ἣν ἂν πόλιν εἰσέλθητε* (10:11; Mark 6:10; Luke 9:4; 10:5); *ἐκτινάξατε τὸν κονιορτόν* (10:14; Mark 6:11; Luke 9:5; 10:11). Although more detailed, these instructions of the twelve missionaries displayed by Matthew in block 4 are comparable to the shorter instructions retained by Mark and Luke in block 6, and even greater is the similarity with the instruction of the seventy missionaries according to Luke in block 8.

In the middle of Matthew's commission speech, the editors have introduced a prophecy on a coming persecution of the apostolic church (Matt. 10:17–25). The same Gospel presents fragmentary counterparts to this prophecy in the passion narrative of block 11, and in contextual parallelism Mark and Luke there contain a rather detailed analogy to this Matthean doublet (Matt. 24:9–14 // Mark 13:9–13 // Luke 22:11–19). As was observed above with regard to the Sermon on

the Mount, and as will be demonstrated below, the Matthean circle has, in this case too, advanced a piece of tradition but at the same time retained a couple of reminiscences within the older context.

After that announcement of a persecution, the conclusion of the Matthean commission speech is displayed (Matt. 10:26–42). Here the twelve apostles receive instructions about their conduct in the world. In the first instance, this part of the commission speech consists of three Q traditions (Matt. 10:26–33, 34–36, 37–39), and the corresponding analogies found in Luke belong to the travel report of block 8. At the end, the Matthean commission speech implies a special tradition (10:40–41) and a double tradition with a later analogy in Mark (Matt. 10:42; Mark 9:41).

Whereas the Matthean commission speech in block 4 forms a logical composition in itself, the comparison of its elements with analogous passages in other parts of Matthew as well as with various elements of Mark and Luke yields a highly complicated picture. *Alibi* analogies to elements of Matthew's speech in block 4 are found in block 3 of Matthew, even more in blocks 5 and 6 of Mark and Luke, in block 8 of Luke, and in block 11 of Matthew, Mark, and Luke. These intricate relationships between Matthew's block 4 and numerous elements of blocks 3, 5, 6, 8, and 11 need to be studied more in detail. They are listed on pages 98–99.

The multilateral analogies here illustrated are too complicated to be explained on the basis of any utilization theory. It is, rather, a question of an interplay between traditional structures and redactional tendencies, and on these principles the following explanation may be suggested: Among the many *alibi* analogies involved, those connected with Matthew's sermons in blocks 3 and 4 have been inserted there because of specific Matthean interests; those belonging to blocks 5, 6, and 11 owe their context to more traditional circumstances; and those *alibi* analogies which are scattered within Luke's travel narrative in block 8 have been placed there because of particular Lukan interests. By means of such an explanation it becomes possible to count upon observable, constructive factors, while any efforts toward a literary derivation implies that one evangelist would have disapproved and distorted extant units and sequences of another, and this for no sensible reason.

The well-documented concern of the Matthean circle for apostolic instruction can thus be regarded as the reason for the incorporation of the relevant *alibi* analogies in the compositions here called blocks 3 and 4; and the notorious interest of Luke in the mission to the nations as the reason for the absorption of several comparable elements in block 8, as will also be demonstrated below in the analysis of the travel narrative.

Concerning the *alibi* analogies quoted in the list as belonging to block 5, essential facts that indicate their traditional connection with this context were pointed out above (p. 89): (1) Matt. 12:15–16 is a fragmentary duplicate to 4:23–25 without substantial importance, and must therefore be understood to be a

Main Topics of Matthew's
and Analogies in Blocks

Block 3	Block 4	Block 5
Mt 4:23—7:27 Introduction + Sermon on the Mount[1]		Mt 12:15–16 Introduction Mk 3:7–12 Lk 6:12–19 Introduction + election of the Twelve Lk 6:20–49 Sermon on the Plain[4]
	Mt 9:35—10:16 Introduction + sending of the Twelve, first part[2]	
	Mt 10:17–25 Persecution of the early church	
	Mt 10:26–42 Sending of the Twelve, last part	
	a. Mt 10:26–39 confession, division, conditions of discipleship	
	b. Mt 10:40–42 Reception of messengers, fresh water[3]	

1. Matt. 4:23 in block 3 has a doublet at Matt. 9:35 in block 4, and Mark 6:6b in block 6 forms a short *alibi* analogy to both. Matt. 4:24–25 in block 3 corresponds to Mark 3:7–12 // Luke 6:12–19 in block 5. The Sermon on the Mount in Matt. 5:1—7:27 contains elements to which there are counterparts in Luke's Sermon on the Plain in block 5, but also in several passages of Luke's travel narrative in block 8.

2. Matt. 9:35 in block 4 is a doublet of Matt. 4:23 in block 3, and Mark 6:6b in block 6 represents a shorter analogy to both passages. The counterpart to the apostle list in Matt. 10:2–4 is found in block 5 of Mark and Luke. The commission of the Twelve in Matt. 9:35—10:16 is partly comparable to their sending according to Mark and Luke in block 6, but more verbally to the commission of the Seventy according to Luke in block 8, so that it also represents a Q tradition.

3. Matt. 10:40–41 in block 4 is comparable to a triple tradition in block 7, Matt. 18:5 with par. Matt. 10:42 represents a Matthean-Markan double tradition, to which Mark 9:41 in block 7 offers the counterpart.

4. Matt. 12:15–16 in block 5 is just an introduction, whereas Mark's and Luke's contextual parallels to this passage include a list of the Twelve, to which Matthew presents a counterpart in block 4. Luke proceeds in block 5 to the Sermon on the Plain, which partly corresponds to Matthew's sermon in block 3, but Mark has no counterparts to these sermons.

5. Mark 6:6b in block 6 is a shorter analogy to the doublets represented by Matt. 4:23 in block 3 and Matt. 9:35 in block 4.

Commission Speech in Block 4
3, 5–8, and 11

Block 6	Block 8	Block 11
	Lk 14:34–35, 11:33; 16:18; 11:2–4; 12:33–34; 11:34–36; 16:13; 12:22–31; 11:9–13; 13:23–27[7]	
Mk 6:6b–13 Lk 9:1–6 Introduction + sending of the Twelve[5]	Lk 10:1–12 Sending of the Seventy[8]	
		Mt 24:9–14 Mk 13:9–13 Lk 21:12–19 Persecution of the early church[10]
	Lk 12:2–12, 49–53; 14:25–37[9]	
Block 7		
Mt 18:5 with par. Reception of messengers, Mk 9:41 fresh water[6]		

6. In block 7, Matt. 18:5 with par. can be compared with Matt. 10:40–41. Mark 9:41 in block 7 is a Matthean-Markan double tradition, the counterpart to which is Matt. 10:42 in block 4.

7. All of these elements of block 8 belong to Luke's travel narrative. Together with elements of Luke's Sermon on the Plain in block 5 they are comparable with elements of Matthew's Sermon on the Mount in block 3.

8. In block 8, Luke 10:1–12 describes the commission of the Seventy shortly after the beginning of the travel narrative. The instructions given to them partly correspond to what Jesus told the Twelve according to Mark's and Luke's commission speeches in block 6. Even more evident, however, is that elements of Luke 10:1–12 and scattered passages of Luke 12 and 14 (see note 9) are comparable to parts of Matthew's commission speech in block 4, so that Matt. 9:35—10:42 mainly comprises Q traditions not supported by Mark.

9. These passages are scattered elements of Luke's travel narrative in block 8, inserted here in continuation of the instructions given at the sending of the Seventy according to Luke 10:1–12. Analogous quotations are found in Matthew's speech addressed to the Twelve in block 4 (cf. note 8).

10. Matt. 24:9a in block 11 corresponds to the first part, and Matt. 24:9b–14 to the last part of the contextual parallels Mark 13:9–13 // Luke 21:12–19. The counterpart to its middle part is formed by Matt. 10:17–21 in block 4. At the same time, there are overlappings.

reminiscence of a preliterary tradition reflected in contextual parallelism by Mark 3:7–19 and Luke 6:12–19. (2) On other accounts, Mark 3:7–19 must be said to reflect this fundamental tradition in a form that is merely incomplete. The audience here described is not offered any instruction afterward, even if the reference to a boat enabled the redactor to create a connection with the parable speech presented in a later chapter. (3) It is Luke 6:12–19 and 20–49 that reflect the preliterary tradition in the closest way, for here the audience is allowed to hear the anticipated sermon. Since one cannot derive the passages of Matthew and Mark at issue from the present text of Luke without ascribing strange destructive ambitions to the editors of these Gospels, the only possibility is to regard their fragmentary notes as reminiscences of a given tradition.

Focusing again on Matt. 9:35—10:16, which is the first half of Matthew's commission speech in block 4, it appears that its next counterparts are Mark 6:6b–13 and Luke 9:1–6 in block 6. Like the speech in Matthew, these passages also deal with the sending of the twelve apostles, using several analogous phrases, as indicated above (p. 96). Matthew, however, has given the speech a more detailed, expressive, and even more consistent form than Mark and Luke, who have indeed presented incomplete and perforated summaries. Furthermore, the Matthean commission speech is not only to be studied in the light of these Markan and Lukan analogies. It must also be compared with Luke 10:1–12, which belongs to block 8 and contains a very similar instruction of seventy missionaries. The latter pericope also includes elements reminding of Mark 6:6b–13 and Luke 9:1–6 in block 6, but its general similarity with Matt. 9:35—10:16 in block 4 is more important and really striking.

Attempts to explain this confusing picture of similarities and varieties by means of literary source theories lead to precarious results. If the text of Matthew were the source of the analogies involved, then both Mark and Luke would have moved and spoiled it, although Luke 10:1–12 brings a more adequate version just afterward. Were the text of Mark the source, then Matthew would have dislocated, enlarged, and clarified it with remarkable accuracy, while on the other hand Luke would have taken over Mark's text without any scruples but also used Matthew's text for an improved version in a subsequent chapter.

It is merely natural to start from a preliterary tradition supposed to have comprehended Christ's instructions when sending out his disciples as missionaries. Matthew may be said to have preserved this tradition especially well, as is easily understandable with regard to the interest taken by the Matthean circle in apostolic instruction. For the same reason, the speech was given an early place in the Matthean text, so that it appears in block 4 immediately after the sequence of ten healings in block 3 where the conversion of the tax collector is the center. Seeing that Mark was less concerned about instruction of disciples, it becomes conceivable that he presented the instructions of Jesus in a summarized form. Luke also took over this abbreviated tradition, but for him a further reason was that in general he was less occupied with traditions coming from Peter and

Galilee. Since his special interest was in Christ's missionary activity in Transjordan, to be described in the travel narrative of block 8, Christ's instructions to the missionaries were inserted there in a more complete form on the basis of a tradition corresponding to that reflected by Matthew in block 4. The elements common to Matthew in block 4 and Luke in block 8 without support in Mark may be regarded as Q traditions based on similar reminiscences of instructions given by Jesus.

Compared with Mark's and Luke's reports in block 6, Matthew's introduction to the commission speech in block 4 has been increased by the insertion of the apostle catalogue (Matt. 10:2–4). Interestingly enough, the list is given in the present tense (10:2): "The names of the twelve apostles *are* these," implying that hearers and readers were here informed about names of contemporaries. The corresponding list appears in Mark and Luke within block 5 as part of a report on the calling of the apostles upon a mountain, which in Luke is later followed by the Sermon on the Plain. It was evidently because the Matthean circle had a special interest in apostolic instruction, and wanted to stress the participation of the newly converted publican Matthew in the subsequent mission of the Twelve, that it presented the apostle catalogue here in block 4.

By the use of the present tense, "The names of the twelve apostles are these," the readers were in fact treated as contemporaries of that group of twelve apostles in Jerusalem whose leader was Peter (Acts 1:13). A primary concentration of the activity on Israel was characteristic of this circle (Acts 2:36; 5:31; 6:2; 8:1; 10:14; Gal. 2:9). In a corresponding way, the First Gospel has emphasized that Jesus, already in Galilee, sent out his apostles exclusively to the lost sheep of the house of Israel (Matt. 10:6). Among the participants in this Jewish mission the apostle Matthew was pointed out by the epithet "tax collector" (10:3).

In the middle part of Matthew's commission speech its actuality for the church in Jerusalem is further testified (Matt. 10:17–25). What is stated here on the persecution of the disciples through local councils and synagogues, governors and monarchs did happen to the Christians in Jerusalem in the first decades after the death of Christ (Acts 4:1—12:19 passim; 1 Thess. 2:14; Acts 21:27; etc.). However, to this section of block 4 according to Matthew there are detailed *alibi* analogies in block 11 according to Mark and Luke, where Jesus, sitting on the Mount of Olives, describes a similar persecution of the Jerusalem church (Mark 13:9–13 // Luke 21:12–19). And to the last-mentioned units of Christ's farewell discourse Matthew also offers a context-parallel, equally localized to the Mount of Olives (Matt. 24:9–14). Characteristic topics and terms are present in both Matthean texts. From the triple tradition reflected by Mark and Luke in block 11, the editors of Matthew have thus detached a section and combined it with the mission speech in block 5, but at the same time retained a fragmentary parallel to Mark and Luke in their version of the Mount of Olives discourse. As was observed above (p. 89), Matthew left behind in block 5 (Matt. 12:15–21) a reminiscence of that sequence which in Mark consists of fragmentary informa-

tion and in Luke of detailed information about the multitude, the mountain, the names of the Twelve, and the subsequent Sermon on the Plain (Mark 3:7–12; Luke 6:12–49). In this way, the editors of Matthew have in block 11, too, left behind a reminiscence of the prophecy about a persecution of the apostolic church (Matt. 24:9–14), although they had already inserted a detailed prophecy of the same kind in block 4 (10:17–25). Details are shown in the table on pp. 98–99.

The last part of the Matthean mission speech contains further admonitions given to the apostles. It consists of three double traditions of the Q type (Matt. 10:26–39), then of a special tradition in certain similarity with a triple logion in block 7 (10:40–41; cf. 18:5 with par.), and finally of a double tradition with a Markan parallel also found in block 7 (Matt. 10:42; cf. Mark 9:40). As is the case in the first part of Matthew's commission speech, the editors have thus augmented the report on Christ's instructions particularly by Q traditions, and in both contexts the counterparts represented by Luke are mainly found in the travel narrative. Matthew has arranged these Q elements in a relatively logical order, while Luke has distributed them on several different texts, as demonstrated in the list above. Words of Jesus were thus taken over here and there by Matthew and Luke according to the subject that was to be treated. Matthew's references to Gehenna (in the Hinnom valley), sparrows as temple offerings, and the duty to carry the cross (Matt. 10:28, 29, 38) indicate that some words of Jesus were quoted with preference, for which members of the early church in Jerusalem might possess special resonance.

As a synoptic totality, block 4 is dominated by Matthean pericopes mainly forming *alibi* analogies or special traditions. Several of them have been attached to the report on Matthew's conversion, and thus a series of ten miracles has been allowed to surround the context-parallel triple tradition about his calling (Matt. 9:9–13 with par.). The report on the sending of the twelve apostles to preach in Israel also betrays such a personal concern for Matthew because of his particular identification as the publican (10:3). Evidently the *alibi* analogies and the unique Matthean units found in block 4 have been situated in the magnetic field of Matthew's conversion, and this has been achieved by the editors, yet without any personal glorification.

Block 5
Instruction,
Discussion, and Parables
Matt. 11:1—13:52 with Parallels

Block 5 describes a further teaching of Jesus in Galilee which is overshadowed by criticism and skepticism, and finally replaced by esoteric parables (Matt. 11:1—13:52 with par.). The former activity of Jesus in Galilee has been described as successful, but in block 5 different groups appear who question his person and message. Among those who raise questions or express opposition

there are hesitating disciples of John (Matt. 11:3); Pharisees (12:2 with par.), some of whom decide to attack Jesus (12:14 with par.); scribes who dare to identify him with Beelzebul (12:24 with par.); even representatives of his own family who nourish doubts (12:46 with par.). Confronted with this misunderstanding and opposition, Jesus concentrates his preaching and teaching upon the disciples, that is, persons willing and able to understand his parables (13:11 with par.).

Materially, block 5 consists of triple traditions, Q traditions, other double traditions, and special traditions. Here the contextual parallelism claims a little more space than in block 4 but remains less predominant than in later blocks.

In block 5 the synoptic concord is somewhat reduced because Luke interrupts the parallelism through a sequence of Q and particular traditions including the Sermon on the Plain and subsequent pericopes (Luke 6:20—8:3). A current name for this sequence is the "shorter interpolation" of Luke, alluding to his travel narrative as the longer interpolation. This terminology is misleading insofar as it presupposes a literary priority of Mark, which just with regard to the piece of text at issue cannot be confirmed. In fact, the immediate context before and after the Lukan sequence in block 5 speaks against the idea of any interpolation, whether in relation to Matthew or Mark. Right before the sequence in question (Luke 6:20—8:3), the Third Gospel follows neither the order of Matthew nor that of Mark (Luke 6:12–19). And right after the end of the sequence (at 8:3), Luke proceeds directly to the parables (8:4–18) without referring here to the Beelzebul discussion as do the other Synoptics (Matt. 12:22–37 // Mark 3:22–30; Matt. 12:38–45), whereas *alibi* analogies to the same discussion appear in Luke's block 8 (Luke 11:14–32; 12:10). Thus the Lukan sequence in question should not be called an interpolation, but only a Lukan specialty. Here the interest of Luke in traditions concerning women is also noteworthy (Luke 7:11–17, the widow of Nain; 7:36–50, the anointing; 8:1–3, the ministering women).

Contextual parallelism of triple traditions is represented in block 5 by two narratives about Sabbath healings (Matt. 12:1–8, 9–14 with par.), with a slight inversion by a reference to numerous listeners (Matt. 12:15–16 // Mark 3:7–12 and Luke 6:17–19 just after these parallels), and in full parallelism again by three elements of the concluding parable chapter (Matt. 13:1–9, 10–15, 18–23 with par.). These contextual parallels appear in combination with *alibi*-analogous triple and double traditions which show a remarkable inclination toward correspondence in connection and sequence. Although their order is not exactly the same, they still form distinct figures, so that a fundamental parallelism comes to the fore.

In both Mark and Luke the Master appears with the same large multitude in the vicinity of the sea and calls the twelve apostles on a mountain (Mark 3:7–19 // Luke 6:12–19). The throng of people and the election of the apostles do not appear in the same order, but in combination with each other both reports are

contextually parallel (Mark 3:7–19 = Luke 6:17–19 + 12–16, or Mark 3:13–19 + 7–12 = Luke 6:12–19). A similar transposition is represented by the question of Christ's true relatives, in Matthew and Mark discussed before the parable chapter but in Luke only afterward (Matt. 12:46–50 // Mark 3:31–35; Luke 8:19–21).

Previous surveys have shown that block 3 contains Matthean *alibi* analogies to that Markan and Lukan sequence in block 5 which refers to the multitude, the mountain, the election of the apostles, and in Luke also to their instruction (above, pp. 90–91). The editors of Matthew have advanced the relevant tradition to block 3, but the sequence of the narratives is practically the same as in block 5 according to Mark and Luke. In spite of this, a reminiscence of the reference to the multitude has also been preserved by Matthew within block 5 in contextual parallelism with Mark and Luke (Matt. 12:15–21 with par.). Although it must be expected that the people had gathered here for some instruction, no sermon has been quoted either by Matthew or by Mark, whereas Luke's Sermon on the Plain (Luke 6:20–49) seems to retain a tradition less changed by redactional adjustment. Of course the editors of Matthew were incited to leave out the anticipated sermon, because they had already served a similar purpose by the Sermon on the Mount in block 3. But they also felt they had to cover the vacancy caused in block 5 after the reference to the listeners (Matt. 12:15) and therefore inserted a scriptural quotation (Isa. 42:1–2) dealing with the messianic secret (Matt. 12:16–21). Having less concern for missionary instruction, Mark also left out the sermon to be expected. As indicated above (p. 90), he felt the same vacancy as Matthew and desired to conceal it, and this he did by inserting a boat (Mark 3:9), which he took up later in his presentation of the parable speech (4:1). Thus some common structures of preliterary traditions are reflected in the different sequences now mentioned, even if the order and the details are no more quite equal in their redactional shape.

Similar observations can be made as to the Q traditions about the centurion, which Matthew has presented in block 3 and Luke in block 5 (Matt. 8:5–13; Luke 7:1–10). In both cases the story is attached to a sermon just given, in Matthew to the Sermon on the Mount and in Luke to the Sermon on the Plain. This likewise points to a traditional correlation, and the reason why Mark did not include the story is that he did not quote any sermon in the relevant context.

Another example of preestablished connections between Q traditions is offered by two pericopes dealing with John the Baptist and presented by Matthew in block 5, by Luke in block 8 (Matt. 11:1–6, 7–19; Luke 7:18–23, 24–35). In both Gospels they are two units but form one sequence. They also serve as practical illustrations of instructive sermons presented shortly before, and these are Matthew's commission speech and Luke's Sermon on the Plain. Being sent out as missionaries, the apostles should according to both Gospels subsequently be informed about the relationship between the Baptist and the Savior.

Further examples of Q traditions, forming corresponding structures though

distributed on block 5 in Matthew and block 8 in Luke, are found in two sequences characterized by the names of "Chorazin" and "Beelzebul." The first sequence (Matt. 11:20–30; Luke 10:13–15, 21–22) consists of the Lord's complaint about Chorazin and other cities and is followed by his rejoicing over the innocent. In blocks 5 and 8, respectively, Matthew and Luke present these topics in the same order. The second sequence (Matt. 12:22–50; Luke 11:14–32) deals with the following topics: the Beelzebul accusation; the defense against it; the danger of relapsing; the definition of Christ's true relatives (in Luke referred only to Mary and not to the brothers); and finally, the demand for a miraculous sign with the counterargument "greater than Jonah and Solomon." Here also the sequence has a comparable structure in block 5 according to Matthew and in block 8 according to Luke. To the second sequence Mark also represents a few analogies in block 5 (Mark 3:22–35), introduced by an extra item, a short reference to the skepticism of Christ's relatives (3:20–21). One must admit here that although the two Matthean-Lukan sequences are dominated by traditions of the Q type, parts of the second one figure as triple traditions. This change of frequency types is no evidence of a combination of different sources but is due to the fact that Mark was content with a shorter version. With regard to Luke, his double reference to the question of Christ's true relatives is noteworthy. A first time, the family of Jesus appears in block 5 (Luke 8:19–21), and this corresponds to a sequence preserved in block 5 by Matthew and Mark, although Luke has mentioned the relatives not before but after the parables (8:3–18). A second time, Luke has touched upon the problem of Christ's true relatives by referring to Mary in his Beelzebul sequence of block 8 (11:27–28), and in analogy to a corresponding unit found in Matthew's Beelzebul sequence of block 5 (Matt. 12:46–50) Luke has also actualized the question immediately after the warning against backsliding (Luke 11:24–26). When the Lukan traditionists used the Q sequence beginning with the Beelzebul accusation for the complex here called block 8, the problem about Christ's true relatives followed along, though Luke varied it a little because a similar discussion had been mentioned in block 5.

After the Beelzebul sequence represented by Matthew and partly by Mark in block 5, while reserved by Luke for block 8, a contextual parallelism of all the Synoptics occurs again in the last part of block 5, which is a speech given in the form of parables (Matt. 13:1–52 with par.).

Even if the pericopes comprised in the parable speech alternate between triple, double, and single traditions, an inclination toward contextual parallelism is dominant. Three context-parallel triple traditions dealing with the sower and the use of parables are found at the beginning of the speech (Matt. 13:1–9, 10–15, 18–23 with par.), and later a triple tradition dealing with the mustard seed appears of which the contextual parallelism is represented only by Matthew and Mark but is traceable in Luke's Transjordanian context because of a reference to the Galilean sowing (Matt. 13:31–32 // Mark 4:30–32; Luke 13:18–19). Otherwise there are double traditions of different types, among them two Q units

(Matt. 13:16–17 and Luke 10:23–24; Matt. 13:23 and Luke 13:20–21) and two other context-parallel double traditions, one common to Mark and Luke (Mark 4:21–25 // Luke 8:16–18) and one to Matthew and Mark (Matt. 13:34–35 // Mark 4:33–34). The rest consists of single units, in Matthew including four special parables and two commentaries (Matt. 13:24–30, 36–43, 44–46, 47–50, 51–52) and in Mark the parable about the seed (Mark 4:26–29). In spite of this constant variation in the frequency, the parable speech is a comprehensive structure of which several elements represent contextual parallelism in the synoptic perspective.

The program of the parable speech is also consistent and in coherence with the preceding elements of block 5. Jesus is explicitly said to have passed on to parables in order to permit his disciples to understand the secrets of heaven in distinction to those outside (Matt. 13:11 // Mark 4:10 // Luke 8:10). This implied a concentration of his teaching activity on persons willing to hear and follow him. In the preceding units of block 5, including those sequences to which Luke has presented analogies in block 8, the intention was to show that different groups of people had begun to question or even attack that Son of Man who had first been welcomed as having admirable power and spiritual authority. He was exposed to questions asked by disciples of the Baptist and members of his own family. Chorazin and other cities in Galilee showed inclinations to reject him. Most disappointing and deplorable were the attacks on him arranged by Pharisees on account of his activity on a Sabbath or his warfare against evil spirits. Block 5 demonstrates in a dramatic way how this skepticism and criticism were intensified and led Jesus to concentrate his activity on the disciples, which he did by addressing them in parables supposed to be understood by them alone.

Certainly the integrity of block 5 is reduced by the oscillating *alibi* analogies. Several elements are included here, to which more extensive counterparts are found in other blocks. In such cases, however, particular interests can be regarded as reasons for redactional movements of elements away from a traditional structure to be supposed behind what is treated here as block 5. This has been demonstrated above with regard to Matthew's Sermon on the Mount in block 3 which is comparable to Luke's Sermon on the Plain in block 5, and with regard to several passages and sequences of Luke in block 8 which correspond to units of Matthew and partly of Mark in block 5. Matthew's concern for the instruction of the twelve apostles in Galilee and Luke's for that of the seventy missionaries in Transjordan (see below) were redactional factors which caused the transfer of some traditional items from a context here called block 5 to block 3 (Matt. 4:23, etc.), while others were moved to block 8 (Luke 10:1, etc.). The traditional contents of block 5 are mainly represented by manifest contextual parallels but partly also by short *alibi* analogies to more extensive counterparts in other blocks of Matthew and Luke. Mark contributes to the picture insofar as it shares in contextual parallels, but since the author of this Gospel had less concern for the instruction of missionaries, several traditional elements of instruction have been left out.

Behind block 5 one must not suppose there ever was any fixed literary composition but should realize that traditional units are here kept together in different ways and sustained by a common occupation with problems of importance for the Lord himself and his missionaries. There is a noticeable alternation between discussion with different groups who ask questions or raise opposition, and instruction of messengers sent out to announce the kingdom of heaven and to invite people to it. The experiences and communications of Jesus are here described in such a way that his disciples should be taught how to behave in corresponding situations when going out to preach and teach in their environment.

Another comprehensive factor determining the material in block 5 is the general intention to portray the increasing hesitation and opposition in Galilee as leading to that concentration of the teaching on the disciples which is the topic of the parable chapter. In this regard, the redactors of Matthew have provided the reader with the richest material. Yet several contextual parallels are found in Mark, and they represent the same program. And although the evangelist Luke has integrated some corresponding sequences in his block 8 to exemplify the instruction of the seventy missionaries, his contextual parallels in block 5 also support the program, and his addition of the episode with the anointment criticized by a Pharisee (Luke 7:36–50) enforces the dramatic tension.

Block 6
Excursions in Various Directions
Mark 4:35—9:29 with Parallels

For the most part, block 6 comprises narrative pericopes, and in fundamental correspondence between the Gospels these describe an expansion of the Lord's activity from Capernaum and Gennesaret to various countries around the Lake of Galilee. Here the units of Mark are more numerous and more consistent than what is found in the parallel texts (Mark 4:35—9:29), for both Matthew and Luke present a limited amount of contextual parallels to Mark in this block (Matt. 13:53—17:21; Luke 8:22—9:43), and each of them deviates from the other Gospels in different sections of the block. Exceptionally, the survey may therefore begin with the Second Gospel, yet without presupposing that Mark was the literary source of the other Gospels.

According to Mark in block 6, Jesus undertook six excursions after having delivered the parable speech. Starting from the west coast of the lake, he went out in six different directions:

1. Over the lake in a southeastern direction to the country of the Gadarenes (Mark 4:35; 5:1).
2. Back over the lake and then in a southwestern direction to Nazareth (5:21; 6:1).

3. Over the lake again in a northeastern direction to the shore east of Bethsaida (6:31, 45).
4. Having walked on the lake back to Gennesaret, from there in a northwestern direction to Phoenicia (6:49, 53; 7:24).
5. Passing the lake (cf. Matt. 15:29), in a southern direction to Decapolis (7:31).
6. Starting from the west coast again, in a boat to Bethsaida and from there in a northern direction to the region of Caesarea Philippi (8:13, 22, 27).

According to block 7, Jesus then dwells again in Galilee and Capernaum, the home of Peter (9:30, 33).

To facilitate the survey of block 6, the topographic scheme unconsciously developed by Mark may be illustrated by this sketch:

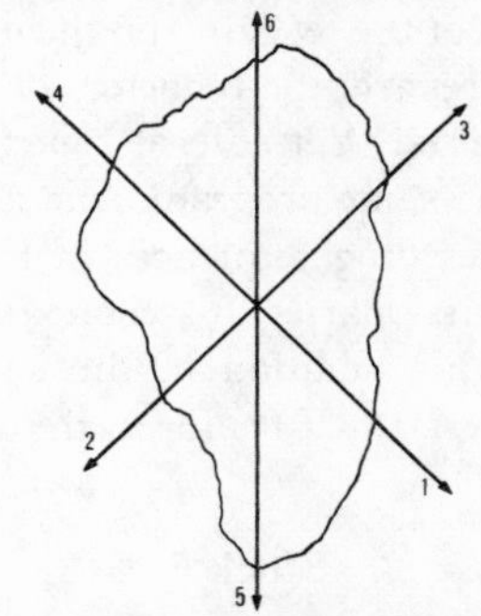

With regard to frequency types, no Q traditions are found in block 6, only triple traditions and in the middle a row of Matthean-Markan double traditions (Matt. 14:22—16:12 // Mark 6:45—8:21), increased by one Markan special tradition (the blind man of Bethsaida in Mark 8:22–26).

To the middle section of block 6, which includes Matthean-Markan double traditions, there are no Lukan counterparts anywhere. It is usual here to speak of the "great lacuna" in the Third Gospel, implying that Luke, right after its counterpart to the third excursion according to the Markan pattern (Mark 6:30–44 // Luke 9:10–17), presents a parallel to the sixth excursion (Mark 8:27–30 // Luke 9:18–21) without touching upon the fourth and fifth travels in Mark's scheme. This will be studied more closely below.

In the first instance, Matthew deviates from Mark and Luke at the beginning of block 6, for this Gospel has in block 4 already reported on the miracles connected with the storm at sea, Gadara, Jairus, and the sending out of the Twelve (Matt. 8:23–34; 9:18–26; 9:35—10:16). As was pointed out in the analysis of block 4, the prolepsis was connected with an interest of the redactors in the publican Matthew. The miracle narratives just mentioned surround the story about his calling which is told in the middle of the Matthean block 4, and in the report on the sending of the Twelve Matthew's participation is emphasized by the identification of the apostle with the publican (10:3). In spite of this Matthean

dislocation in relation to the Markan and Lukan analogies in block 6, the order of the miracle stories in question is the same in Matthew as in Mark and Luke, and the sending of the Twelve is introduced in Matthew with the same words as in Mark (Matt. 9:35; Mark 6:6). A certain relationship of the traditions must thus be assumed, and the deviation of Matthew from Mark and Luke can be understood as an expression of the interest taken by the redactors in the person of Matthew. The prolepsis of the story on the sending of the Twelve in Matthew also involves an interruption of a logical sequence found in the corresponding texts of Mark and Luke. In these Gospels the sending of the Twelve, which implies an intensified activity in Galilee, leads to the reaction of the Galilean tetrarch Antipas against Jesus (Mark 6:12–14 // Luke 9:6–7). Matthew has only indicated that Antipas heard about the visit of Jesus to Nazareth and therefore was led to believe that John the Baptist had reappeared in Jesus (Matt. 14:1–2). This yields an insufficient explanation, and Matthew has evidently caused the abridgment here by advancing the sending of the Twelve to block 4. Doubtless the early location of Matthew's parallels to the narratives of the storm, and so forth, and the sending of the apostles, which appear in block 6 of Mark and Luke in connection with excursions numbers one and two according to the Markan scheme, was due to Matthean redaction.

Within block 6 the result has become that Matthew has introduced the series of excursions with Christ's visit to Nazareth (Matt. 13:53–58), which corresponds to the second half of number two in the Markan pattern. From this point on, Matthew and Mark follow nearly the same order in the block. There are only two slight exceptions insofar as Matthew has not mentioned the sending of the Twelve after the visit to Nazareth (Matt. 9:35—10:16 as against Mark 6:6b–13) and Mark has inserted a special tradition about the blind man of Bethsaida (Mark 8:22–26). Luke also participates in this parallelism, apart from the pericopes on the execution of John and the visit to Nazareth, on which Luke had already reported in his blocks 2 and 3 (Luke 3:19–20; 4:16–30), and the so-called great lacuna in Luke (between 9:17 and 9:18). With these exceptions, there is a homologous sequence in the three Gospels between the second half of Mark's excursion number two and its excursion number six.

Matthew, Mark, and Luke thus follow a common pattern in the middle and the last part of block 6. This, however, is only true of the order in which the pericopes occur. With regard to details, there is a really labyrinthian distribution of similarities and discrepancies. Analogies and differences of style and vocabulary are constantly alternating, so that an irrational zigzag pattern emerges. On this account, all theories of literary dependence become ambiguous, for the interrelationships can always be understood in both directions. It must, for example, be observed that Mark presents more words and details in the stories about the execution of John and the feeding of five thousand persons than what is found in the parallel reports, but with regard to the storm at sea, the woman in Phoenicia, and the confession of Peter, the situation is reversed. The flexibility is

by no means bound to any system, but can only be explained on the assumption of a common dependence on traditions kept in mind.

Seeing that Mark presents more elaborate and consistent material in block 6 than do Matthew and Luke, it only follows that in this context the available traditions were particularly close to him. In each case the excursions depicted by Mark go out from Capernaum and its surroundings, and the Master finally returns to this city in order to teach in the house of Peter, as dealt with in block 7 (Mark 9:33). Because of this concentration upon Capernaum and the house of Peter, the pattern of Mark developed in block 6 may especially be traced back to personal contacts between Peter and Mark, and such contacts have been indicated by Luke and confirmed by Papias (Acts 12:12; Eusebius, *EH* III.39.15).

Other factors contributed to Luke's deviations from Matthew and Mark in block 6.

1. In the first part of the block, Luke did not report either about the execution of John or about the Lord's visit to Nazareth, because these topics had already been dealt with in blocks 2 and 3 (Luke 3:19–20; 4:16–30). The evangelist was generally inclined to pay special attention to John the Baptist and the mission to the Gentiles and therefore decided to give such early records on the martyrdom of John and the discussion in Nazareth.

2. As to the second part of block 6, Luke abruptly deviates from Matthew and Mark by what is called the great lacuna. It implies that between Luke 9:17 and 9:18 there is no counterpart to Matthew's and Mark's descriptions of excursions four and five in the Markan scheme, because Luke has passed directly from the Matthean-Markan excursions three to six (cf. the sketch above). The reason for this apparent omission was the special orientation of the traditions that Luke took over, as will be explained below.

On the whole, Luke's narratives show that his subject matter was less bound to Peter, Capernaum, and east Galilee than what is found in Matthew and Mark. Luke instead paid much attention to the activity of Jesus in Transjordan, which is the scene of his extensive travel narrative in block 8. In the Lukan pericopes of the blocks 3 to 7, one rarely finds explicit references to Capernaum and its surroundings (Capernaum mentioned as scene only in Luke 4:23, 31; 7:1, and Galilee in 4:14, 31). On the other hand, as is evident from the table above (pp. 98–99), Luke has inserted many *alibi* analogies to Matthean-Markan units of these blocks in his block 8. The analysis of block 8 will later show that Luke used traditions imparted to him by the Hellenists of Jerusalem, for whom he, in the Book of Acts, has betrayed a particular interest. A primary group of the Jerusalem Hellenists had arrived with Jesus from Transjordan, so that reminiscences from this eastern neighborhood were important for them. In the northern part of Transjordan there was the region of Caesarea Philippi and Bethsaida, governed by the tetrarch Philip; in the middle the Greek confederacy of Decapolis; and in the southern part Perea around the city of Livias, founded by the tetrarch Antipas. Decapolis was completely Hellenistic, and though northern and southern Trans-

jordan had been influenced by Judaism, they were still dominated by Hellenism. Seeing that Luke did not have such direct access to Petrine and Galilean traditions as Matthew and Mark, but instead was able to adopt traditions of Hellenistic disciples with a background in Transjordanian countries, it becomes understandable that he was led to depict several events in a Transjordanian perspective.

From Transjordanian points of view, the excursions corresponding to numbers four and five in the Markan scheme were less important, since they extended west of the river Jordan, whereas numbers three and six remained connected with northern Transjordan. With the report on the feeding of the five thousand (Luke 9:10–17), which forms a counterpart to excursion number three of Mark, although it contains Lukan variants, the region of the Hellenistic city of Bethsaida had been reached (mentioned in Mark 6:45 and Luke 9:10; indicated by John 6:5 in comparison with 1:44). In consequence of Luke's dependence on Transjordanian reporters, it seems probable that his version of the feeding narrative came from disciples especially connected with Bethsaida, among whom one may think of the apostle Philip (cf. John 1:44; 6:5), since he was very likely identical with the evangelist Philip, whom Luke met in Caesarea (Acts 21:8).

On psychological grounds, it thus appears natural that after the reference to the feeding of the multitude near Bethsaida (Luke 9:10–17), the Lukan traditionists continued the story by telling about the confession of Peter located to the same area (9:18–21). To use the numbers of the Markan scheme, this implied a direct transition from excursion three to six, leaving out excursions four and five, and the reason was the connection of the relevant traditionists with northern Transjordan.

No literary source theory is able to explain this gap in the Lukan report. If Luke worked on the basis of a written source that contained references to excursions four and five, no reasonable arguments can be found to explain why he deleted these journeys, and they would in no way have been uninteresting to him. On the other hand, any supposition of a source without information about excursions four and five, no matter whether this is termed pre-Markan or something else, remains pure imagination and makes the increase of the material in the other Gospels a further puzzle.

3. In the third part of block 6, the subject is the excursion here called number six following Mark's arrangement (Matt. 16:1—17:21 with par.). According to Matthew and Mark, Jesus and his disciples moved from the lake in a northern direction to the countryside of Caesarea Philippi (Matt. 16:13 // Mark 8:27), and until the end of block 6 all pericopes are referred to different places in the north. The Gospel of Luke is somewhat different insofar as it does not mention Caesarea Philippi but merely indicates a lonely neighborhood of Bethsaida (Luke 9:18, linked up with 9:10) and has only a short counterpart to the dialogue following upon the transfiguration (9:36b–37a). Otherwise the sixth excursion has been described in contextual parallelism by all the Synoptics.

The reason for the contextual harmony concerning excursion number six is easy to find. It is throughout a matter of themes that were of current significance for the early church. All passages in question, here to be quoted from Matthew, represent triple contextual parallels of which the topics are the following: Peter's messianic confession in the name of the disciples (Matt. 16:13–20); the suffering of the Son of Man in Jerusalem (16:21–23); the necessity to follow Christ on the path of tribulation (16:24–28); the transfiguration of God's Son before the eyes of three disciples (17:1–8), later known as the leading apostles of the early church (Acts 1:13; 3:1, etc.; 12:2; Gal. 2:9); finally the martyrdom of the Baptist in the function of a new Elijah (17:9–13) and the question of healing demoniacs (17:14–21). Owing to the significance of the topics for the kerygma, the traditions here quoted remained consistent in three Gospels.

As a totality, block 6 represents a considerable harmony. The relations of journeys one to five are somewhat shifting, but the traditions reflected in Mark's detailed scheme, probably based on Peter's remembrances from Capernaum, do also remain perceptible in the other Gospels. In the first part of block 6 it is Mark and Luke that move parallel. While the Matthean circle has transferred the miracles connected with the storm at sea, Gadara, and Jairus back to block 4 because of its concentration on the calling of Matthew, the episodes were still kept in the same order as in Mark and Luke. In the second part of block 6 it is Matthew and Mark that proceed in a parallel manner, whereas Luke deviates on account of his great lacuna. The latter may be ascribed to the interest of Luke's traditionists in Bethsaida, which led them not to separate excursions three and six, since both were connected with this region. Hence the Matthean and Lukan deviations in comparison with the Markan scheme in the first and second parts of block 6 were based upon personal interests of Matthew's translators and Luke's traditionists. In the third part of block 6, however, the contextual parallelism is throughout dominant.

A reminiscence of events portrayed in the synoptic block 6 is also found in the Gospel of John. Short counterparts to the Matthean-Markan journeys three, four, and six form a sequence here. Like the synoptic writers, when dealing with journeys three and four, John made reference to the feeding of the five thousand (John 6:1–13), then to Christ's withdrawal (6:14–15), and subsequently to his walking across the lake back to the west coast again (6:16–25). With representatives of Judaism, Jesus there discussed the meaning of the bread and the signs offered by him (6:26–65), and both topics are reflected in Matthew's and Mark's reports on excursion number six (Matt. 16:1–12 // Mark 8:11–21). Similar to the synoptic writers (Matt. 16:13–20 with par.), John allowed Peter's messianic confession to follow upon these discussions (John 6:66–71). In spite of formulation differences, the synoptic block 6 accordingly finds counterparts in John, and this must be understood to be an effect of preliterary traditions.

Within the framework of the common synoptic presentation of Christ's ministry, his journeys depicted in block 6 signify an extension of his activity

beyond the areas of Capernaum and Gennesaret. This has definite theological implications. Jesus came into contact with regions mentioned in the Old Testament as conquered or at least invaded by the ten northern tribes of Israel (Judg. 1:2–33), and characteristically enough the Phoenician woman called Jesus the Son of David (Matt. 15:22). However, in the days of the Lord most of these regions were politically non-Jewish and culturally Hellenistic. The foreign countries mentioned in Mark's chiastic scheme were the land of the Gadarenes, the vicinity of Bethsaida, the southern part of Phoenicia, the region of Decapolis, and the tetrarchy of Philip. An anticipation of the Christian mission among the Gentiles was thus understood to have been established. The synoptic writers presented this as resulting from that lack of understanding which had recently encountered the Master in Galilee (Matt. 11:1—12:50 with par.). As was indicated by the parable of the sower (Matt. 13:8 with par.) and by the image of the light under the bushel (Mark 4:21 // Luke 8:16), all people of goodwill should now become acquainted with the gospel, in contrast to those impenitent. The excursions of Jesus depicted in block 6 actually touched upon countries that were later reached by the first gentile mission of the church, that is, Phoenicia and Syria (Acts 11:19).

Block 7
Teaching in Capernaum
Matt. 17:22—18:35 with Parallels

The pericopes found in the relatively short block 7 deal with the Lord's final teaching in Galilee, and particularly in Capernaum. In accordance with its general didactic program, the Gospel of Matthew has reported about this in detail (Matt. 17:22—18:35), while Mark and Luke have retained somewhat less material (Mark 9:30–50; Luke 9:43b–50). Jesus begins with a second prediction of his passion (Matt. 17:22–23 with par.; cf. 16:21–23 with par.). What follows is a discussion of questions important for the early church. There is a question about the temple tax, addressed to Peter (Matt. 17:24–27); then discussions about the highest rank among the apostles (18:1–5 with par.); the correct attitude toward a foreign exorcist (Mark 9:38–41 // Luke 9:49–50), caused by John the son of Zebedee and later actualized in Samaria just for him (Acts 8:9, 14). Finally, there are problems of church discipline later significant for the early church and especially for Peter, concerning the following topics: the eventual necessity of an excommunication (Matt. 18:6–9 with par.; cf. 16:19); the duty of saving every lost sheep (18:10–14; cf. the word to Peter in John 21:15–17); the obligation to admonish and forgive an erring brother (Matt. 18:15–35).

With regard to frequency types, the material of block 7 is subject to great variation. Context-parallel triple traditions are found in two pericopes, dealing with the passion and the question of rank (Matt. 17:22–23; 18:1–5 with par.). The pericope about excommunication is a non-context-parallel triple tradition

where the Lukan parallel is found in the travel narrative (Matt. 18:6–9 // Mark 9:42–48; Luke 17:1–2). Furthermore, there are these units: three Q traditions to which the Lukan parallels also occur in the travel report (Matt. 18:10–14, 15, 21–22; Luke 15:37; 17:3, 4); one context-parallel double tradition common to Mark and Luke, namely, the pericope on the exorcist (Mark 9:38–41 // Luke 9:49–50); three special units of Matthew dealing with the temple tax (Matt. 17:24–27), with the admonition of an erring brother (18:16–20), and with the forgiveness of debts (18:23–35). At the end of the block, Mark has quoted a logion about salt, the parallels to which are found in Matthew's Sermon on the Mount and Luke's travel narrative (Mark 9:49–50; Matt. 5:13; Luke 14:34–35).

Topographically, the Gospels of Matthew and Mark agree with each other in block 7 insofar as they have connected the Master's last teaching in Galilee with Capernaum. After having described his visit to countries north of the lake in the concluding section of block 6, they have mentioned his return to Galilee (Matt. 17:22 // Mark 9:30), and let him enter a house in Capernaum (Matt. 17:24–25; Mark 9:33). Because this house was simply called "the house," it was assumed to be well known, and evidently the house of Peter's mother-in-law was alluded to, where Jesus had stayed during his beginning activity in Galilee (Matt. 8:14 with par.). There are two references in Matthew to Peter as the receiver of the teaching in this house (Matt. 17:24–25; 18:21), while Mark has mentioned only Capernaum, the house, and the Twelve (Mark 9:33).

Luke differs from the other Synoptics in block 7 by his vague topography. This already affects block 6, where Luke's contextual parallels to Matthew and Mark contain no indication of Caesarea Philippi and its surroundings (see pp. 110–11). In block 7, too, counterparts to the geographical indications of Matthew and Mark are missing in Luke where neither Galilee nor Capernaum, neither the house nor Peter, are mentioned.

Only in the first half of block 7 has Luke presented contextual parallels to Matthew and Mark. These concern the following themes: (1) the second prediction of the passion (Luke 9:43b–45); (2) the question of rank among the apostles (9:46–48), which is further illustrated by an important *alibi* analogy explicitly referring to the sons of Zebedee (Matt. 20:20 // Mark 10:35); and (3) the question about the exorcist, asked by John the son of Zebedee (9:49–50). The latter here learns to be tolerant of foreign exorcists, and immediately afterward the same disciple and his brother learn to moderate their indignation over a village in Samaria (9:51–56), the country where John was later confronted with the exorcist Simon Magus (Acts 8:9, 14). In all of these cases a gradual enlightening of the apostle John is the subject, and this seems to have been what caused Luke to preserve the traditions in question.

Within the second half of block 7 according to Matthew and Mark, there are no elements to which Luke offers contextual parallels. But in Luke's travel narrative of block 8, which actually implies a continuation of the instruction given by Jesus in the Lukan elements of block 7, the evangelist has included several

alibi analogies to passages found in Matthew's and Mark's second half of the block (counterparts to Matthew and Mark in Luke 14:34–35; 17:1–2; and to Matthew in 15:37; 17:3–4).

These particularities, displayed in block 7 by Matthew and Mark on the one hand and by Luke on the other, can be explained with reference to the different authorities from whom the evangelists took over their material.

It is noticeable that Matthew has explicitly referred to Peter as the mediator of those lessons on questions of church discipline which were offered by Jesus in Capernaum (Matt. 17:24; 18:21). To some extent, Mark has taken over corresponding material and referred it to a house in Capernaum which must be understood to be that of Peter (Mark 9:33). Matthew's and Mark's material in block 7 was therefore most likely based on remembrances of Peter from Capernaum. Later the questions and the answers involved received concrete importance for Peter and the apostles in Jerusalem, and so the assumption is also justified that Peter's well-known instructional speeches (called διδασκαλίαι by Papias in Eusebius, *EH* III.39.15) were behind the teaching units collected in block 7 by Matthew and Mark, in which connection there is special reason to think of Peter's teaching activity in the Jerusalem temple (Acts 2:46; 3:11; 5:12, 21, 25).

Luke's differences from Matthew and Mark in block 7 can be ascribed to another background of the traditions adopted. In this section the Third Gospel contains no reference to Peter and Capernaum, and only some contextual parallels to Matthew's and Mark's first half of the block, while some *alibi* analogies to their second half are inserted among Transjordanian narratives in Luke's block 8. This proves that Luke did not base his information so much on reminiscences of Peter from Capernaum but rather on communications of traditionists connected with Transjordan. Among them, Philip was evidently of central importance for Luke, as will be demonstrated in chapter 7. This is confirmed by a circumstance observed above, namely, that Luke's contextual parallels to Matthew and Mark in the first half of block 7 have to do with instructions particularly given to John the son of Zebedee, whose later missionary activity in Samaria around A.D. 37 had been prepared just by Philip (Acts 8:5, 14).

Chapter Six

Part III: Jesus in Transjordan and Jerusalem

Luke 9:51—18:14 + Matt. 19:1—28:20 with Parallels

The last section of the synoptic material, which is here called part III, contains pieces of tradition designated as blocks 8 to 12. They describe a journey of Jesus from the north to the south, his activity in Judea and Jerusalem, his passion, crucifixion, and resurrection.

What is handled as block 8 in the present context deals with the first part of the journey from Galilee to Judea and is found only in Luke as the so-called travel narrative which, because of its size and weight, is here treated separately (Luke 9:51—18:14). In blocks 9 to 12 there is a fundamental parallelism between all the Synoptic Gospels (Matt. 19:1—28:20 with parallels).

An essential difference between the first three Gospels and the Fourth Gospel appears in connection with this move of Jesus from Galilee to Judea. While the Gospel of John has alternately connected its account with Judea and Galilee and has referred to more visits of the Master in Jerusalem, the Synoptic Gospels have indicated only one coherent activity in Galilee and one definitive journey to Jerusalem. This difference cannot be leveled out by any literary harmonization. Originally the units of tradition existed independently from each other and were meant to illustrate various topics, and when they were comprehended into larger structures, the result became somewhat different compositions. The synoptic and Johannine pictures of the Master's life may therefore be understood as complementing each other.

First of all, the synoptic reports contained in part III are characterized by the presupposition just mentioned, implying that Jesus had concluded his activity in Galilee and then passed to Perea and Judea in order to fulfill his destiny in Jerusalem. Block 8, or the travel narrative (Luke 9:51—18:14), amplifies this layout and at both ends is attached to material common to the Synoptics in the adjacent blocks. Its purpose was to fill the gap between the synoptic traditions clustered in blocks 7 and 9, one of which refers to Galilee and the other to Perea in the southern part of Transjordan. For some reason Matthew and Mark have not described any wandering between these areas. To give a more complete

picture of Christ's journey through different parts of Transjordan, Luke collected Q traditions and special units in his travel narrative. He reported here that messengers of Jesus first visited Samaria without success (9:51–56) and that he then sent out missionaries and instructed disciples in Transjordan, where he was accompanied by an imposing and enthusiastic multitude (9:57—18:14). Without interruption the wandering is afterward continued in the Lukan elements of block 9 (18:15—19:31), and in this context the story of Luke runs again in parallelism with that of the other Synoptics (Matt. 19:1—20:34 // Mark 10:1–52).

An interesting point is the simple device by which Matthew and Mark have passed in their story from block 7 to block 9, for they have only indicated the move from Galilee to southern Transjordan by introducing block 9 with a sudden reference to Perea (Matt. 19:1 // Mark 10:1). It was the material that brought them to connect block 7 and block 9 in this fragmentary manner, because in both cases the contents were examples of Christ's teaching activity, so that block 9 just continued what had been the subject of block 7. Since block 8 is also based on instructive material, Luke's addition of it meant that two didactic blocks, separated in Matthew and Mark only by that topographic notice, were completed and combined by inserting further instructive material of different origin. In block 9 the synoptic parallelism, which has been studied above in the analysis of block 7, is to be observed again (Matt. 19:1—20:34 with par., increased by Luke 19:1–27).

After having mentioned a visit to Jericho at the end of block 9, the synoptic writers have described the conclusive drama with a maximum of contextual parallelism in the last sections of part III, which include blocks 10 to 12 (Matt. 21:1—28:20 with par.). These blocks contain the passion story, and the records of the entry into the city, the cleansing of the temple, and the disputations in Jerusalem are designated below as block 10, the farewell speech on the Mount of Olives as block 11, and the reports on the trial, the eucharist, the crucifixion, and the resurrection as block 12.

In its totality part III thus consists of the Lukan travel report, of the common synoptic sequel of information about the journey, and of the passion story (Luke 9:51—18:14 + Matt. 19:1—28:20 with par.).

Block 8
Teaching in Transjordan
Luke 9:51—18:14

Luke's travel narrative, here called block 8, comprises an entire third of the largest Gospel and for that reason is treated as a special unit (Luke 9:51—18:14). It is exclusively Lukan, and while it consists of a few nonparallel triple traditions, all of its other components are Q traditions and special pericopes.

The triple, double, and single traditions contained in the travel narrative are of

a pronouncedly didactic type. It is alternately a question of instructing disciples and discussing with opponents. The purpose of the whole block, however, is to establish a transition of the Lord's Galilean teaching according to block 7 (Matt. 17:24—18:35 with par.) to his Perean and Judean teaching in block 9 (Matt. 19:1—20:34 with par.). In block 7 the tradition represented Jesus as teaching in Capernaum, and in block 9 Matthew and Mark have described a direct continuation of this teaching but referred it to Perea by a sudden notice at the beginning of the block (Matt. 19:1 // Mark 10:1) without any reference to the journey between the areas in question. Luke's travel narrative in block 8 forms a bridge between the didactic traditions located in Galilee in block 7 and Perea in block 9.

Through scattered remarks Luke has made it clear in block 8 that he wanted to shed light upon a journey of the Master and his disciples from Galilee to Judea (Luke 9:51, 57; 10:1, 38; 13:22, 33; 14:25; 17:11). No place-names were mentioned, but various details indicate that Luke had in mind a journey through different parts of Transjordan, and one may think of the tetrarchy of Philip in the north, Decapolis in the middle, and Perea in the south.

In the introductory report on the disappointment of the sons of Zebedee concerning a Samaritan village, the presupposition is that Jesus had sent a couple of messengers over the northern border of Samaria while he remained with the apostles on the border (Luke 9:51–56). There is a later retrospective on this situation in the episode about the ten lepers (17:11–19). Here v. 11 is literally to be translated in the following manner: "while he was on the point of crossing (διήρχετο, imperfect) over the border between Samaria and Galilee." The reason for the insertion of this retrospective was the catchword "thankfulness" (17:9), which the traditionists wanted to illustrate by the story of the thankful Samaritan (17:16). In any case, the disappointment of James and John concerning the village in Samaria (9:53) represents the beginning of Christ's pilgrimage to Jerusalem (9:51).

After this Samaritan episode Jesus is said to have passed through other regions (9:56). There he was able to gather a powerful multitude of followers with the aid of seventy (according to a variant reading seventy-two) disciples (10:1, seventy disciples sent out; 10:17, 21, 23, the messengers and Christ rejoice over the success; 11:29, great crowds gathered; 12:1, even myriads; 14:25, new multitudes).

For the following reasons, the activity implies an extension to Hellenistic areas. (1) The reference to seventy or seventy-two disciples corresponds to the number of nations in the world mentioned in Gen. 10:1–32 by the Hebrew and Greek texts, respectively. (2) Those sent out were admonished two times not to refuse any food offered to them (10:7 and 8), so they were entrusted with a mission among the heathen independently of Jewish laws about clean and unclean food. (3) They reported later about a general defeat of the demons (10:17), and this indicates a victory over idolaters (similar connections between

demons and idolatry in Deut. 32:17; Ps. 96:5; Acts 17:18, 22; 1 Cor. 10:20–21; 1 Thess. 1:9). In the travel narrative the great multitudes who followed Jesus and the disciples in the course of their journey to Judea and Jerusalem were therefore considered mainly to have consisted of converted Gentiles.

Concerning the homelands of those converted, there is reason to think of (1) northern Transjordan, (2) Decapolis, and (3) southern Transjordan as the closest Hellenistic neighborhoods of Palestine. (1) Followers coming from northern Transjordan and even Syria may be supposed to have been involved because of the success Jesus had already had in these countries. In block 6 Luke's traditionists have betrayed special connections with the surroundings of Bethsaida (above, p. 111). According to Matthew, people in Syria had already heard of Jesus (Matt. 4:24), and according to Luke in Acts a proselyte called Nicholaus of Antioch belonged to the earliest church in Jerusalem (Acts 6:5). (2) In different contexts, Decapolis has also been mentioned or indicated as a region where Jesus had previously had success (Matt. 4:25; 8:28 // Mark 5:1 // Luke 8:26; Mark 5:20 // Luke 8:39; Mark 7:31). (3) According to Josephus, the middle and southern parts of Transjordan were called Perea and included the area from Pella to Machaerus and from the Jordan to Philadelphia (Josephus, *War* III.44–47). This corresponds to parts of Decapolis, and to the southern area of Transjordan which belonged to the Galilean tetrarch Herod Antipas and was called Perea in a narrower sense. When the evangelists Matthew and Mark spoke of the country "across the Jordan" (*πέραν τοῦ Ἰορδάνου*), they meant Perea in that wider sense (Matt. 4:15, 25; Mark 3:8; Matt. 19:1 // Mark 10:1). Luke has never used any such expression, and evidently it was due to the fact that his traditionists belonged to this region and did not regard it as being on the other side of the river. At any rate, the Pharisaic warning concerning plots to be expected from Herod Antipas (Luke 13:31–33) points toward Perea, because this region was governed by the same tetrarch and its capital was the Hellenistic city of Livias or Julias, which Antipas had named after the wife of Augustus. The warning in question depended on the fact that Antipas had recently arrested and beheaded John the Baptist in Perea (Josephus, *Antiquities* XVIII.119). Moreover, the utterance of Jesus about his approaching visit to Jerusalem (Luke 13:33) is meaningful only if localized to Perea. Finally, one has to observe that in block 9 Luke's travel narrative of block 8 is directly prolonged in contextual parallelism with Matthew and Mark, and so the reference of the First and Second Gospels to the country across the Jordan (Matt. 19:1 // Mark 10:1) proves that Luke's story in blocks 8 and 9 was generally connected with this area.

To sum up, the Lukan travel narrative indicates a journey of Jesus from Galilee through Decapolis and Perea, countries dominated by Hellenism. Luke has not quoted any place-names except the introductory reference to Samaria (Luke 9:51–56), but the circumstances standing out in the rest of block 8 as well as in block 9 point in this direction. The traditionists behind the travel narrative looked back upon the words and works of Jesus in a Transjordanian perspective.

As to the multitudes who followed Jesus according to Luke in block 8, the great crowd of pilgrims going with him is mentioned by all the Synoptics in block 9 with regard to his passage through Jericho (Matt. 19:2 // Mark 10:1; Matt. 20:29 // Mark 10:46; Luke 18:46; 19:3) and in block 10 with regard to his entry in Jerusalem (Matt. 21:9 with par.). Since the pilgrims had followed Jesus from Perea, a Hellenistic background is to be presupposed concerning several of them. John has also mentioned this crowd (John 12:12, 17), and in addition referred to Greek-speaking pilgrims who came to Jesus in Jerusalem and with the help of Philip and Andrew were informed by Jesus about following him in stewardship (John 12:20–26). According to a former notice of John, both mediators came from the city of Bethsaida in northern Transjordan (1:44), and by mentioning the city again when describing the Jerusalem episode (12:21), John in fact intimated that the God-fearing Hellenists came from this area. They asked Philip and Andrew to introduce them to Jesus, because they knew that these disciples were their countrymen. It is also evident that John was aware that Philip would become entrusted with the task of stewardship, for at the feeding of the five thousand in the region of Bethsaida Jesus was said to have made Philip especially amazed by his intention of feeding such a great crowd (6:5–6). This furnishes a background of Philip's later service at the tables in the early church, as described by Luke in another context (Acts 6:1, 5).

In a similar way there is reason to see a connection between the interest of Luke in the Hellenistic followers of Jesus during his journey through Transjordan and the same evangelist's detailed information about the activity of the Hellenistic group and especially Philip in Jerusalem and on the mission field (Acts 6:1—8:40). A particular aspect of block 8 is the numerous scenes and metaphors connected with meals (Luke 10:38–42 e.p.), which stamp the entire travel narrative, as will be demonstrated below. They correspond to the emphasis of Acts on the charity meals arranged by Stephen, Philip, and the other Hellenists of the early church (Acts 6:1–6).

According to an inscription from the first Christian century and discovered in Jerusalem, a certain Theodotus had founded a synagogue for the Hellenistic Jews on the Ophel south of the temple.[1] The Hellenistic Christians in Jerusalem may be supposed to have met in the same area, and the discussions of Stephen with Hellenistic Jews in Jerusalem (Acts 6:9) can also have taken place there.

In any case, Luke's conspicuous insistence on the great multitudes of mainly Hellenistic pilgrims following Jesus to the Holy City suggests from which persons the evangelist took over the traditions contained in his narrative of block 8. There is reason to think of authorities who may have been known to Luke and inclined to report on the journey of Jesus from Galilee to Jerusalem from the points of view characteristic of the extant travel narrative.

1. W. Schrage, "συναγωγή," *Theologisches Wörterbuch zum Neuen Testament* 7 (1964): 811, 818, 820, 844.

Luke told Theophilus in his prologue that he wanted to record what original eyewitnesses and servants of the word had delivered to him orally (Luke 1:2). For him, the eyewitnesses were particularly the Galilean apostles (Acts 1:21–22). The other category of traditionists important for him, those whom he said had been servants of the gospel from the very beginning, were obviously witnesses to Christ of whom Luke had personal knowledge, and these were, according to Acts, the Hellenists of the early church. Luke was able to report in detail about charity meals in favor of the Jerusalem widows, the installation of seven Hellenistic social workers, the martyrdom of Stephen, and the subsequent missionary activity of Philip (Acts 6:1—8:40). Later he told about Peter's conversion to a mission among Hellenists in Caesarea (10:1—11:18), and described on the basis of personal experiences the expansion of the gospel from Antioch (11:19–30) as well as the sending of Paul to distant Hellenistic countries (13:1—28:31). The so-called "we" reports and other elements of Acts prove that Luke came into personal contact with several of the Hellenists in Jerusalem, such as Barnabas, Mark, Silvanus, Philip, and Mnason (4:36; 12:12; 13:2, 5; 15:22, 35, 40; 21:8, 16). Among these persons, Mnason came from Cyprus but had a house in Jerusalem where he offered hospitality to Paul and the company, including Luke according to the "we" (21:16–17), and by calling him "an old disciple" Luke indicated that Mnason belonged to those who had been "servants of the word from the very beginning" (Luke 1:2). Especially remarkable is the notice on an encounter with Philip in Caesarea, which is also part of a "we" report (Acts 21:8). On the basis of Paul's letter to Philemon, it becomes evident that Luke, like Mark, served as a fellow worker of Paul during the latter's captivity in Caesarea from A.D. 58 to 60 (Mark and Luke mentioned together in Philemon 24, as also in Col. 4:10, 14). The location to Caesarea is necessitated by the expression "now also a prisoner of Christ Jesus" (Philemon 9). Numerous details thus illustrate associations with Hellenists who had belonged to the Jerusalem church.

On the assumption that Luke's material collected in block 8 came to him from traditionists in Jerusalem with a background in Hellenistic parts of Transjordan, it becomes conceivable why Luke has referred so many units of his travel narrative to this area. Except single traditions, Luke has accumulated here a few non-context-parallel triple traditions and especially a great number of non-context-parallel double traditions, to which Matthew and Mark offer analogies localized to Galilee or Judea. Thus, for instance, Matthew has presented the Lord's prayer within a sermon of Jesus in Galilee (Matt. 6:9–15), but Luke has traced it back to a disciple's request during the journey through Transjordan (Luke 11:1–4). Matthew and Mark have told of a scribe in Jerusalem wanting to discuss the greatest commandment (Matt. 22:34–40 // Mark 12:28–34), while Luke took up the same topic right after the beginning of the pilgrimage to Jerusalem (Luke 10:25–28). Originally such teaching units, named διδασκαλίαι by Papias with regard to Mark, were built up on a topic and not on local circumstances. In the early church of Jerusalem they were quoted to illustrate the

teaching activity of Jesus with regard to extant problems. Here the Galilean apostles, led by Peter, were inclined to remind the audience of Christ's teaching in Galilee and Capernaum, while the Transjordanian members of the Hellenistic group preferred to speak about his teaching in Transjordan. Certainly some *alibi* analogies can possibly be explained on the suggestion that analogous situations in Galilee, Transjordan, or Judea have led Jesus to use similar words in different contexts. However, insofar as most quotations were not originally localized, one has to presuppose a fundamental mobility. Depending on the interests of the traditionists in Jerusalem, several quotations came to the fore as reminiscences either from Galilee, Transjordan, or Judea.

Whereas the framework of the journey presupposed by the travel narrative is Transjordan, the details contained in the block are based on interests of the Jerusalem church. As will be shown with regard to blocks 9 to 12, practical concerns of the early church were a starting point for the formation of many traditions, and this is also true of block 8. In the latter case, one has to think not so much of apostolic teaching in the temple (Acts 2:42–46, etc.) as of a partly analogous teaching presented by Stephen, Philip, and the other Hellenists. The seven Hellenists were elected among persons able to speak with spirit and wisdom (Acts 6:3, 10), and Philip later developed a successful preaching activity (8:5–40).

A survey of the travel narrative will illustrate such connections between units of block 8 and practical concerns of the early church.

In the first half of block 8 (Luke 9:51—13:35), the introductory notice about the Lord's "going up" (ἀνάλημψις) to Jerusalem (9:51, 53) was clearly formulated in a Jerusalem perspective. The lesson given to the sons of Zebedee about the right attitude toward Samaria (9:55) was of importance with regard to the later activity of Philip and John the son of Zebedee in Samaria (Acts 8:5, 14). Numerically the seventy (or seventy-two) missionaries in Transjordan (Luke 10:1) form a counterpart to the members of the Sanhedrin in Jerusalem. In spite of the Transjordanian localization, the question of the scribe concerning the greatest commandment (10:25) remains in a Jerusalem perspective, because in the reply Jesus describes events on the road from Jerusalem to Jericho (10:30). According to John, the sisters Mary and Martha lived in Bethany (John 11:1). Luke mentioned the sisters without any localization quite early in the travel narrative (Luke 10:38–42), because the interest of the traditionists was to let the episode shed light on a problem important for the early church. This was the relationship between liturgy and diacony in Jerusalem, where the Hellenists had to serve at the tables as did Martha (Acts 6:2) but were also eager to serve the word as was Mary (6:10; 8:5–40). Considering the following sequence of instructions about prayer for daily bread (Luke 11:1–4), willingness to feed the hungry (11:5–8), and divine providence (11:9–13), one will find it was apt to encourage social workers and missionaries such as the Hellenists of the early church. The answer given to the woman who praised the Lord's mother because of her blood

relationship to Jesus (Luke 11:27–28) illustrated a problem in the early church, to which Mary and the brothers of Jesus belonged (Acts 1:14) and in which Hebrew widows were easily preferred to Hellenistic ones (Acts 6:1). In a speech containing Q traditions and special units, Jesus then warns the disciples not to be anxious, to have trust, to be prepared, and so on (Luke 12:1–56), and the selection of the topics shows that he was understood to have visualized difficulties familiar to the early church. Characteristic are the references to a martyrdom like that of Stephen (12:4), to provision of food (12:24), to patient table service (12:42), and to divisions among relatives (12:52–53). The catastrophes, which had occurred in the temple and at Siloam (13:1, 4), must especially have been remembered by Christians in Jerusalem, and the complaint about the city (13:34–35) was of concrete importance for Hellenistic believers there.

The second half of block 8 (Luke 14:1—18:14) contains further reminiscences of the Lord's teaching, and these are in particular applicable to the activity of the Hellenists in Jerusalem with regard to the common meals. At the very beginning there are instructions about places at the table and the invitation of poor and sick people (14:7, 13, 21). The three parables about the lost sheep, the lost coin, and the prodigal son (15:1–32) were suitable to justify the presence of non-Jewish elements at the charity meals, as practiced by the Hellenists in Jerusalem. Charity toward the poor is also the topic of two subsequent parables (16:1–13, 19–31). Within the instructions about life in the church (17:1–19) and waiting for the Parousia (17:20–37) allusions to the meals of the disciples are found again (17:8, 27, 28, 34), and thus an interest of the Hellenistic group is considered, as even in the retrospect on the thankful Samaritan (17:11–19). At the end of block 8 two example stories have been appended, one about the judge and the widow and one about the Pharisee and the publican in the temple (18:1–14). These pericopes are not misplaced, for like the whole travel narrative they represent concerns of the Hellenists in Jerusalem who took special care of widows (Acts 6:3), opposed Jewish pretentiousness (7:51), and possibly had a center on the Ophel near the temple (above, p. 120).

Further evidence for the didactic purpose of the material collected in block 8 is found in the general distribution of the pericopes on two alternating themes: (*a*) discussion with outsiders, sometimes with believers; (*b*) instruction of disciples. Luke has produced a nearly rhythmic variation of these items:

a. Discussion about Samaria (9:51–56) and condition for discipleship (9:57–62)
b. Instruction of the seventy missionaries (10:1–24)

a. Discussion about the greatest commandment (10:25–37), then about diacony and liturgy (10:38–42)
b. Instruction on prayer and on providence (11:1–13)

a. Discussion with opponents and dissenters (11:14–54)
b. Instruction on confession, on confidence, and on preparedness (12:1–59)

a. Discussion about catastrophes and healing on the Sabbath (13:1–17)
b. Instruction on the expansion of the kingdom and on the exclusion of unbelievers (13:18–30)

a. Discussion about Antipas, and complaint on Jerusalem (13:31–35); another discussion about healing on the Sabbath (14:1–6)
b. Instruction on the order at the tables, on invitation of guests and conditions for discipleship (14:7–35)

a. Discussion about inviting the lost (15:1–32)
b. Instruction on generosity (16:1–31), on church discipline (17:1–10) and thankfulness (17:11–19)

a. Discussion about the parousia (17:20–37)
b. Instruction on prayer and on repentance (18:1–14)

The suggested connection between the travel narrative and the Hellenists in Jerusalem is especially illustrated by the numerous scenes and metaphors dealing with meals (above, p. 123). A summary of the relevant items may clarify this.

Within block 8, references to meals emerge when the following topics are treated: the service of Martha (Luke 10:40); the providing of daily bread (11:3, 5, 11–12); a dinner in a Pharisee's house (11:37); the concupiscence of the rich man (12:19); satisfaction through divine providence (12:24); diacony practiced by the heavenly bridegroom (12:37); distribution of daily food by Peter and the apostles, and even by "all" servants of the word (12:41–42); table communion of the converted, together with the patriarchs (13:25–29); another dinner in a Pharisee's house (14:1); the order at the tables (14:7–14); the invitation to the great banquet (14:15–24); the joy about the return of those lost (15:6, 9, 22–32); hospitality as a recompense for the remission of debts (16:4–7); the banquets of the rich man and the hunger of Lazarus (16:19–21); table service of a faithful servant (17:8); sudden destruction of the world during a meal (17:27, 28, 34).

Moreover, two comprehensive sections of block 8 portray the Lord's teaching as continuous table-talks (11:37—12:59; 14:1—18:14). In the first case Jesus is briefly said to have been invited by a Pharisee for a meal (11:37); in the second case a leading Pharisee is expressly said to have invited him for a Sabbath meal (14:1), that is, for a Jewish qiddush arranged to inaugurate the Sabbath. What follows upon the two indications of meals is presented in both cases as examples of instruction and discussion given during these meals. An exception is only the retrospect on the thankful Samaritan (17:11–19), which has been inserted to illustrate the topic of thankfulness (17:9).

No doubt the many references to meals as well as the two prolonged table-talks found in block 8 prove that Christian communion at the tables was the basis for the collection of the traditions in question. Seeing that Luke had special contacts with the Hellenists in Jerusalem, who organized such a table communion, the conclusion must be that he took over his material in block 8 from this group.

In the same way that the Lukan elements of block 7 (Luke 9:43b–50) are directly continued in block 8 (9:51—18:14), so the latter block is also immediately continued by the Lukan elements of block 9 (18:15–30).

A certain similarity to Deuteronomy may be said to arise in this broader context. Deuteronomy has described how Moses led the elect people through Transjordan to the region of Jericho (Deut. 3:12–22; 34:1–3), and in block 8 Luke has permitted Jesus to lead his people through Transjordan to Jericho which is mentioned in block 9 (Luke 18:35). However, it was the connections of Luke's traditionists with Transjordan which caused the accumulation of the didactic material in block 8, whereas a comprehensive analogy between the exodus of Moses and the pilgrimage of Jesus may appear on a theological level when block 8 is studied together with block 9.

Block 9
Teaching in Perea and Activity at Jericho
Matt. 19:1—20:34 with Parallels + Luke 19:1–27

In block 9, the subject is the Lord's further teaching and continued activity in Perea and near Jericho. The main part of the block is dominated by context-parallel triple traditions (Matt. 19:1—20:34 with par.), while at the end are two Lukan units also referring to Jericho (Luke 19:1–27).

The arrangement of Matthew and Mark implies that Christ's teaching in Galilee and Capernaum described in block 7 (Matt. 17:22—18:35 // Mark 9:30–50) is directly continued by what is comprised in block 9. A short notice about Perea (Matt. 19:1 // Mark 10:1) is the only indication of a new scene, but attention remains focused on similar problems of the church as those treated in block 7.

Between the teaching sections represented by the blocks here called 7 and 9, Luke has inserted the travel narrative in his block 8 (Luke 9:51—18:14). Since its contents are likewise didactic, Luke has in fact presented three didactic sections in a row. In his elements of block 9, Luke has not mentioned Perea but has twice referred to Jericho (18:35; 19:1). As in block 8, Luke has in block 9 repeatedly mentioned the great multitude that accompanied Jesus on his pilgrimage to Jerusalem (18:15, 36, 43; 19:3, 11). The interest of Luke in table communion is also represented in the notice on the meal celebrated at the conversion of Zacchaeus (19:7).

In correspondence with Christ's approach to Jerusalem through Perea, the synoptic material contained in block 9 implies a much stronger frequency of context-parallel units than is found in the blocks 3 to 7 which deal with Galilee. Among the pericopes of block 9 are four context-parallel triple traditions (Matt. 19:13–15, 16–30; 20:17–19, 29–34 with par.) and two context-parallel double traditions (Matt. 19:1–12 // Mark 10:1–12; Matt. 20:20–28 // Mark 10:35–45), to which Luke presents elementary *alibi* analogies. In addition, there is one special tradition in Matthew (Matt. 20:1–16), one in Luke (Luke 19:1–10), and finally a Q tradition in Luke (19:11–27).

As was observed with regard to blocks 7 and 8 and as will become clear in blocks 10 to 12, the instructive material of block 9 was also meant to comply with practical concerns of the early church. Traditionists in Jerusalem (Matt. 20:17 with par.) recalled episodes during Christ's pilgrimage through Perea (Matt. 19:1 // Mark 10:1) and Jericho (Matt. 20:29 with par.; Luke 19:1) as replies to problems of importance for the community.

Questions were answered here concerning the exemplary attitude of Jesus toward marriage and divorce, infant children, and great wealth (Matt. 19:1–30 with par.). After the entry of Jesus with an imposing multitude of adherents from Transjordan, the equality of the old and new collaborators became a problem, and the answer to this was the parable of the workers in the vineyard (Matt. 20:1–16).

The logia of Jesus about his suffering in the capital and the need for the sons of Zebedee to follow him in suffering (Matt. 20:17–28 with par.) were relevant to the early church in Jerusalem, because here Peter and the apostles spread the testimony about the crucifixion and the resurrection of the Messiah (Acts 2:23, etc.) and here the church experienced attacks upon the apostles John and James (3:11; 12:2). The blind man Bartimaeus and the chief publican Zacchaeus lived at Jericho (Matt. 20:29 with par.; Luke 19:1), but the stories about them were told in Jerusalem. Bartimaeus had come with Jesus into the city (Matt. 20:34 with par.) and was known there. Zacchaeus was a pioneer of benevolence in the service of Jesus, and such welfare activity was a primary concern of the Hellenists in Jerusalem (Acts 4:36–37, Barnabas; 6:3, the Seven).

The parable of the pounds (Luke 19:11–27) was at the same time associated with Jericho and with Jerusalem. It is a Q tradition, and its Lukan form comprises a framework that implies both topographical aspects. Whereas the Matthean analogy is part of Christ's farewell speech in Jerusalem (Matt. 25:13–20), Luke has presented the parable just after the report on Zacchaeus in Jericho (Luke 19:1, 11) and said that Jesus intended to reject a rapturous eschatology (19:11). The particular framework of the parable in Luke's version opens three perspectives in which the pericope is to be studied. (1) In his parable Jesus has mentioned a claimant to the throne who made a journey to a distant country to be acknowledged (19:12), while his citizens sent an embassy to demonstrate against him (19:14). On his return he called his servants to account (19:15–26) and

punished his opponents (19:27). The central point here is the story of the account, to which there is a counterpart in Matthew. (2) Luke has surrounded this fundamental subject with a framework in which Jesus tells about the journey of the claimant, the opposition against him, and other details that do not seem to have been motivated by the central topic. It is possible, however, to explain the framework as based on reminiscences of historical events related to Jericho. Here was the favorite palace of Archelaus, the son and successor of Herod in Judea (Matt. 2:22), and his career was stamped by events like those told in the parable. Archelaus went to Rome with the ambition to get acknowledged by Augustus, but leading Jews complained about his nomination by an embassy sent to Rome, and when the prince had returned to Judea he punished the opponents severely (Josephus, *War* II.22, 37, 57, 80, 111). Recollections of this drama inspired the framework of the story which Luke has explicitly referred to Christ's ascent from Jericho to Jerusalem (19:11), just where the palace of Archelaus was located at the beginning of the mountain road. (3) The didactic purpose of the story, however, was to show what Christ will require from his messengers when he returns to judge the world. As in the Matthean parallel, the point is that Jesus wanted to make clear that he expects a profitable administration from his servants. It means they must expand the message of the kingdom, let it bear fruit and not remain isolated. This alternative was a problem for the apostles and the Hellenists in Jerusalem, and it was also exemplified by the Cornelius discussion (Acts 10:1—11:18).

It is thus evident that both the context-parallel traditions of block 9 and the other units of the section contain material collected for the information of the apostolic and Hellenistic church in Jerusalem.

Block 10
Entry Into Jerusalem, Temple Cleansing, Discussions Matt. 21:1—23:39 with Parallels

Block 10 depicts events taking place in Jerusalem during the first days of the passion week: the entry of Jesus over the Mount of Olives, traditionally dated to Palm Sunday; the cleansing of the temple area; discussion with various groups (Matt. 21:1—23:36 with par.); and in addition the Lord's lamentation on Jerusalem (Matt. 23:37–39) as well as the episode with the widow in the temple (Mark 12:41–44 // Luke 21:1–4).

As in block 9, context-parallel triple traditions are dominant, but there are sporadic examples of the other frequency types as well. Among them are two context-parallel double traditions, one in Matthew and Mark (the fig tree in Matt. 21:18–22 // Mark 11:12–14 + 20–26) and one in Mark and Luke (the widow in Mark 12:41–44 // Luke 21:1–4), then also three *alibi*-analogous Q traditions in Matthew (the wedding in Matt. 22:1–14, the woes against the

Pharisees in 23:13–36, the lamentation over Jerusalem in 23:37–39). Furthermore, a couple of special traditions are found: a shorter pericope and elements of a larger pericope in Matthew (the two sons in Matt. 21:28–32 and parts of the Pharisee speech in 23:2, 3, 5, 7b–12, 15–22, 27, 32), and a short pericope in Luke (the lamentation on Jerusalem known as "Dominus flevit," Luke 19:39–44).

With regard to frequency types, Matthew's anti-Pharisaic speech (Matt. 23:1–36) is an extraordinarily complicated aggregate. It begins with a context-parallel triple unit (below indicated as T), followed by a row of alternating special units (S) and Q traditions (Q) which is divided twice by a context-parallel triple unit (T):

Matt. 23:1 = T, vv. 2–3 = S, v. 4 = Q, v. 5 = S, v. 6 = T, v. 7a = Q, vv. 7b–12 = S, v. 13 = Q, v. 14 *var. lect.* = T, vv. 15–22 = S, vv. 23–27a = Q, vv. 27b–28 = S, vv. 29–31 = Q, vv. 32–33 = S, vv. 34–36 = Q.

In spite of this variation of frequency types, the Matthean composition forms a logical structure, as will be demonstrated below.

With remarkable consistency, all pictures developed in block 10 represent the perspective of the Jerusalem church. In this context, the material collected by Matthew is particularly rich.

The enthusiasm of the multitude expressed at the entry of Jesus over the Mount of Olives (Matt. 21:1–9 with par.) was recalled in order to emphasize the contrast to the skepticism later unfolded by various circles in Jerusalem against the son of David. As will be explained in chapter 7, the Lukan report on Christ's lamentation over Jerusalem when seeing the city from the Mount of Olives ("Dominus flevit," Luke 19:39–44) is no prophecy *ex eventu* about the Roman siege of the city in A.D. 70, but accentuates with the aid of prophetic quotations the disappointment of the early church over the official resistance against the gospel and the reserves of Stephen and other Hellenists against the popular veneration of the temple (Acts 6:13; 7:48, 51). The cleansing of the temple (Matt. 21:10–17 with par.) was reported in view of the later activity of the apostles in the temple (Acts 2:46; 3:1, 11; 5:12). Concerning the parabolic act practiced on the barren fig tree, there is a difference of context insofar as Matthew has told of it after the cleansing of the temple, while Mark has first mentioned it before and then after this event (Matt. 21:18–22 // Mark 11:12–14 + 20–26). In any case, there is reason to see the fig tree in the light of a similar parable in Luke where a barren fig tree symbolizes countrymen who disappoint Jesus (Luke 13:6–12), a feeling shared by the Christians in Jerusalem.

The following disputations in the temple, in which Jesus defeated high priests, Pharisees, Sadducees, and scribes (Matt. 21:23–27 with par.; 22:15–46 with par.), were likewise supposed to serve as visual instruction of the post-Easter church in Jerusalem. In the vicinity of the temple, the church was confronted with the same groups, negatively with high priests and Sadducees (Acts 4:1; 5:17), in part also positively with Pharisees and scribes (5:34; 15:5). Form

criticism has called such disputations *Streitgespräche* and made them a special genre. Although reports on disputations also occur in other contexts (Matt. 15:1–20 with par.; John 5:16–47 e.p.), the Synoptic Gospels, especially Matthew, have accumulated examples of the kind in the passion story. Reminiscences of the intellectual victories of the Master during the holy week had to strengthen the early church when its members were debating with such critics. Stephen was especially known as being successful in this regard (Acts 6:9–10).

Between the reports on the altercation with high priests and Pharisees appears the parable about the wicked husbandmen, which is a context-parallel triple tradition (Matt. 21:33–46 with par.). In the First Gospel it is encompassed by two further parables, of which the one about the two sons is a special tradition (Matt. 21:28–32) and the one about the wedding a Q tradition (22:1–14). The three parables deal with the same topic, that is, the disobedience of those first commissioned and the forwarding of the assignment to others.

By means of these parables, the relationship between the mission to the Jews and that to the Gentiles is elucidated (cf. the discussion in Gal. 2:7–9). According to Matthew and Mark, Jesus had demanded a primary approach to the Jews (Matt. 10:6; 15:24, 26 // Mark 7:27), and this particularism was first represented by Peter and his group in Jerusalem (Acts 2:14, 22; 10:28). In a prophetic way, the parables in question indicate an extension of the mission to all nations. Matthew has permitted his report to culminate in this universalism (Matt. 28:19), and in spite of Peter's hesitation the early church gradually accepted the program of a foreign mission (Acts 8:5; 10:35; 11:20; Gal. 2:9).

As were the preceding examples of discussion, so also were the critical remarks of Jesus against the Pharisees and the scribes, clustered in the final part of block 10 (Matt. 23:1–39, partly with par.), intended to guide the early church in controversy with such opponents.

Jesus is first quoted as warning his listeners in the temple against difficult adversaries by whom the church of Jerusalem was later to be attacked. According to Matthew the Pharisees were especially meant, according to Mark and Luke generally the scribes (Matt. 23:1–12, with fragmentary parallels). Matthew has then cited seven (eight, according to a variant reading) woes of Jesus spoken against the Pharisees and concluded by a general indictment on them (Matt. 23:13–36). An *alibi* analogy to this series of woes is found in Luke's block 8 (Luke 11:39–52), here introduced by a reference to Jesus as being a guest in a Pharisee's house during his journey through Transjordan (11:37–38) and concluded with a description of Pharisaic indignation against him (11:53–54). Luke has presented six of the woes found in Matthew, but in a different order. Three of them are directed against the Pharisees (11:42–44) and three against the scribes (11:45–48, 52). Before the last woe (11:52), there is a counterpart to the indictment which summarizes the speech in Matthew (Luke 11:49–51). Thus similarities and differences are completely mingled in the two Gospels. Matthew and Luke have preserved the same theme and the same components of the speech, but the context

is different and the order of the woes divergent. Even if the variation in context can eventually be explained on a redactional level, this is not possible with regard to the deviation in order. Whether the one Gospel is understood as the source of the other, or a logia source is supposed to be the source of both, the absurd picture of a redactor emerges who cuts up his copy into small pieces out of sheer arbitrariness and produces a new pattern. The only possible explanation is furnished by the tendency of many oral traditions to combine a constancy of the topic with a flexibility of the structure. With regard to the woes, it seems most plausible that Matthew and Luke were dependent on a common tradition, which developed in two directions while allowing contingency and variation to complement each other.

The background of the woes quoted by Matthew and Luke were logia of Jesus of which the apostles and other servants of the gospel were reminded in order to enforce themselves and the believers when discussing with antagonists in Jerusalem. It is evident from the references to the building of tombs for the prophets and to the murder of Zechariah in the temple that Matthew's and Luke's traditions had a background in Jerusalem (Matt. 23:29, 35; Luke 11:47, 51). Luke, however, has inserted the woes in his travel narrative of block 8, because his Hellenistic traditionists liked to trace back such words of Jesus to the Lord's journey through Transjordan, as has been observed several times in block 8 (pp. 120–25).

At the end of Matthew's anti-Pharisaic speech in block 10, a Q tradition concerning the lamentation of Christ over Jerusalem was added (Matt. 23:37–39), and the *alibi* analogy to this is also found in Luke's travel narrative (Luke 13:34–35). In both cases the Lord's disappointment over Jerusalem's impenitence has a bearing on the disappointment of the early church when confronted with the Jewish opposition. Luke's dependence on Hellenistic traditionists led him to incorporate this dirge into his travel narrative. Without a doubt, however, both in Matthew's critical speech and in Luke's travel narrative the grievance of Jesus was quoted because of negative experiences of Christians in Jerusalem.

In the last portion of block 10, a context-parallel double tradition of Mark and Luke appears which concerns a widow's offering in the court of the women on the temple area (Mark 12:41–44 // Luke 21:1–4). Why this pericope finds no counterpart in Matthew remains a question. Mark and Luke depict the episode with different expressions but quote the words of Jesus almost in verbal agreement. This tendency occurs frequently in the synoptic traditions, for the action is often told with freedom, while agreement is maintained in the words of Jesus (e.g., Matt. 9:1–8 with par., the Paralytic). Literary criticism cannot explain this phenomenon, but one can resort to experiences of tradition history which imply that narrative elements should be varied and sayings of the hero be treated with reverence. Since the Lord is said to have observed the widow in the temple and since the young church had special concern for widows (Acts 6:1), the transmission of the story was also based on activities of the early Christians in Jerusalem.

On the whole, problems and duties of the early church in Jerusalem led to the formation of traditions collected in block 10. These traditions recalled actions and sayings of Jesus connected with the temple in Jerusalem, and the purpose was to strengthen and encourage the activity of the Christians at the temple and near it. It is especially evident that Matthew has allowed the pericopes of block 10 to serve as such encouragement and guidance of the apostolic church.

Block 10 forms a consistent structure even though different frequency types occur in the synoptic texts. Seven context-parallel triple traditions constitute a basic framework, and the ten representatives of the other frequency types never break off the message of the triple traditions but, rather, supplement them. This is true particularly of the double and special traditions preserved in Matthew but even of the other double and special traditions found in block 10. Christ's conflict with the Jewish public is here the golden thread insofar as he offers an image for the church that was exposed to similar confrontations in Jerusalem.

Block 11
Farewell Speech on the Mount of Olives
Matt. 24:1—25:46 with Parallels

In block 11, quotations of logia illustrate a teaching offered by the Master shortly before his passion (Matt. 24:1—25:46, partly with parallels). Here again, as in block 10, the most detailed presentation of the material is found in Matthew, but the logia form a continuous speech in all three texts. According to Matthew and Mark, Jesus instructed the apostles or a few of them on the Mount of Olives (Matt. 24:4 // Mark 13:3), while Luke has connected the speech directly with the episode of the poor widow (Luke 21:1–4), so that according to him a further teaching of those present followed in the temple (21:5, 37). Since all texts report on the last speech of Jesus and their contents are the fate of the disciples after the Lord's death, the complex may be called a farewell speech. In the perspective of form criticism, the function of the synoptic farewell speech makes it a counterpart to the Johannine farewell speech given at the Lord's last meal (John 13:31—17:26).

With regard to the structure, the Mount of Olives speech in Matthew and Mark as well as its counterpart in Luke consists of three paragraphs dealing with the following topics: (1) the destiny of the temple and the experiences of the early church after Christ's death (Matt. 24:1–28 with par.); (2) the end of the world (24:29–35 with par.); (3) the need for watchfulness (24:36—25:46, partly with par.).

The first two paragraphs of the speech (Matt. 24:1–28, 29–35 with par.) are supported by context-parallel triple traditions which actualize the following themes:

1. No stone of the temple will remain on top of another (24:1–3). Many will pretend to be the Messiah, and war rumors will be spread (24:4–8). The church in Jerusalem will be persecuted, and must flee into the mountains of Judea when the so-called abomination comes (24:9–28).

2. When the world is destroyed, the Son of Man will return in a cloud from heaven (24:29–31). A fig tree will be a sign of the approaching end (24:32–33). Heaven and earth will pass away, but not the words of Christ (24:34–35).

Most quotations given here from Matthew include contextual parallels in Mark and Luke. On the other hand, the synoptic harmony is reduced by the following circumstances.

a. In the first paragraph of block 11 the Matthean circle has depicted a Jewish persecution of the early church in contextual parallelism with Mark and Luke (Matt. 24:9–14), but it has in addition presented an even closer analogy to this description in the commission speech of block 4 (10:17–21). Characteristic expressions common to both Matthean texts (*παραδώσουσιν, εἰς μαρτύριον τοῖς ἔθνεσιν*) show that two versions of the same tradition are found here. As noted in block 4 (above, p. 101), the Matthean circle wanted to inform as early as possible about coming tribulations of the apostles. By inserting the epithet "the publican" (10:3), the presence of the apostle Matthew among those first initiated was underscored. In spite of this anticipated prophecy, very analogous to the relevant passages of Mark and Luke in block 11, the persecution topic was also treated by Matthew in block 11 in the form of a less analogous but context-parallel counterpart to the announcement in Mark and Luke. The latter fact must be understood to imply a reminiscence of a common oral tradition.

b. Two logia of Jesus quoted by Matthew in the first paragraph of block 11 do not form context-parallel triple traditions. This is true of the sayings introduced by the words "here is the Messiah" (Matt. 24:23–26) and "as the lightning" (24:27–28). A contextual parallel to the first one is found only in Mark ("here is the Messiah" in Mark 13:21–23), while Luke has brought in a fragmentary *alibi* analogy in his travel narrative ("he is here" in Luke 17:23). The second logion just mentioned as quoted by Matthew is of the Q type, since it does not find any counterpart in Mark, while Luke's travel narrative contains a parallel together with the saying "as in the days of Noah" quoted by Matthew in the third paragraph ("as the lightning," "as in the days of Noah": separate in Matt. 24:27–28, 37–41, coherent in Luke 17:24–37). Once again the comparison merely shows that Mark was less concerned with apostolic instruction and parenesis than Matthew and that Luke, under the influence of Hellenistic traditionists, preferred to trace back such didactic material to the journey of Jesus through Transjordan.

3. The third paragraph of the Mount of Olives speech, which contains admonitions to watchfulness, is largely dominated by Matthew (Matt. 24:36—25:46). Well-known special traditions of Matthew are here the parables of the ten virgins and the great judgment (Matt. 25:1–12, 31–46). Apart from them,

Matthean-Markan and Matthean-Lukan double traditions are found, in which a couple of elements even figure as triple traditions.

Matthew has arranged its special and double traditions of this paragraph in three rows. Each of them contains a general admonition to watchfulness, substantiated by concrete applications that display the following topics: (*a*) The end is incomputable, for it sets in like the flood (Matt. 24:36–41); (*b*) the believers must be watchful, for the Parousia comes like a thief in the night, and in the meantime the "servants" have to care for the household and the "virgins" to be prepared for meeting the bridegroom (24:42—25:12); (*c*) watchfulness is also necessary in view of the account for the "talents" and the judgment of all nations (25:13–46).

Mark presents three almost contextual parallels to the admonitions introducing each of the three rows in Matthew, and short applications of the two latter admonitions citing arguments that seem to be fragments of the more detailed applications in Matthew. In the travel narrative, Luke has preserved some *alibi* analogies to Matthew's applications but no explicit counterparts to the admonitions.

A table illustrating this parallelism of Matthew and Mark and their *alibi* analogies in Luke may be serviceable. (See p. 134.)

The collation reveals a remarkable circumstance, and this is that Mark offers very similar counterparts to Matthew's three admonitions, followed by short applications that partly resemble the pictures and parables developed in Matthew's applications. A considerable parallelism of the context is also found, with the exception only that Mark has given items *b* and *c* a reversed order. Luke is not represented by such contextual parallels within the paragraph in question, but there are some important *alibi* analogies to Matthew's applications in the travel narrative of block 8.

Here it becomes evident again that Mark did not serve as the source, for the very tight and laconic intimations of Mark could not possibly have produced the rich and expressive parables of Matthew. Nor could the present text of Matthew in block 11 have served as the source, for shortly before the context in question Mark and Luke have depicted a persecution caused by the synagogue (Mark 13:9–13 // Luke 21:12–19) to which there are two different counterparts in Matthew. On the one hand there is the *alibi* analogy in block 4 (Matt. 10:17–21) which has an extensive similarity to Mark's description in block 11 supported by an essentially identical parallel in Luke; on the other hand there is the contextual parallel in block 11 of which only some fundamental elements correspond to Mark's and Luke's descriptions in the same block. It is not conceivable that Mark and Luke would have amalgamated Matthew's *alibi* analogy in block 4 and the same Gospel's contextual parallel in block 11, letting the former suppress the latter. Rather, one is led to the conclusion that Mark's exhortations to watchfulness, items *a*, *b*, and *c*, and in the two latter cases the adjacent short applications, which resemble fragments of the pictures displayed with more details in Mat-

Matthew	Mark	Luke (esp. in Block 8)
	a	
	Admonition	
Matt. 24:36 But about that day and hour nobody knows . . .	Mark 13:32 But about that day or hour nobody knows . . .	Lukan analogy in Acts 1:7
	Application	
24:37–41 *for* as in the days of Noah . . .	Cf. *c*	Q tradition with analogy in Luke 17:26–27, 34–35
	b	
	Admonition	
24:42a Thus be watchful	13:35a Thus be watchful (referring to 13:34, see below)	
	Application	
24:42b *for* you do not know on which day . . . in which part of the night, . . . (pictures of the thief, the household the virgins) (in 24:43—25:12)	13:35b–37 *for* you do not know when . . . in the evening or at midnight or in the morning	Partly a triple tradition mostly Q traditions with analogies in Luke 12:35–46
	c	
	Admonition	
25:13a Thus be watchful	13:33a See to it that you stay awake (referring to 13:32, see above)	
	Application	
25:13b–14 *for* you do not know the day nor the hour. *For* it is like a man going abroad . . . (parables of the talents and the judgment in 25:15–46)	13:33b–34 *for* you do not know when the moment comes. It is like a man going abroad . . .	Matthean parable of the talents a Q tradition with analogy in Luke19:11–27

thew, were abbreviated reminiscences of a common tradition. In view of his readers, Mark was often inclined to shorten parenetic traditions. Nevertheless the Second Gospel has emphasized that Christ's exhortations to watchfulness should be applied to the early church in general: "But what I say to you, I say to all—be watchful" (Mark 13:37). This motive is also found in the Third Gospel (Luke 12:41), and it confirms the importance of the logia for all disciples and believers.

Luke has presented three *alibi* analogies to the parables or metaphors that, in Matthew, carry out the warnings to watchfulness. In his travel narrative a nearly literal analogy to the Matthean metaphor of the thief in the night is to be found, and because of the above-mentioned abbreviated counterpart in Mark, it forms a fragmentary triple tradition (Matt. 24:43–44 = Luke 12:39–40; tendency to analogy in Mark 13:35b–37). Directly afterward Luke offers a practically literal analogy to the Matthean parable on the feeding of the household, which implies a Q tradition (Matt. 24:45–51 = Luke 12:41–46). Later in the travel narrative the evangelist has inserted a nonliteral and yet unmistakable analogy to the Matthean parable of the talents—namely, his parable of the pounds, which is another Q tradition (analogy between Matt. 25:14–30 and Luke 19:11–27). With regard to these parables, Luke's contacts with reporters from Transjordan explain why, in comparison to Matthew's order, Luke's pericopes have been referred to the journey of Jesus through Transjordan and the region of Jericho.

Although the three Matthean and Markan admonitions found no direct parallels in Luke, the third evangelist has at least quoted an exhortation to watchfulness in the last part of his parallel to the Mount of Olives speech: "Beware. . . . Stay awake . . ." (Luke 21:34–36). The topic makes this exhortation comparable to the above-mentioned warnings to watchfulness in the other Gospels (Matt. 24:42; 25:13; Mark 13:35 and especially 13:33a, "See to it that you stay awake"). In spite of the difference in context, the Lukan warning is partly a triple tradition. However, it also reiterates motifs that Luke had already touched upon in his travel narrative and to which there are analogies in the Mount of Olives speech according to Matthew and Mark. Similarities of contents and wording occur in connection with the following items: warning against revelry (Matt. 24:49; Luke 12:45 and 21:34); breaking in of the last day "as the lightning" or "like a trap" (Matt. 24:27; Luke 17:24 and 21:34); warning to avoid being surprised (*ἐξαίφνης* in Mark 13:36 like *αἰφνίδιος* in Luke 21:34); exhortation to watchfulness (*γρηγορεῖτε* in Matt. 24:42 // Mark 13:35a like *γρηγοροῦντες* in Luke 12:37; *βλέπετε ἀγρυπνεῖτε* in Mark 13:33 like *προσέχετε . . . ἀγρυπνεῖτε* in Luke 21:34a, 36a); account required by the Son of God (Matt. 24:50; Luke 12:36 and 21:36b). Among the comparable passages quoted here, some appear in Luke's travel narrative of block 8, and some belong to his conclusive exhortation in block 11 (Luke 21:34–36). Whereas the former analogies were inserted in block 8 under the influence of Transjordanian reporters, the latter must be regarded as fragmentary reminiscences of the same tradition as the one found in connection with the Matthean-Markan exhortations to watch-

fulness in block 11. Luke's contacts with the Hellenists in Jerusalem have also found an expression in the formulation of the conclusive exhortation, for the point is a warning against revelry (Luke 21:34), which must have been particularly important for those who organized common meals (Acts 6:3).

The dependence of Luke upon Hellenistic traditionists is also confirmed by the fact that in the Lukan parallel to the Mount of Olives speech (Luke 21:5–38) neither the apostles nor this mount are mentioned (in comparison to Matt. 24:3 // Mark 13:3). Luke's traditionists may have taken over the tradition of the speech from the apostles but could not claim to have heard the words of Jesus on the Mount of Olives. For that reason their version of the speech was delivered without any explicit localization, and just connected with the teaching of Jesus in the temple as indicated by the episode with the widow (21:1–4). In a final note Luke also mentioned the temple as the place where Jesus taught during the days of the holy week, while he spent the nights on the Mount of Olives (21:37–38). Luke or his traditionists wanted to display the eschatological farewell speech of Jesus not as an esoteric instruction but as a public communication also heard by foreigners within the temple area.

On the whole, sections 1 to 3 in the Mount of Olives speech and its Lukan counterpart deal with problems and duties of the early church. Partly they refer to a near future and partly to a distant end time. The apostles and other disciples are strengthened by Jesus in a threefold respect: (1) in view of tribulations soon coming upon the church while still living among the Jews near the temple (Matt. 24:4–28 with par.); (2) in view of the world's destruction that will take place in an entirely incalculable future (24:29–41 with par.); (3) in view of the watchfulness of the church without interruption until this end of time and space, and until the judgment expected to follow thereupon (24:42—25:46, partly with par.).

1. In the first major part of the Mount of Olives speech (Matt. 24:1–28 with par.), Jesus announces dramatic experiences of the early church which, to a certain degree, correspond to concrete Christian experiences during the first decades after his crucifixion. This partial affiliation of the prophecies with circumstances historically known does not entitle interpreters to degrade the entire Mount of Olives speech to a prophecy constructed afterward, or what is generally called a prophecy *ex eventu*. Certainly the traditionists did formulate their reports on the Lord's words in the post-Easter period, at first in Hebrew or Aramaic and then in Greek, and inevitably their choice of quotations was influenced by recent experiences of their own. During the first decades after the death of Jesus the early church was exposed to different temptations and tribulations similar to those predicted by Jesus according to the first section of the speech. However, the correspondence is not systematic and refers only to punctual occurrences during the very first years, as will be illustrated below point by point.

In noticeable agreement with the twofold warning against false messiahs that introduces and concludes the first part of the speech (Matt. 24:1–5 with par.;

24:26 with par.), messianic pretenders are known to have appeared in the 30s and until the 50s of the first century. Several have been indicated by Josephus, and the New Testament mentions among them Simon Magus, Theudas, and the Egyptian (Acts 8:9; 5:36; 21:38). The subsequent reference to a time of insecurity owing to rumors of a world war (Matt. 24:6 with par.) was actualized in the years 35 to 36 when a war between the world powers of Rome and Parthia was fought (Josephus, *Antiquities* XVIII.96–104; Tacitus, *Annals* VI.31–44). Jesus is literally quoted as having mentioned a war between great nations and kingdoms in the world (*ἔθνος ἐπ' ἔθνος, βασιλεία ἐπὶ βασιλείαν*), and this cannot be applied to the local revolt of the Zealots in A.D. 66–70. The persecutions depicted immediately afterward (Matt. 24:9–14 + 10:17–21; Mark 13:9–13 // Luke 21:12–19) are expressly ascribed to Jews and Judean authorities. On this account, they point to such oppressive measures as those befalling Peter and John in A.D. 34–35 (Acts 4:1; 5:18), Stephen in A.D. 36 (6:9), the apostle James around A.D. 42 (12:2), the Jewish Christians in A.D. 52 (1 Thess. 2:14), and Paul in A.D. 58 (Acts 21:27; 22:30; 23:24). These and similar experiences of the apostles, made during the first three decades of the early church, may have affected the formulation of the prophecies contained in the first part of the speech under consideration.

Yet the catastrophes of the following period have not colored the texts. During the revolt against the Romans in the years 66–70 and afterward, Jewish persecutions of Christians such as those described in the apocalyptic speech were out of question, because the Christians had left the holy country around A.D. 64 (Eusebius, *EH* III.5.3) and the Jews were concerned with other problems. Only until A.D. 60, but not later, can the present formulation of the warnings against Jewish measures of oppression have been influenced by experiences of the traditionists.

Contrary to a current opinion, the expectation of the so-called "abomination of desolation" (Matt. 24:15 // Mark 13:14) and of Jerusalem's siege (Luke 21:20) must be recognized as real prophecy. For the following reasons, it cannot be ascribed to acquaintance with the Jewish war of the years 66–70 and with the final capture of Jerusalem by Titus in A.D. 70: Jesus bade the church of Jerusalem to flee (Matt. 24:16 with par.) when seeing the temple profaned by the abomination (Matt. 24:15 // Mark 13:14) as prophesied by Daniel (Dan. 9:27; 11:31; 12:11), or when finding the city surrounded by enemies (Luke 21:20) as Ezekiel had indicated (Ezek. 4:2–3). Indeed, a flight of the early Christians from Judea was known to the church historian Eusebius, but he said it occurred sometime before the Jewish war broke out, that is, around A.D. 64 (*EH* III.5.3). There are both chronological and topographical differences between the flight described in the synoptic texts and the one testified by Eusebius. According to Matthew-Mark-Luke, the Judean Christians were ordered by Jesus to flee southward from Jerusalem into the mountains of Judea when the profanatory abomination would appear (Matt. 24:16 with par.), and this was obviously

conceived in accordance with the flight of the Maccabean heroes (1 Macc. 2:2–9). Standing on the Judean mountains, the refugees would be the first to see the Son of Man returning from heaven (Matt. 24:30 with par.). But according to Eusebius, the historical flight of the Judean Christians occurred before the war, that is, when the Romans had not yet profaned the temple. Furthermore, Eusebius did not say the Judean Christians fled southward up on the mountains of Judea, but northward to Decapolis, where they established a new center in Pella (*EH*, ibid.), an important Hellenistic city on the east side of the Jordan Valley. The words of Jesus quoted by the synoptic writers do not agree either with that flight to Decapolis or with other historical events known from the New Testament period. Based on traditional elements of prophecy or apocalypticism, they evidently refer to a future still lying before the traditionists and their first readers.

2. The second main part of the Mount of Olives speech (Matt. 24:29–35 with par.) deals with events that merely belong to an unknown future. No historical experiences can possibly have influenced the scenes here depicted. The subjects of the pericopes involved are the end of the world and the parousia of Christ, the ripening of a fig tree, and the destruction of heaven and earth. Everything is seen in a purely eschatological perspective, and one cannot find any traces of a prophecy *ex eventu* in these pericopes. Attempts to explain the Mount of Olives speech as based on knowledge about later events do not find support in the middle section.

3. The third major section of the speech contains several exhortations to watchfulness and to pictures, parables, or metaphors illustrating the necessity of being prepared for the final judgment (Matt. 24:36—25:46, with sporadic parallels). Its message is neither prophetic nor quasi-prophetic, but exclusively parenetic. Therefore the last section of Christ's farewell speech is just as unsuitable as the middle one for dating the speech in the present form to any specific post-Easter period.

As was demonstrated above, it has to be admitted that in the first part of the synoptic apocalyptic speech (Matt. 24:4–24 with par.) there are details that indicate a convergence of Christ's prophecies with the church's experiences during the first decades after his death. Several of the quotations were selected in order to exhort and strengthen the Christians in a period when they were exposed to difficulties similar to what the Lord had told his disciples. This really has importance for dating the extant text of the speech, but since no influence of the dramatic conflicts that dominated the 60s is perceptible, it must be supposed that the speech received its present shape before that period.

In chapter 7 the chronology of the Synoptic Gospels will be studied in detail. Some points may be emphasized in advance here, after the analysis of the Lord's farewell speech. Essentially the modern preference for dating the Synoptics about A.D. 70 and later depends on artful endeavors to derive the predictions of tribulations in the apocalyptic speech from calamities known to have been caused

by the Jewish war of 66–70. On closer examination it becomes clear that no such correlations are presupposed in the speech quoted by the Synoptics. In addition, two other texts of Matthew and Luke are often adduced in order to give both Gospels a postwar date, and these are the Matthean parable of the wedding (Matt. 22:1–14) and the Lukan pericope "Dominus flevit" (Luke 19:23–44). As will be shown in chapter 7, the king sending his troops against the disobedient city in the Matthean parable is God, not Vespasian, and the siege of the city foretold in the Lukan pericope is throughout depicted on the basis of well-known Old Testament prophecies without the slightest reference to historical details of the Jewish war. In fact, no post-event prophecies at all can be found in these passages of Matthew and Luke. With regard to the Mount of Olives speech, it must be acknowledged that in the first third of it several quotations were selected and formulated in the years after the death of Christ, but to pass beyond the time around A.D. 60 is possible only through shrewd assumptions of prophecies *ex eventu*. This has a bearing upon the whole question of the synoptic chronology, which will be discussed in the last chapter.

Block 12
Trial, Eucharist, Crucifixion, and Resurrection
Matt. 26:1—28:20 with Parallels

In the final part of Matthew, Mark, and Luke, which is treated here comprehensively as block 12, a culmination of the christological drama is reached. The story deals with the plot and trial against Jesus, his last supper, crucifixion, and resurrection (Matt. 26:1—28:20 with par.).

Several narratives and quotations found in blocks 1 to 11 indicate a move toward the drama told in block 12. The entire flow of action as well as individual passages in the texts (e.g., Matt. 1:21; Mark 2:20; Luke 2:30) alludes to a culmination in the passion story. It is also made evident by Jesus himself in four prophecies on his suffering. Three of them are found as context-parallel triple traditions in blocks 6, 7, and 9 (Matt. 16:21; 17:22–23; 20:18–19, all with parallels), while a fourth prophecy of suffering occurs at the opening of block 12 as a Matthean unit which forms a transition from the Mount of Olives speech to the passion story (Matt. 26:1–2).

Under the aspect of contextual parallelism, block 12 occupies a singular position. In no section of the Synoptic Gospels do context-parallel triple traditions play such a dominant role as here, being supported even by Johannine parallels.

The table of the synoptic pericopes presented above (pp. 43–44) shows that block 12 consists of twenty-nine text units. Among them no fewer than fifteen pericopes form extensive context-parallel triple traditions (framed in the table). In addition, there are four triple pericopes that are nearly context-parallel, the

parallelism being slightly reduced by Lukan deviations in sequence (Luke 22:21–23, 24–30, 31–34, 56-66). The ten remaining units are as follows: one double tradition of Matthew and Mark, to which Luke has at least preserved a topical counterpart (the mocking of Jesus ordered by Pilate according to Matt. 27:27–31 // Mark 15:16–20, by Antipas according to Luke 23:11); and nine unique traditions partly found in Matthew, partly in Luke (Matt. 27:3–10, 62–66; 28:11–15, 16–20; Luke 22:35–38; 23:27–31; 24:13–35, 36–49, 50–53). Of these special units the last one in Matthew and the last one in Luke (Matt. 28:16–20; Luke 24:50–53) are certainly different in form but not quite in content. The short final remark of Luke about the ascension of Jesus into heaven (Luke 24:50–53) has been abbreviated only in order to be further elaborated in the beginning of Acts (1:6–12). In this perspective the same fundamental motif as in the final pericope of Matthew emerges (Matt. 28:16–20), for in both contexts the point in question is a mountain on which the disciples are commissioned to spread the gospel to the entire world (Matt. 28:19; Acts 1:8). By the way, a context-parallel is also offered in the secondary Markan ending (Mark 16:19–20). At any rate, the conclusive special traditions of Matthew and Luke stand close to the category of context-parallel triple traditions, even if they differ from each other in form and localization.

As a totality, block 12 is thus dominated by context-parallel triple traditions and text units comparable to them. Here the agreement is much stronger than in the preceding blocks, and the synoptic passion narratives come near to being a threefold harmony, which indicates that a relatively homogeneous and established tradition lies in the background.

This homogeneity of the tradition behind the synoptic passion texts becomes even more impressive by a comparison with the passion narrative of John. Up to the passion story, the Synoptic Gospels and John diverge so much in sequence and topography that no harmonization is feasible. In its description of Christ's passion, however, John actually keeps pace with the synoptic reports, and in this context a number of context-parallel quadruple traditions can be observed. The essential agreement between the main elements of the drama according to the Synoptic and Johannine Gospels comes to the fore in a convincing way, if a synopsis of all Gospels is studied—for instance, the one published by Kurt Aland. In spite of occasional differences, John has formulated several reports in a similar manner and in the same order as the Synoptics. (1) This is the case with regard to the conspiracy against Jesus (John 11:47–57), his anointing in Bethany (12:1–8), his entry into Jerusalem (12:12–19), his predictions about the betrayal of Judas (13:21–30), and the denial of Peter (13:37–38). (2) Similar analogies to the Synoptics are found concerning the arrest of Jesus, the interrogation by the high priest and the denial by Peter (18:1–27), the interrogation by Pilate and the release of Barabbas, and the extradition and mocking of Jesus (18:28—19:15). (3) Finally, his crucifixion (19:16–30) and burial (19:38–42), the discovery of the

empty tomb by Mary Magdalene (20:1–13), the revelation of the risen Lord before the Eleven and the bestowal of the charge to evangelize upon the apostles (20:19–29, corresponding to Luke 24:36–49) are topics that have also been presented in a similar manner and the same order by John and the Synoptic Gospels.

Certainly various degrees of similarity appear in the passion narratives, if each Gospel is compared with the others. At the beginning the agreement is relatively consistent between the three Synoptics (Matt. 26:1–19 with par.), but from the eucharist report and beyond, the similarity becomes more prominent between Matthew and Mark (Matt. 26:20—28:10 // Mark 14:17—16:8), whereas Luke disagrees in some points by the sequential deviations and unique traditions mentioned above. At this very point, on the other hand, Luke is occasionally found in remarkable parallelism with John (cf. Luke 22:27 and John 13:12–16; Luke 23:4 and John 18:38; Luke 24:12 and John 20:4–5; Luke 24:36–49 and John 20:19–23).

In its entirety the passion story is nevertheless stamped by a topical and structural concord between all four Gospels. As if it were through a *harmonia praestabilita,* a common architecture of the four passion narratives was preserved, although individual circumstances and points of view have affected their development.

Secondhand adoption of material already edited can be observed only in the epilogue of Mark, which is missing in the oldest manuscripts (Mark 16:9–20). It implies a redactional addition of traditions found in Luke about Mary Magdalene, the two disciples going to Emmaus, and the eleven apostles gathered for a meal in Jerusalem (Mark 16:9, 11, 12, 14; Luke 8:2; 24:11, 13–35, 36–49). Even a certain acquaintance with events recorded in Acts is noticeable, insofar as the Markan epilogue contains allusions to the Pentecost miracle in Jerusalem and Paul's adventure with the viper (Mark 16:17–18; Acts 2:4; 28:3).

In the actual passion narratives of the four Gospels, however, no literary employment of material already fixed in documents is provable. Although there are fundamental agreements between the descriptions, these are so frequently combined with differences of style and variations of particulars that every assumption of a literary elaboration involves serious difficulties. Similar to what has been observed in earlier sections of the Synoptic Gospels, the analogous descriptions and expressions contained in the passion narratives constantly alternate with variations and synonyms. The comparison of parallel texts shows that elements corresponding verbally to each other are spread haphazardly, so that a zigzag pattern emerges which prevents any consistent derivation of one Gospel from another.

Examples chosen from two pericopes found in the Synoptic Gospels at the beginning of block 12 may illustrate how the distribution of corresponding expressions yields an irrational zigzag arrangement even in short context-parallel triple units:

Matt. 26:1–5	Mark 14:1–2	Luke 22:1–2
μετὰ δύο ἡμέρας	μετὰ δύο ἡμέρας	
	τὸ πάσχα	τὰ ἄζυμα
	καὶ τὰ ἄζυμα	λεγομ. πάσχα
	καὶ ἐζήτουν	καὶ ἐζήτουν
	οἱ ἀρχιερεῖς	οἱ ἀρχιερεῖς
	καὶ οἱ γραμματεῖς	καὶ οἱ γραμματεῖς
	πῶς αὐτὸν	τὸ πῶς . . . αὐτόν
ἵνα ἐν δόλῳ	ἐν δόλῳ	
κρατήσωσιν	κρατήσαντες	
καὶ ἀποκτείνωσιν	ἀποκτείνωσιν	
μὴ ἐν τῇ ἑορτῇ	μὴ ἐν τῇ ἑορτῇ	
ἵνα μὴ θόρυβος	μήποτε . . . θόρυβος	

Matt. 26:14–16	Mark 14:10–11	Luke 22:3–6
	εἷς τῶν δώδεκα	ἐκ . . . τῶν δώδεκα
	ἀπῆλθεν	ἀπελθών
πρὸς τοὺς ἀρχιερεῖς	πρὸς τοὺς ἀρχιερεῖς	
	ἐχάρησαν	ἐχάρησαν
	ἀργύριον δοῦναι	ἀργύριον δοῦναι
εὐκαιρίαν		εὐκαιρίαν

In both pericopes the structure of the narrative is the same, but identical or nearly identical vocables and phrases are found in only two of the Gospels at a time. Similarities oscillate either between Matthew and Mark, Mark and Luke, or Matthew and Luke in an unpredictable way. The picture is too complicated to be explained as the result of copying and variation applied to a text found in any of the Gospels. Rather, one is driven to presume that a background existed in traditions based on common recollections but intentionally varied in the choice of words and occasionally increased by some addition of details. Such a dichotomy is characteristic of preliterary traditions in general.

Another specimen of free variations on a common topic is offered by the four reports on the mocking of Jesus. Two of them form contextual parallels in Matthew and Mark, and one appears in John within a similar context (Matt. 27:27–31 // Mark 15:16–20; John 19:1–3). Luke has told about the mocking of Jesus in a slightly different context, and not ascribed it to Pilate but to Antipas (Luke 23:11); yet he evidently meant a similar event. In any case, the essential features of the four narratives are common, and variations are found only in subordinate details. According to Matthew, Jesus was given a scarlet cloak (χλαμύς), according to Mark and John a purple robe (ἱμάτιον), and according to

Luke a white dress (ἐσθής). In all these cases there is an organic mixture of correspondence and deviation which can be explained only in a psychological way, not by any literary criticism. The references to different colors would not have emerged if one evangelist had copied directly from the written text of another. It must be presumed, rather, that in the mind of the traditionists or the evangelists the elaboration of the circumstances was exposed to variation, so that an objective homogeneity of the recollections was combined with a subjective fluctuation in particulars. Here again that dichotomy characteristic of preliterary traditions becomes apparent.

Similar observations can be made on all passion narratives which the Gospels have preserved in relative analogy with each other. The contextual parallelism of the Synoptics is many times more prominent in block 12 than in the preceding blocks, and strengthened as well by the Johannine narrative. Here the ultimate agreement of four witnesses cannot possibly have emerged from the literary workshops of three evangelists, who suddenly felt a common need to follow the extant text of a fourth one, no matter which of the four is supposed to have been primary. The fundamental reason for the extensive harmony between the four Gospels in their passion narratives was rather the actual history, about which the traditionists and the evangelists had to report.

It was thus in principle the importance and holiness of the Golgotha drama which caused the exceptionally solid formation of the relevant traditions in the early church. Owing to a general reverence for the passion history, the community's recollections of it were the first to be molded into traditions. The latter had a relative similarity from the very beginning and did not change much in the course of time. What kept them intact was the subject of the report, preeminent and hallowed as it seemed to the disciples. It is only under these aspects that it becomes possible to explain the extensive harmony of the passion narratives, including the Fourth Gospel though its previous narratives advance several points of view different from those of the Synoptic Gospels.

Moreover, it has to be taken into account that a number of adherents to Christ are mentioned as participants in the passion history and therefore may be regarded as eyewitnesses. Reminiscences of these men and women can be understood as the matrix of the relatively uniform traditions.

With regard to the beginning and the end of the passion narratives, the eyewitnesses indicated were the apostles, who took part in the eucharist just before the crucifixion of their Lord (Matt. 26:20 with par.) and were confronted with him at meals and in other ways after his resurrection (Matt. 28:16; Luke 24:36, 50; John 20:19; 21:7; Acts 1:3–4, 6–9).

On the other hand, the inner circle of the apostles is said to have abandoned Jesus at Gethsemane (Matt. 26:56 // Mark 14:50), and they are not mentioned as witnesses of the Golgotha drama. Even when Peter had sneaked into the courtyard of the high priest, he remained there and could not follow the interrogation personally (Matt. 26:58 with par.; John 18:15). Instead, the texts allude to

other eyewitnesses of the trial and the subsequent Golgotha drama.

The four Gospels tell unanimously of a councillor named Joseph of Arimathea who had become a disciple and had arranged the burial of Jesus (Matt. 27:57 with par.; John 19:38). Since he was a member of the Sanhedrin, this disciple had actually been present at the trial of Jesus. Luke confirms it by his remark that Joseph of Arimathea had not voted for the death sentence (Luke 23:51). In view of the fact that he took charge of the Lord's corpse, it becomes obvious that he also had witnessed the crucifixion. This councillor was certainly able to inform the other disciples about the trial before the Sanhedrin and the drama on Golgotha.

John has also told about Nicodemus, a second councillor and disciple who contributed to the funeral by offering a hundred pounds of myrrh and aloes (John 19:39). This adherent of Jesus is also known through other traditions (John 3:1; 7:50; a Jewish baraita in Paul Billerbeck, *Kommentar,* 2, pp. 417–18). He was said to be not only a member of the Sanhedrin, as was Joseph of Arimathea, but even an "archont," which means that he belonged to the ministerial cabinet led by the high priest (in John 3:1 he is called an archont, in 7:48 one of the archonts). Nicodemus was therefore most probably the anonymous disciple who helped Peter to enter the residency of the high priest (John 18:15). Some information given by the councillor Nicodemus about the interrogation by the high priest and the Sanhedrin may very well have complemented that given by Joseph of Arimathea. However, according to John the interrogation of Jesus by Pilate took place inside the praetorium, where the councillors refused to enter (John 18:28). Perhaps the Roman officer converted under the cross (Matt. 27:54 with par.) may have told fellow believers about this part of the trial.

The redactors of John have also written that the disciple whom Jesus loved accompanied the mother of Jesus and was an eyewitness of the crucifixion (John 19:26, 35). Although this notice is not supported by the other Gospels, its solemn form ("he knows that he speaks the truth") makes it worthy of consideration.

In any case, all four Gospels tell about some women associated with Jesus who saw the crucifixion (Matt. 27:56 with par.; John 19:25). According to the Synoptics, they also saw the interment (Matt. 27:61 with par.), and Mary Magdalene is unanimously mentioned as the first one among those who followed Joseph of Arimathea at the burial and found the tomb empty after the Sabbath (Matt. 27:61; 28:1 with par.). John has not mentioned any women in connection with the burial and only Mary Magdalene at the empty tomb (John 20:1), but all the same this Gospel has emphasized her importance. In all extant reports on the discovery of the empty tomb, Mary Magdalene is the protagonist, and she was certainly a leading witness of the burial and the empty tomb.

Convergent indications of such eyewitnesses to the passion drama thus contribute to explaining why context-parallel quadruple traditions dominate the passion narratives. In addition, however, more comprehensive structural factors have evidently influenced the formation of the traditions, and these factors will now be studied.

The great passion report of block 12 contains narratives that have not been interpolated by didactic units such as those of the previous blocks. It is true that words of Jesus are often quoted, but they go along with the story, and so their purpose is narrative, not didactic. Although the whole passion report of block 12 can be divided into pericopes as with the previous material in the Gospels, it differs from the other blocks insofar as here the pericopes form a coherent story. The center which keeps the story together is the record of the crucifixion. All preceding accounts, dealing with the conspiracy, the eucharist, Gethsemane, the arrest and conviction of Jesus, point toward the Golgotha drama. Likewise do all subsequent accounts, on the burial of Jesus, the discovery of the empty tomb, and the appearances of the risen One, depend on that drama. No single piece can be regarded as having ever been a separate unit of its own. All pericopes form a chain of narratives intimately linked one to the other, and their continuous subject is what happened before the crucifixion, during the crucifixion, and after the crucifixion.

One has also to seek a life setting or a practical basis for this coherence of the narratives in block 12, where the cross is the center and where contextual parallels occur in all four Gospels. Such a basis is found in the community meal of the early church.

The oldest common meals of the Christians were arranged in private houses, in Jerusalem daily (Acts 2:42, 46; 6:1), in the Diaspora on Sundays (Acts 20:7; 1 Cor. 16:2; *Didache* XIV.1). Corresponding to the principle *"pars pro toto,"* the apostles called the meal the "breaking of bread" (Acts 2:42, 46; 20:7) and their successors the "thanksgiving," or the "eucharist" (*Didache* IX.1.5; Ignatius, *Letter to the Ephesians* XIII.1 e.p.). That does not mean there was no drink at the breaking of bread or no bread and wine at the thanksgiving, for the expressions referred only to characteristic moments. According to the *Didache,* which has preserved traditions of the first century, the breaking of bread and the thanksgiving were two aspects of the same meal (*Didache* XIV.1). Paul called the common meal of the Christians "the Lord's supper" (1 Cor. 11:20) in order to emphasize that it ought to actualize the death of the Lord (11:26).

Very soon after the death of Jesus the apostles began to lead the breaking of bread in Jerusalem (Acts 2:42, 46). The ceremony thus did not depend upon any influence of foreign cultic meals but derived from Christ's institution of it before his death. Matthew and Mark on the one hand and Luke and Paul on the other have given fundamentally concordant reports about this last will and testament of Jesus (Matt. 26:26–28 corresponding to Mark 14:22–25; Luke 22:15–20 corresponding to 1 Cor. 11:23–25). Their statements, supported by other testimonies, imply that at the meal the bread solemnly broken was meant to actualize the sacrifice of Christ's body (Matt. 16:26 with par. and 1 Cor. 11:24, "this is my body"; John 6:51, "the bread that I shall give you is my body"; 1 Cor. 10:16, "the bread that we break implies communion with the body of Christ").

Consequently the crucifixion of Jesus Christ was to be proclaimed and

recounted at the community meals of the early church. Drawing the attention of the believers to the accomplishment of salvation in Christ's sacrifice on the cross, the leaders of the meals portrayed the drama. This is how the recollections of the passion history were developed into traditions.

An embryo of the traditions behind the passion narratives may accordingly be seen in the reports on the last supper of the Lord. The meal participants were always to bear in mind what Christ had meant in the eucharist, and therefore were reminded repeatedly of his acts and words on the night he was betrayed.

It is possible to elucidate this function of the report on the institution by considering the following analogies:

1. During the last supper of Jesus and the apostles, as well as during the early Christian breaking of bread in Jerusalem and in the Diaspora, a characteristic element of the Jewish Passah ceremony was practiced, implying that a so-called *maṣṣah* or unleavened bread was broken at the beginning of the meal. According to the Mishnah tractate *Pesachim* (Easter), the host started the meal by taking a *maṣṣah,* breaking it, and dipping the pieces, or "morsels" (John 13:27), in a dish with bitter herbs, and then passing the morsels to each of the guests (Mishnah, *Pesachim* X.3a). Just after the eating of the Passah lamb the host pronounced a benediction over a cup of wine and then passed it to the others (ibid.). The last meal of Jesus was also held with bread and wine. Although it evidently took place on the evening before the preparation day (Matt. 27:62; Mark 15:42; Luke 23:54; John 19:1, 14, 31), when the lambs to be slaughtered in the temple were not yet available, the two elements administered by Jesus were in fact treated as counterparts to the bread and wine of the Passah (Matt. 26:17; Mark 14:12; Luke 22:15).[2] Paul has also used Passah traditions to illustrate the meaning of the Christian eucharist (1 Cor. 5:7–8, unleavened bread symbolizing a pure mind of the guests for whom Christ himself is the Passah lamb; 10:16, the cup of the eucharist called the "cup of blessing" in analogy to the Jewish name of the cup passed around after the main Passah dish). The apostolic breaking of bread, the Pauline supper of the Lord, and the postapostolic eucharist thus preserved essential moments of the Passah meal.

Inevitably it must be supposed that the breaking of bread in the early church included a counterpart to the solemn explication of the Passah ceremony which the host was expected to give, the so-called Passah Haggadah. According to the Mishnah, at each Passah meal the host should answer the following question addressed to him by one of his sons: "What distinguishes this night from other nights?" His task was to explain the elements of the meal with reference to the biblical reports about Israel's exodus from Egypt and to praise God for the salvation of the people (Mishnah, *Pesachim* X.4–6). At the breaking of bread celebrated in the early church and at the eucharist administered in the missionary

2. B. Reicke, *The New Testament Era: The World of the Bible from 500* B.C. *to* A.D. *100* (Philadelphia: Fortress Press, 1968), 176–83.

churches, the participants needed a similar explanation concerning the importance of the elements and the liturgy. This practical need led to the formation of a report about the institution of the eucharist on the night of the betrayal. As a liturgical kernel this report, with slight variations, has been quoted by the synoptic evangelists and Paul.

2. The report on the institution of the eucharist has found an organic extension in the narratives that cover Christ's arrest and condemnation, his crucifixion, burial, and resurrection. A comparison with Paul may illustrate that there was such a pertinent relationship between the eucharist tradition and the other elements of the passion narratives.

Paul reminded the Corinthians of the tradition imparted to him about the institution of the eucharist. His purpose was to ascertain the importance of the two elements and the whole sacrament (1 Cor. 11:23–26). Tracing his tradition back to Christ himself (11:23), he referred to the night of the betrayal in analogy to the night of Passah (ibid.), and presented the relevant acts and words of Jesus as a binding rule for each eucharistic celebration (11:26). It is probable that Paul had become acquainted with traditions about the institution of the eucharist through contacts with older disciples such as Ananias in Damascus and Barnabas in Jerusalem (Acts 9:17, 27), and later with Luke, whose report on the last supper of Jesus is rather like that of Paul.

With regard to elements of the passion history surrounding the institution of the eucharist, there is special reason to recall what Paul defined as the topics of his very first preaching in Corinth (1 Cor. 15:1–7). He referred to matters that he personally had received as oral tradition (15:3) and forwarded to the Corinthians (*παρέλαβον*, *παρέδωκα*). The tradition received involved accounts of Christ's crucifixion, his burial (15:3–4), and his resurrection as confirmed by eyewitnesses (15:5–7). Paul emphasized that his preaching was based on these topics from the beginning. A modern technical expression for such a summarized message is "kerygma." The apostle may have taken over the kerygma in Damascus, in Jerusalem, or in other contexts, and in any case was accustomed to promulgating it when he came to Corinth (15:1). In his letter to the Galatians, Paul has also reminded the readers of the fundamental message called *εὐαγγέλιον* which they had received (Gal. 1:6–9) and which consisted in "vividly portraying" Christ as the crucified one (3:1).

Since very much the same topics as those mentioned by Paul with regard to his kerygma in Corinth form the constitutive elements of the passion history described by the four Gospels, it seems reasonable to regard the Gospel reports on Christ's suffering as based on such fundamental preaching and teaching in the early church. The analogies found in 1 Corinthians between Paul's approach to the eucharist and the kerygma, especially his emphasis in both cases on authentic Christian traditions, will also support the assumption that for the development of the passion narratives in the Gospels the eucharistic tradition was a starting point.

In the missionary preaching and baptismal teaching of early Christianity, traditions on the passion history could only be spread in the form of summaries such as the so-called kerygma. Nevertheless the eucharist offered an opportunity for imparting more details. Luke has alluded to this in a "we" story about Paul in Troas (Acts 20:5–12). In connection with the breaking of bread on a Sunday, the apostle is said to have taught until midnight (20:7), and in view of the meal it must be supposed that an essential subject of his speech was the passion of Christ. Paul certainly did not start a new practice in Troas, but just continued what had been done from the beginning of Christian preaching and teaching. These features confirm the original relationship between the holy meal and the passion tradition.

3. Oral traditions of the passion history were also retained carefully in the postapostolic period, as is evident from what Ignatius of Antioch has stated in a letter of A.D. 114. Against dissenters who refused to believe what they could not find written in documents (ἀρχεῖα), he assured that for him the only relevant document was Christ himself, active through inviolable reports of his crucifixion, death, and resurrection (Ignatius, *Philadelphians* VIII.2).

The texts of Paul, Luke, and Ignatius here referred to show that Christ's last supper, crucifixion, and resurrection were fundamental topics of a sanctified tradition spread in the early church, primarily in the form of that summary nowadays called kerygma. Since the report of the last supper accompanied the celebration of the eucharist, the other elements of the kerygma were probably also developed in connection with the holy meal. For natural reasons the reports were then broadened, so that Christ's arrest, trial, and other items of the passion history were included.

Because there must have been a need for such information from the very beginning, the development of eucharistic and related traditions certainly took place in the earliest Christian community. The authors of the Synoptic Gospels and the Fourth Gospel thus had relatively congruent passion traditions of the early church at their disposal when they wrote down their passion narratives. On this basis it can be explained that, in contrast to other sectors of the Synoptic Gospels, the passion reports are throughout dominated by context-parallel triple traditions and that several of the units are even supported by parallels in the Fourth Gospel. The *harmonia praestabilita,* which has led to considerable fourfold parallelism of the passion narratives, is to be understood in the light of these empirical circumstances.

In conclusion, the following historical factors turn out to have been influential on the development of the oral traditions that led to the passion narratives of the four Gospels:

1. Apostles and other eyewitnesses were able to remember substantial features of the passion history. Their personal communications became a basis for the materialization of traditions in the church. At this stage, a rather short interval

between the original course of events and the primitive narration may be presumed.

2. The concrete incentive for this formation of traditions, or its life setting, was the holy meal which Luke called the breaking of bread and Paul the Lord's supper. Insofar as the participants had to be reminded in solemn terms of the new covenant inaugurated by Jesus at his last meal, the report on the institution of the eucharist received a liturgical function and shape.

3. As administered in remembrance of Christ's sacrifice, the eucharist gave the impulse to a further development of narratives about the crucifixion and resurrection of Christ.

4. Thus a complex of narrative communications arose which formed a unity from the beginning and, unlike other Gospel traditions, had never consisted of separate pericopes.

5. In early oral traditions the passion story had the value of a most hallowed sanctuary, as testified by Paul and Ignatius. Thus it was memorized with special care, and therefore many fewer variants of the subjects and their order came up here than in other parts of the Gospels—except the story of Christ's baptism and a couple of units around it (see remarks above on block 2).

6. Although the Gospel of John offers a considerable parallelism with the other Gospels in connection with Christ's suffering, it has not directly told about the institution of the eucharist. This interesting particularity is due to John's report being addressed to outsiders and catechumens (John 20:31: "These signs are recorded so that you may believe that Jesus is the Christ"), while knowledge of the eucharistic mystery should be reserved for the initiated. Nonetheless there are unmistakable indications of the eucharist in the Fourth Gospel. The reference to the farewell meal of Jesus celebrated immediately before the Passah occupies the same context in John as in the Synoptic Gospels (John 13:1–2), and several particulars mentioned afterward implicitly allude to the mystery of the eucharist. Having presented himself as the host of the apostles by washing their feet (13:3–17), Jesus identifies the traitor by a piece of bread, as in the Synoptic Gospels. The dish of bitter herbs mentioned here connects the description even more clearly with the Passah ritual (13:18–30). Jesus finally elucidates the new communion with him in an instructive dialogue (13:31—17:26), to which there is a certain parallel in the Third Gospel (Luke 22:24–38). No doubt the Johannine description of the farewell meal and speech depended on a tradition in which the institution of the eucharist had been central. John has refrained from quoting the eucharistic text because it was a sublime mystery reserved for the believers. His caution actually confirms the unique sanctity of this liturgical tradition in the early church.

Chapter Seven

Matthew, Mark, and Luke as Redactors

In the actual texts of the Synoptic Gospels the evangelists have not, as did Paul in his epistles or John in his Revelation, presented themselves by name as the authors or redactors. The names of Matthew, Mark, Luke, and John are only found outside the text in titles added by copyists. Nevertheless these titles are found in the manuscripts from a very early period on, and they are confirmed by an important early witness, as will be shown below. Therefore they appear to be relatively trustworthy.

The Traditional Titles

All manuscripts available support the familiar attribution of the Gospels to Matthew, Mark, Luke, and John by their *inscriptiones,* that is, titles placed above the texts. In the four Gospels the titles have a common form, which runs like this in Greek:

εὐαγγέλιον κατὰ Μαθθαῖον
εὐαγγέλιον κατὰ Μᾶρκον
εὐαγγέλιον κατὰ Λουκᾶν
εὐαγγέλιον κατὰ Ἰωάννην

The literary meaning of the formulas is: "The Good News According to (or, in the Version of) Matthew," and so forth.

Certainly these formulas depended upon a collecting of the four texts into a corpus, so the inscriptiones were not produced by the evangelists but must be ascribed to some later redactors of the collection. On the other hand, this does not make the statements worthless. As will be demonstrated here, the titles may be dated to around A.D. 100 when historical information was still available. It will also be demonstrated that two names of the evangelists mentioned in the inscriptiones are confirmed by reminiscences of veteran Christians interviewed by Bishop Papias of Hierapolis around A.D. 110. No other authors or redactors of the canonical Gospels have been quoted in the traditions of the old church. From

these points of view it seems possible and even probable that persons known as Matthew, Mark, Luke, and John were responsible for the Gospels named after them. On the other hand, the function of the names must be understood in different ways, and this will also be discussed below.

The earliest technical evidence for a general dispersion of the titles in question is found in documents from the years before A.D. 200. It is two papyri belonging to the Bodmer Library in Cologny near Geneva which prove this. They were published by Victor Martin under the names of Papyrus Bodmer II and XIV–XV, and in current lists of New Testament manuscripts their numbers are P66 and P75.[1] On paleographical grounds they are dated to around A.D. 200 or even before.[2] P66 contains the Gospel of John from 1:1 to 21:9, with some lacunae caused by damage. Above the first verse, and with the same hand as in the main text, this inscriptio can be read: **εὐαγγέλιον κατὰ Ἰωάννην**.[3] With similar lacunae, P75 contains the Gospel of Luke from 3:18 until the end, as well as the entire Gospel of John which begins on the last page of Luke after a space. The text of Luke is concluded by a subscriptio, reading **εὐαγγέλιον κατὰ Λουκᾶν** and written by the same hand as the text. After the space mentioned, the Gospel of John begins with an inscriptio, reading **εὐαγγέλιον κατὰ Ἰωάνην** *(sic)*, also written by the same hand.[4] The copyist of this papyrus, which is a codex, has preserved a usage characteristic of earlier Greek scrolls when he defined the preceding text by that subscriptio, and to help the readers he also introduced the subsequent text by an inscriptio.[5]

Other remains of Gospel papyri available from the second and third centuries are so fragmentary that no inscriptiones are found in them, and therefore no comparable documentation is possible with regard to Matthew and Mark. The two Bodmer papyri, however, are parts of manuscripts in which it must be supposed that the Gospels of Matthew and Mark preceded those of Luke and John, and their explicit naming of the later writings proves that in second-century papyri the four canonical Gospels were generally called "The Good News According to Matthew," and so forth. In the same way the titles **εὐαγγέλιον κατὰ Μαθθαῖον**, and so forth, are constantly found in the New Testament parchments that became dominant in the fourth century. The codices Sinaiticus and Vaticanus have partly left out the word **εὐαγγέλιον**,[6] but this is an unimportant exception, and even so the idea of **εὐαγγέλιον** remains fundamental. On

1. V. Martin, *Papyrus Bodmer II. Evangile de Jean,* 1 (Geneva: Bibliotheca Bodmeriana, 1956); 2 (1962); V. Martin and R. Kasser, *Papyrus Bodmer XIV–XV. Evangiles de Luc et Jean,* 1-2 (1961).

2. Martin, *Bodmer II,* 1, pp. 17–18; Martin and Kasser, *Bodmer XIV–XV,* 1, pp. 13–14.

3. Martin, *Bodmer II,* 1, pp. 21–23; plate IX, p. 37.

4. Martin and Kasser, *Bodmer XIV–XV,* 1, p. 150; 2, p. 6; plate 61–61 bis.

5. Martin, *Bodmer II,* 1, pp. 21–23.

6. K. and B. Aland, *Novum Testamentum graece,* 26th ed. (Stuttgart: Deutsche Bibelstiftung, 1979), 1.

the whole, there are no hesitations about the names of the evangelists. From the second century on, the habit of giving the Gospels titles like those found in the Bodmer papyri was generally established.

In fact, the formula *εὐαγγέλιον κατὰ Μαθθαῖον*, and so forth, has a meaning that even makes it necessary to date its origin back to the beginning of the second century. Literally the formula means: "The Good News in the Version of Matthew," or "Mark," and so on, and this implies that each evangelist had given the general Christian presentation of Jesus an individual expression. Here the conception *εὐαγγέλιον* has a collective function, whereas the attributes *κατὰ Μαθθαῖον*, and so forth, are meant to particularize. This collective use of *εὐαγγέλιον* in the singular, granting the common Christian preaching and teaching historical superiority over the written documents, corresponds to the use of the expression in the New Testament and the Apostolic Fathers until around A.D. 120. By the middle of the second century, the word changed its meaning, so that it began to denote *any* canonical or apocryphal gospel, but the collective sense found in the titles of the four Gospels was a peculiarity of the period before and shortly after A.D. 100.

In the New Testament, *εὐαγγέλιον* is found seventy-seven times, and the word is always used in a collective sense about that oral message which the audience knew from preaching and teaching (e.g., in Matt. 4:23; Rom. 1:1; Rev. 14:6, and in all other cases as well).

Since the meaning of *εὐαγγέλιον* is so unequivocal in the New Testament, there is every reason to allow no exception for the ingress of the Second Gospel, but also to understand Mark 1:1 within this perspective: "Beginning of the Good News About Jesus Christ." As a summary the ingress indicates that the subsequent report is going to illustrate the beginning (*ἀρχή*) of Christian preaching (*εὐαγγέλιον*). That is, the background of the church's present activity is found in the historical activity of Jesus, which Mark intended to actualize. Here the word "beginning" has to be given a retrospective sense, which is supported by other New Testament passages where "beginning" refers to events in the life of Jesus. This is true of Luke 1:2, "eyewitnesses from the beginning," and 1 John 1:1, "what was among us from the beginning." Even the same phrase as in Mark 1:1, although with regard to Paul's earliest preaching, occurs in Phil. 4:15, "at the beginning of the good news." In this way the "good news" in Mark 1:1 proves to be what the expression always meant in the New Testament. No text-dissecting interpretations of Mark 1:1, by which the "beginning" is only referred to the first verse or the next verses of the first chapter and "good news" is therefore identified with the book of Mark, are compatible with the New Testament vocabulary.

It must thus be observed that whenever the New Testament speaks of *εὐαγγέλιον*, it means the good news announced by Jesus and his witnesses. This collective notion was still basic when the Gospels were given titles such as *εὐαγγέλιον κατὰ Μαθθαῖον*, and so forth.

A direct continuation of the collective New Testament conception of *εὐαγ-*

γέλιον is found in the earliest postbiblical writings up to around A.D. 120, that is, in books of the so-called Apostolic Fathers.

The earliest witness is *Didache,* or the *Teaching of the Twelve Apostles,* a church order generally supposed to have been written in Syria around A.D. 100. In four cases it has quoted moral instructions said to be given in the Lord's Prayer (*Didache* VIII.2; XI.3; XV.3, 4). Approximate analogies to these instructions are found in Matthew, and in *Didache* VIII.2 the Lord's Prayer is quoted in a form reminiscent of the Sermon on the Mount, but the reference is always to the message of Jesus and never to that of Matthew. Furthermore, the instructions referred to were not quoted from a written text but from memory, for striking variations are included. Certainly the authors of *Didache* had a slight knowledge of Matthew's account, but on the basis of hearing rather than of reading. They did not let the evangelist appear overly important to the readers, but treated his book as witness to the common **εὐαγγέλιον** of the church and quoted elements of it from memory in a free way.

In the epistle of Barnabas two passages also mention the εὐαγγέλιον of Jesus as preached by the church (*Barnabas* V.9; VIII.3). Somewhat later Bishop Ignatius of Antioch, writing in A.D. 114 to churches of Roman Asia, characterized the εὐαγγέλιον orally preached in the church as the only reliable authority (Ignatius, *Philadelphians* V.1; VIII.2; IX.2; *Smyrneans* V.1; VII.2). With great emphasis he defined it as the living tradition and actualization of Christ's life and passion, crucifixion and resurrection (*Philadelphians* VIII.2). This is also the topic of the canonical Gospels, but in the last of the passages quoted Ignatius criticized sectarians who exaggerated the importance of written documents (ἀρχεῖα). He referred to the living Christian message as the criterion for any reliability of documents (*Philadelphians,* ibid.). About the same time, Bishop Papias of Hierapolis emphasized the superiority of the living oral tradition (Eusebius, *EH* III.39.4).

In all of these Christian texts from the years shortly after A.D. 100, **εὐαγγέλιον** is found only in the collective sense of the good news preached by Jesus and the early church.

Since the Gospel inscriptiones, judging from the logical structure of the formula εὐαγγέλιον κατὰ, ascribe the same collective sense and superior function to the message, there is good reason to date them back to around A.D. 100.

Only after the middle of the second century, it became customary to speak of εὐαγγέλια in the plural and to use the word for individual Gospels. About the year 160, Justin the Martyr mentioned the liturgical use of the Gospels in the church. For the information of non-Christians he characterized these books as "recollections" written by the apostles and said they were called Gospels by the Christians (Justin, *Apology* I.66.3). In another context, Justin introduced a Scripture reference by these words: "It is written in the Gospel (εὐαγγέλιον) that Jesus says," and then a quotation of Matt. 11:27 follows (Justin, *Dialogue* 100.1). Here the word "Gospel" is explicitly used in the sense of a written

document. Irenaeus also regarded the Gospels as written documents when he discussed heretical movements around A.D. 180. Using older information of Papias, which is treated below, he represented the evangelists as editors of four texts. Going beyond the information of Papias, he connected these texts with Syria, Asia, Greece, and Italy to get an even distribution on four important Christian countries (Irenaeus, *Against Heresies* II.1.1). Although he emphasized the unity of their message, it was mainly the individual formation of the Gospels that interested him (III.11.8–9). Clement of Alexandria, writing around A.D. 200, illustrates a further step in the development of the vocabulary by separating the four Gospels of the canon from the apocryphal Gospel According to the Egyptians (Clement, *Stromateis* III.13). In the years 150 to 200 the four Gospels thus began to be understood as individual documents.

This latter approach differs from the conception that is found in the New Testament and in the writings of the Apostolic Fathers until around A.D. 120. Here *εὐαγγέλιον* is a collective expression, used only in the singular and indicating the apostolic message which is spread and heard among the believers. The characteristic formulation of the Gospel inscriptiones—*εὐαγγέλιον κατὰ Μαθθαῖον*, and so forth—exactly represents such a logical progression from the collective nature of the good news to its individual manifestation in written documents. This is the reason why they can be dated slightly before or after A.D. 100. Since they presuppose the collection of the Gospels in a corpus, a much earlier date will not appear probable, but the particular meaning of *εὐαγγέλιον* in the New Testament and the Apostolic Fathers quoted above requires a dating to around A.D. 100.

At that time, about A.D. 100, it was still possible for Christians to recall the names of those responsible for the redaction of the Gospels. Consequently the traditional attribution of the four documents to Matthew, Mark, Luke, and John does not seem to have been arbitrary.

With special regard to the Synoptic Gospels, their traditional names must even be ascribed to historical factors. Although the early church regarded apostolic dignity as very significant (1 Cor. 12:28 e.p.), the unanimous references to Matthew, Mark, and Luke were not caused by any interest to reserve for the Gospels the names of important apostles. It certainly was (and still is) possible to connect the apostle Matthew with the First Gospel, but this apostle was never reported to have claimed a leading function as did Peter or the sons of Zebedee. At any rate, the connection of the First Gospel with a certain Matthew, whether he was the apostle or not, was not based on the general consideration for the Twelve. Nor can any such consideration explain the attribution of the Second and the Third Gospel to Mark and Luke, since these men were never ranked with the apostles. There is merely one possibility to explain the inscriptive names of the evangelists found in the Bodmer papyri and in all later Gospel manuscripts, and this is to presume recollections of the Gospel origins represented by older Christians until around A.D. 100.

It was also shortly after A.D. 100 that such recollections occupied a witness to whom attention will now be drawn.

Papias on the Origin of the Gospels

The common attribution of the Synoptic Gospels to Matthew, Mark, and Luke around A.D. 100 is reflected in material collected by Bishop Papias of Hierapolis shortly after that year. His investigations were published in five books, but unfortunately only short fragments have been preserved, especially by Eusebius of Caesarea in his erudite *Ecclesiastical History*. In spite of their fragmentary shape, they are sufficient to prove that about A.D. 100 at least the two first Gospels were commonly attributed to Matthew and Mark. No fragment concerning Luke has been preserved, but as will be argued below, Papias has alluded to the Third Gospel in his report on Mark, and there is also reason to believe that no hesitation about the name of Luke was felt at the time. The testimony of Papias on the Gospel origins must be considered to be of unique importance as the earliest available evidence.

Declarations of Papias himself confirm that he collected his material for the study of the Gospel origins shortly after the year 100.

In the preface to his five books, which has been preserved by Eusebius in literal quotation, Papias was presented as having endeavored to show what older Christians had told about the historical background of the Gospels. He called these older Christians **πρεσβύτεροι**, and since the point was their age, which implied contacts with early traditions, they were not mentioned here as "presbyters" or "elders" of local parishes but as "veterans" among the Christians. Irenaeus also used the word πρεσβύτεροι for veterans when referring to what Papias had indicated about representatives of early traditions (*Against Heresies* II.22.5), and in the Latin translation of his work the expression became *seniores*.

Papias further said in his preface that whenever persons came who had been in contact with such old traditionists among the believers, he asked them to share with him the information received from these veterans about what apostles such as Andrew and Peter and other disciples of the Lord had said or used to say concerning the Gospel traditions. In this context Papias did not claim more than to have met fellow Christians who had known some of the veterans, and he literally said he used to interrogate such contemporaries to discover what the veterans had told them.

The witnesses here implied consist of three groups:

1. Apostles and other early disciples of Jesus
2. Veteran Christians who remembered sayings of apostles and early disciples
3. Contemporaries of Papias who had been in contact with the veterans

Between the groups, there are these chronological distances:

(1) The apostolic generation dominated the years 33 to 66, seeing that a definite end of the apostolic period was reached on the one hand by the martyr-

doms of James, Peter, and Paul in the years 62 and 65 (below, p. 178), and on the other hand by the emigration of the Judean Christians about A.D. 64 (p. 137). With one exception only, no historical evidence for a later activity of apostles and other important early disciples is available. The exception in question is the information of the Fourth Gospel that a member of the apostolic group was destined to survive Peter for a considerable time (John 21:22). Called the disciple whom Jesus loved, he was later identified with the apostle John, even though he remains anonymous in the Fourth Gospel. (2) Papias did not claim to have met the so-called veterans to whom he ascribed memories of the apostolic generation, but only to have interviewed people who could tell what such veteran Christians had said with regard to apostolic traditions on the Gospel origins. Accordingly, the veterans must be regarded as believers of the first postapostolic generation. One may suppose they lived from A.D. 30 or 40 until about A.D. 100. Irenaeus also thought of this period with regard to the πρεσβύτεροι or *seniores* mentioned by Papias (Irenaeus, *Against Heresies* II.22.5). (3) The interviews of Papias with people who had met such veterans would therefore have begun about A.D. 100 and been going on for the next years, but not later than A.D. 110. Of course Papias may have published his study on some later occasion, for the Byzantine historian Philipp of Side wrote about A.D. 435 in a chronicle based on Eusebius that Papias had told stories about people who lived until the days of Hadrian (A.D. 117–38). But this does not refer to the interviews, which Papias must have undertaken during the very first years of the second century, since the veterans in question cannot have lived much longer.

The date is confirmed by the place that Eusebius, without apologetic intentions, has given his references to Papias in the general chronological framework of his *Ecclesiastical History*. Irenaeus also dated Papias to the beginning of the second century, but his judgment was not based only on historical information. For when he wrote that Papias had been a hearer of the apostle John who lived until the days of Trajan (Irenaeus, *Against Heresies* II.22.5), he was led by a concern for apostolic succession, which is not found in the words of Papias quoted by Eusebius. No such interests determined the selection of the quotations from Papias by Eusebius, who, on the contrary, was inclined to criticize the bishop of Hierapolis. Therefore his quotations may suffice here to demonstrate that Papias collected his material shortly after A.D. 100.

After all, the information supplied by Papias concerning the Gospel origins is of exceptional value. His interlocutors conveyed to him reports of veteran Christians who had spent their life or the main part of it before A.D. 100. Such representatives of the second Christian generation certainly had access to living recollections of the Gospel origins.

The material that Papias wanted to illustrate was defined in the title of his five books: λογίων κυριακῶν ἐξήγησις (Eusebius, *EH* III.39.1). Here ἐξήγησις has the normal meaning of "commentary." On the other hand, the λόγια κυριακά are not simply to be understood as "sayings of the Lord," but in the broader sense of

"reports about the Lord." This is evident from the way Papias has used the same expression in his discussion of the Second Gospel (ibid., 39.15). With regard to Mark, he emphasized two circumstances: (1) that Mark wrote down scattered utterances (διδασκαλίαι) of Peter concerning "what had been either said or done by Christ"; and (2) that Peter himself did not produce any compilation (σύνταξις) of the **λόγια κυριακά**. Both observations are confirmed by modern form criticism insofar as it has become obvious that Mark's Gospel is a compilation of pericopes that may be subdivided into quotations of the words and narratives about the works of Jesus. Since the remark on the **λόγια** implies that it was not Peter but Mark who compiled them, the expression in question covers the elements of the Second Gospel, including both quotations and narratives. The **λόγια κυριακά** written down by Mark are no doubt to be understood as both types of "reports about the Lord," that is, "what had been either said or done by Christ." Seeing that Papias used the same expression in the title of his five books, the literal sense of the title must accordingly be "Commentary on the Reports About the Lord." By "Reports" the author meant nothing but the Gospels, for which the word **εὐαγγέλια** in the plural was introduced only fifty years after his days.

The fact that Papias spoke of **λόγια** in the sense of Gospel reports in general is of decisive importance for the understanding of his statements on Matthew and Mark, which will now be studied in detail. It will also be pointed out below that Papias's apology of Mark includes a slight allusion to Luke.

Matthew

According to Eusebius, Papias had received a threefold piece of information about Matthew and his book: "(1) Matthew compiled (συνετάξατο) the **λόγια** (2) in the Hebrew language, and (3) everyone translated them as [well as] he could" (Eusebius, *EH* III.39.16). These three items are to be understood in the following way:

1. Eusebius did not quote any utterances showing who the evangelist Matthew was supposed to be, but Papias must have meant the tax collector Matthew, who, in the First Gospel, has expressly been identified with the apostle Matthew (Matt. 9:9 and 10:3). In his preface Papias mentioned Matthew among the most important apostles, and the veterans he quoted were said to know what these apostles had reported about the Gospel origins (Eusebius, *EH* III.39.4). When later touching upon the **λόγια** compiled by Matthew, Papias certainly meant the apostle. Nor did Eusebius indicate any doubts with regard to this identity, although he was inclined to find two authors called John in the utterances of Papias (Eusebius, *EH* III.39.5–7).

The **λόγια** said to have been compiled by Matthew cannot have the limited meaning of "sayings," as Schleiermacher believed (above, p. 8). Instead, they must be understood in that wider meaning of "reports" in which Papias used the expression first in the title and then in his passage on Mark (as observed above).

Eusebius quoted the words of Papias on Matthew (*EH* III.39.16) immediately after his words on Mark (*EH* III.39.15), which define the λόγια as "what had been either said or done by Christ." Thus the λόγια refer not only to "sayings" but to "reports" in general. It is evident that Eusebius did not quote Papias in the subsequent passage on the λόγια of Matthew in any other sense than what is found immediately before in his reference to the λόγια κυριακά compiled by Mark. Eusebius merely summarized the view of Papias on Matthew, and therefore let the breviloquence λόγια replace the full expression λόγια κυριακά used in the passage on Mark. Another common element is the reference of Papias to a "compilation" that gives both passages a corresponding meaning: It was not Peter but Mark who produced a "compilation" (σύνταξις) of the reports about the Lord available to him, and Matthew had also "compiled" (συνετάξατο) such reports. What the evangelist Matthew collected was not λόγια in the narrow sense of sayings but in the broader sense of reports consisting of quotations and narratives.

Thus the declaration of Papias on Matthew did not deal with any collection of sayings like the pretended source Q, but with a Hebrew Gospel which contained units of tradition representing quotations and narratives in combination. Both kinds of tradition units, in combination with each other, are essential to Matthew in Greek as well as to Mark and Luke, and there is no reason to understand the Hebrew compilation of Matthew mentioned by Papias as representing a different sort of literature. The latter referred to nothing less than a book that Matthew had written in the genre of a gospel, so that it may be called a proto-Matthew. Certainly, before the units were collected by Matthew, they existed as preliterary traditions, and in his preface Papias underlined the general superiority of a living tradition (ζῶσα ψωνή, *vox viva*) in relation to written documents (Eusebius, *EH* III.39.4). But in the present context Matthew was said to have collected such traditional units into a book.

2. Papias spoke of "Hebrew" as the language in which Matthew published the reports. In analogy to the New Testament, which has used the expression Hebrew instead of Aramaic (Acts 21:40; 22:2; 26:14), Papias may have meant a proto-Matthew written in Aramaic, as this was the vernacular language of the Jews. With regard to the characteristic interest taken by the First Gospel in the fulfillment of the Old Testament, however, it can also be assumed that proto-Matthew was based on Hebrew as the religious language of Israel, and this would correspond to the preference for Hebrew in the Qumran texts.

3. The concluding remark of Papias about the reports collected by Matthew, that "everyone translated them as he could," was meant in a positive way. No indication of any criticism is found in the extant fragments, and the general intention of Papias was to illustrate the reliability of the Gospel traditions. The expression "as he could" must thus be supposed to mean "as well as possible."

In this connection Papias was dealing only with Matthew, and he did not trace

any other Gospel back to the reports collected by Matthew. Eusebius also introduced the quotation in question with an explicit reference to the Gospel of Matthew by writing: "Concerning that of Matthew [i.e., the Gospel of Matthew] this was said [by the informants to Papias]." Therefore, when Papias stated that different persons translated the Hebrew reports of Matthew to the best of their ability, he saw the issue of their activity just in the Greek Matthew. He had learned that proto-Matthew was transposed from Hebrew or Aramaic into Greek by a team. Disciples in contact with Matthew were said to have translated and edited his collection as correctly as possible. The result here indicated was nothing but the canonical Gospel of Matthew, as was also indicated by Eusebius when he introduced the notice on the translation with an express reference to this Gospel.

Really the First Gospel is to be understood as the fruit of a conscious translation and edition. It pays attention to scriptural instruction, and it betrays endeavors to present a relatively cultivated form of Greek with rather few Semitisms. This is exactly what must be expected from a regular translation and edition such as the one indicated by Papias when dealing with Matthew. Whereas the diction of Mark remains on a popular level and shows dependence on the speaking habits of people accustomed to Aramaic and Greek (and familiar with some Latin), the language of Matthew is characterized by inclinations to correctness and concentration in narrative sections as well as by diligence and erudition in didactic contexts. The preference for Septuagint formulations of the Old Testament quotations is another indication of a resolute translation activity behind the Greek Matthew.

At the same time, the Greek vocabulary includes numerous similarities between Matthew and Mark, and in the Q material also between Matthew and Luke. This shows that oral translations into Greek of separate Hebrew or Aramaic tradition units had been made and spread in the early church before the Greek redaction of Matthew, Mark, and Luke took place. No doubt the redactors of Matthew as well as the evangelists Mark and Luke used similar elements of preliterary Greek traditions when they gave their material a literary shape.

Remarkably enough, the editors of the First Gospel have also indicated a special familiarity with the apostle Matthew, the one who must have been meant when the book received the title *εὐαγγέλιον κατὰ Μαθθαῖον*. (1) Only the First Gospel has mentioned the tax collector Levi, who had been converted by Jesus, under his later Christian name of Matthew (Matt. 9:9). (2) In the list of the Twelve the First Gospel has confirmed the identity of this tax collector with the apostle Matthew by adding the epithet "the tax collector" (10:3). That the First Gospel has especially marked out the former profession of this apostle is a significant exception, and in all four available lists of the apostles no other name has been characterized in such a personal way. (3) In another connection the editors of the First Gospel have enforced the importance of Matthew's conversion

that was accomplished by Jesus as the great physician sent to heal the sick (9:12): Bringing the call of Matthew (9:9–13) into focus, they have inserted a sequence of ten healings and miracles (8:1—9:34) between the Sermon on the Mount (5:1—7:29) and the commission of the Twelve (Matt. 9:35—10:40). These ten stories consist mainly of double and single units, and their sequence implies a strong deviation from Mark and Luke, but they surround the context–parallel triple tradition of Matthew's conversion (9:9–13) and were evidently gathered here to illustrate Matthew's healing by the great physician Jesus (above, pp. 95–96). In these points the tax collector and apostle Matthew turns out to have been especially important for the redactors of the First Gospel.

Thus the Greek style of the Gospel According to Matthew, its Septuagint quotations, and the interest taken in the tax collector Matthew indicate that Papias had received a relatively adequate picture of the Gospel's background from those older traditionists he was able to interview. Eusebius (*EH* III.39.12) criticized Papias because the latter believed in the millennium (Rev. 20:49), and modern scholars have often impugned Papias because his sayings are not compatible with their own ideas. But one should not doubt the honesty of his investigations, and internal factors do confirm several of his assessments.

In any case, there is reason to identify Matthew, the one who is mentioned in the title of the First Gospel, with the former tax collector and later apostle Matthew to whom the redactors paid special attention. He may have compiled available traditions in Aramaic or perhaps Hebrew, as Papias asserted, but it was collaborators of his who produced a Greek version and probably a completion of his outline. In this connection they adapted the Old Testament quotations to Septuagint traditions.

At the same time, a harmonization with units of Jesus traditions already circulating in Greek may be assumed, for this will explain several convergences in the Greek of Matthew with that of Mark or Luke. Such common elements of the vocabulary may partially be traced back to communications of Peter, who, in Matthew even more explicitly than in Mark, receives instructions of Jesus as the leader of the apostles (Matt. 4:18; 10:2; 14:28; 15:15; 16:18, 23; 17:1, 4, 14, 15; 18:21; 19:27; 26:37).

Historically, the title defining the writing as "Good News According to Matthew" is therefore adequate insofar as it refers to units of early traditions essentially based on communications of Peter and collected by the apostle Matthew in Hebrew or Aramaic. Following the structure of his compilation, but probably with additions, members of Matthew's community presented the pericopes in Greek under the influence of translations already circulating in the early church. When doing this editing, they also reduced inclinations to Semitisms and harmonized quotations with the Septuagint. The name of Matthew can thus be used individually for the apostle who stood behind the First Gospel and collectively for the redactors who gave the compilation of this author Greek contours.

Mark

Before the short notice on Matthew treated above, Eusebius quoted an instructive remark of Papias concerning the Gospel of Mark (*EH* III.39.15):

> And this is what the veteran [ὁ πρεσβύτερος, referring to the veteran John mentioned in *EH* III.39.14] used to say [ἔλεγεν, imperfect]:
> "Mark became Peter's reporter [ἑρμηνευτής, here in the sense of a secretary, as the next clause shows]. Insofar as he could remember it, he wrote down exactly (ἀκριβῶς)—though not in order (τάξει)—what had been said or done by Christ. He had not heard or accompanied the Lord, but later Peter, as I said. The latter used to present [ἐποιεῖτο, imperfect] the pieces of information (διδασκαλίαι) according to occasional needs, yet without delivering any written compilation [σύνταξις, in contrast to what Matthew had done] of the reports about the Lord (τὰ κυριακὰ λόγια). Mark therefore did not commit any fault when in this way he wrote down some material as he remembered it. For he only cared about one thing: neither to leave out nor to distort anything of what he had heard."
> This was reported to Papias about Mark.

In the statement quoted above, the introductory notice on "the veteran" (ὁ πρεσβύτερος, elative) as well as the concluding remark on what had been reported to Papias indicates that the latter claimed to have received his information on Mark from John, that old disciple of Christ mentioned by Eusebius in the preceding summary. For in the preceding text, the disciples Aristion and "the veteran John" (πρεσβύτερος) are mentioned three times as witnesses of special importance for Papias: once in the quotation from the preface of Papias and twice in the report of Eusebius on the research work done by Papias (*EH* III.39.4, 7, 14). The presentation of "the veteran" at the beginning of the above-quoted text is directly attached to the last of these passages, so that "the veteran" cannot be any other authority than John. And although Eusebius was not willing to identify this veteran John with the apostle John, Papias presupposed this identity, for he quoted the name of John twice in his preface without indicating any reference to different persons (*EH* III.39.4). John first appears together with Andrew and some other apostles, here named in an order influenced by the Fourth Gospel, and is then cited again together with a certain Aristion, obviously known to the contemporaries, though not mentioned in other documents. Both groups were emphatically characterized as personal disciples of the Lord, first the apostles including John, then Aristion together with John (to delete the epithet in the second case, as some of the scholars have done, implies a vicious circle). The point at issue was precisely the identity of the apostle and veteran John. On the other hand, veteran Christians interviewed by Papias had told him what several disciples of the Lord, including the apostle John, had formerly said (εἶπεν, aorist), and, on the other hand, his informants had also told him what two disciples of the Lord, Aristion and the veteran John, were presently saying (λέγουσιν, present tense). Papias did not claim to have met John, but he

mentioned this disciple of the Lord twice in order to confirm the reliability of his material. John had belonged to the circle of the apostles but outlived them, and since he was known to contemporaries as the veteran John, he proved a witness of particular importance for Papias. Eusebius destroyed this point by seeking two Johns in the text, while taking refuge in a subtle manipulation to separate the author of the Fourth Gospel from that of Revelation. Papias did not intend any such division. On the contrary, he referred to the witness of John twice just because this disciple of the Lord had survived the apostolic generation, so that he represented early traditions and recent communications in one person.

In the Johannine writings of the New Testament there are in fact signs of such a disciple who reached an unusually high age. Their author is called John only in the titles, which are secondary. But the Gospel of John especially refers to the witness of the so-called beloved disciple (John 13:23 e.p.) and indicates that he survived Peter for a considerable time (21:22–23). In the Epistles of John the writer presents himself as ὁ πρεσβύτερος, or "the veteran," without feeling any need to inform the readers about his name (2 John 1; 3 John 1). This indicates that Christians, in the last part of the first century, knew a disciple of Jesus who lived much longer than other members of the apostolic circle. Since the name of John is not found in the passages now quoted, it cannot be supposed that Papias took over his references to "the veteran John" from the Johannine writings, but he must have obtained them from living traditions. He summarized his report on the interviews with fellow Christians, who had known the veterans including John, by declaring that he found no written book so trustworthy as the *vox viva* (Eusebius, *EH* III.39.4). So there are independent analogies between the Johannine passages and the notices of Papias, and these analogies make it probable that until around A.D. 100 the apostle John was known among Christians as "the veteran John."

Papias was no doubt conscious of using a first-rate authority when he illustrated the genesis of the Second Gospel by quoting what "the veteran" had declared on Mark. In his eyes the disciple John, who had belonged to the apostolic circle, was identical with that disciple of the Lord whom the environment knew as ὁ πρεσβύτερος, or "the veteran," and whose recollections other veteran Christians had submitted to Papias. An apologetic interest certainly influenced Papias when discussing Mark, but his appeal to "the veteran" has decisive importance, because his contemporaries were still familiar with this authority.

Unless the veteran's judgment on the Gospel of Mark is rejected for aprioristic reasons, it confirms the traditional view of the evangelist Mark in two respects (below, items 1 and 2). Furthermore, the declaration of the veteran John about units of Peter's preaching and teaching as having been written down by Mark is applicable to the pericopes and the structure of the Second Gospel (below, item 3).

1. Without hesitation the veteran John had ascribed the Second Gospel to Peter's assistant Mark. He had not taken over the attribution from the redac-

tional title "The Good News According to Mark," for that was not added to the manuscripts until around A.D. 100 (above, p. 150). Quite to the contrary, the recollections of the veteran legitimate the redactional title of the Second Gospel.

2. The traditional identification of the evangelist Mark with a member of the Jerusalem church by the name of John Mark (Acts 12:12, 25; 13:5, 13; 15:37, 39) is confirmed by two further circumstances: (*a*) that Papias, quoting the veteran John, traced the pericopes of Mark's Gospel back to contacts between Peter and Mark (Eusebius, *EH* III.39.15; more on this below, in item 3); and (*b*) that Luke indicated such contacts in the house-church of Mark's mother in Jerusalem (Acts 12:12).

3. In fact, the topographical structure of the Second Gospel suggests a particular dependence of the evangelist upon communications of Peter.

Mark more than any evangelist has concentrated the Galilean part of his story on Capernaum, where Peter's mother-in-law had a house (Mark 1:29), while Matthew drew attention to other places at the beginning of his Galilean report, and Luke was less concerned with Galilee in general. In contrast to Matthew and Luke, Mark let Jesus visit Capernaum as soon as possible after his baptism (Mark 1:21), then stay in the house of Peter's mother-in-law (1:29, 33; 2:1; 3:30), and work for a considerable time in Capernaum or its closest environment (1:20—4:34). Afterward there is a description of six excursions to countries surrounding the Lake of Galilee, and each time Mark has used Capernaum and its neighborhoods as the starting point (4:35—9:29). Eventually he permitted Jesus to return to Capernaum in order to instruct the apostles in the house of Peter's mother-in-law (9:30–50), before Jesus proceeded with the disciples to Perea and Judea (10:7). This topographical concentration of the Galilean material intimates that recollections of Peter from Capernaum and its neighborhood were available to the second evangelist.

In the Judean part of Mark, as demonstrated above (pp. 146–49), the report on the institution of the eucharist forms the center and served as the starting point for a development of the entire passion story. This happened at holy meals in the house-churches (Acts 2:42), where the participants were informed about the last meal of Christ and events connected with it. In this connection, too, a dependence of Mark upon Peter is likely, because the apostle entertained special connections with the house-church of Mark's mother in Jerusalem (Acts 12:12). It was here and through Peter that Mark became acquainted with the passion story which, from the beginning, was transmitted in a common and coherent way.

At the early Christian meals, further items of belief were also illustrated, as Paul did at length in Troas (Acts 20:7). It may be supposed that in the Jerusalem house-church of his mother and in other places Mark took over from Peter such additional units, especially those individual and disconnected recollections from Capernaum and Galilee which he placed in the Galilean part of his story.

The witness of the veteran John about the dependence of Mark upon the διδασκαλίαι of Peter is thus found to agree with historical facts.

What the veteran John said about the Second Gospel, however, was especially

meant to defend it against critics who found certain deficiencies in Mark. (*a*) It had been observed that in contrast to the apostolic evangelists, Mark was no eyewitness and follower of Jesus. According to Papias, the veteran John emphasized that Mark had been Peter's reporter and written down carefully what the apostle had told, so one should not blame the evangelist for not being an eyewitness. (*b*) Papias then emphasized that Mark had reported exactly (ἀκριβῶς), though not in order (τάξει). Thus the critics had compared Mark with Luke, who, in his prologue, had announced intentions to report exactly and in order (Luke 1:3). In this prologue there are once the same word and twice similar words as those found in the apology of Papias (ἀκριβῶς, "accurately"; ἀνατάξασθαι, "arrange in order"; καθεξῆς, "point by point"). According to Papias, John had neutralized such criticism by stating that Mark wrote down from memory what Peter had made known on different occasions, so that no systematic order could be achieved. (*c*) On the whole, no coherent report (σύνταξις) of the traditions about the Lord should be expected from Mark, for Peter had left no such compilation behind, whereas Matthew had compiled (συνετάξατο) available traditions. Peter had presented such pieces of information (διδασκαλίαι) as occasion demanded, and the oral units thus formed out ad hoc were recorded by Mark as well as he could remember them.

By these declarations based on utterances of the veteran John, Papias has appropriately characterized the structure of the Second Gospel. Except for the coherent passion story, this Gospel actually represents a series of independent pericopes each time dominated by a specific topic, so that Papias's reference to lectures of Peter (διδασκαλίαι), delivered according to occasional needs (πρὸς τὰς χρείας), was totally justified.

Form-critical research has particularly shown that many expressions characteristic of Mark, such as "in those days" or "just afterward" (Mark 1:9, 12), are redactional means of conjunction by which separate pericopes were arranged into a coherent report.[7] Papias's remarks on Mark and Peter thus offer an instructive analogy to the picture which form criticism has established concerning the composition of Mark's Gospel. According to form criticism, the individual pericopes deal with topics that were of current interest for the apostolic church. It is true, for instance, of the reports on Christ's authority to forgive sins (Mark 2:1–12) or his answer to the question about divorce (10:1–12). Everywhere in the Markan pericopes the need for community edification is discernible as an impetus of the formation process. This corresponds to the notice of Papias about "the occasional needs."

Structural features of the Second Gospel thus confirm the picture offered by Papias when he, with an explicit reference to the veteran John, wrote about Mark as the reporter of Peter. By the way, the inquiry of Papias was undertaken

7. K. L. Schmidt, *Der Rahmen der Geschichte Jesu. Literarkritische Untersuchungen zur ältesten Jesusüberlieferung* (Berlin: Trowitzsch & Sohn, 1919).

in that period when apostolic dignity was highly esteemed (above p. 154), and yet the Second Gospel was ascribed not to an apostle but to an assistant of Peter by the name of Mark. Under these circumstances doubts concerning the correctness of the redactional title, "The Good News According to Mark," are not acceptable.

The second evangelist was certainly identical with John Mark of Jerusalem, who is known from Acts and letters of Paul. Since the Gospel of Mark has a completely Palestinian stamp, there is reason to assume that Peter was still in the holy country when the evangelist wrote down what the apostle told or taught according to arising needs, as Papias voiced it. The place where the evangelist got acquainted with the preaching and teaching of the apostle was Jerusalem, where Peter entertained special connections with the house-church of Mark's mother (Acts 12:12). During the meals celebrated in this and other house-churches (Acts 2:46), the communications of the apostle were probably concentrated on the holy eucharist and the passion story (cf. Paul in Troas, 20:7), and the Gospel of Mark also illustrates this priority of the passion report. In addition, the apostle may have offered scattered communications about Christ's earlier preaching and healing activity, and here the circumstance is remarkable that Mark's Galilean narrative is dominated by events taking place in Capernaum and its closest neighborhood. The little city was Peter's home, so that his recollections of Christ's activity in Galilee naturally gravitated toward Capernaum, and this is exactly what is reflected in Mark.

With regard to its language, the Gospel of Mark can indeed be especially well understood against the background of those house-churches to whose edification it may be supposed Peter contributed before Mark wrote down the pericopes in Greek. Even if Peter preferably talked in Aramaic, a Greek paraphrase was no problem in his bilingual environment. In the vocabulary, there are often analogies between Matthew and Mark, and they show that Greek versions of many pericopes were spread in the community, so that Mark's adaptation of the material was already influenced by collective traditions. What is especially characteristic of the Markan narrative, however, is the preference for a popular style, an intimate and visual description, represented, for instance, by the frequent use of the expression "at once" (Mark 1:12, 23, 28, etc.). This stylistic particularity is quite in harmony with the edification of believers in a house-church like that of Mark's mother in Jerusalem to which Peter had special relationships.

Nevertheless the final redaction of the Second Gospel may rather be localized to Caesarea. One has to consider the extensive concord of Mark and Luke in the sequence of such pericopes as they have in common. The best explanation for the parallelism is the personal contacts between the evangelists in Caesarea which are indicated by the Pauline captivity epistles. Evidence for this are the greetings from Mark and Luke in Philemon 24, to be referred to Caesarea and the years 58–60 because of v. 9, "*now* also a prisoner," designating the captivity as a new situation in the apostle's life (similar greetings in Col. 4:10; 2 Tim. 4:11). In his

prologue, Luke expressly mentioned some contemporaries who had at the same time undertaken (ἐπεχείρησαν) to elaborate literary reports on the life of Jesus (Luke 1:1), and he must have thought especially of Mark. The far-reaching harmony in the Gospels of Mark and Luke, which does not exclude variations, is explained in a concrete and practical way if such a personal exchange of experiences during the years of Paul in Caesarea, A.D. 58–60, is regarded as the reason.

Moreover, the striking Latinisms of Mark (centurio, speculator, sextarius, quadrans, and others) do in fact indicate the residence of the Palestinian procurator as the place of redaction, for Caesarea was the official military and mercantile center of the country. Irenaeus suggested a localization of Mark to Italy (above, p. 154), but this was due to his ambition to distribute the four Gospels on each quarter of the heavens. There is certainly a hint of a later connection between Peter and Mark in Rome (1 Peter 5:13), but Papias is not known to have mentioned this. Against the localization inaugurated by Irenaeus severe arguments have to be adduced: (1) Mark exhibits an entirely Galilean and Judean, but not an Italian, perspective. (2) The strong analogies between the Gospels of Mark and Luke are to be explained by personal contacts between the two evangelists during Paul's captivity in Caesarea, as was demonstrated above and will be confirmed by the Third Gospel's connection with Caesarea analyzed below. (3) Papias appealed to what John had declared about Mark, and since this apostle is not known to have visited Italy, his knowledge of Mark's dependence on Peter must rather be referred to Palestine. On account of these circumstances there is good reason to localize the final redaction of Mark to Caesarea and to point out the contacts between the evangelists Mark and Luke during the years 58 to 60.

Structural and textual characteristics of the Second Gospel thus prove that Papias described the background of Mark's Gospel adequately when he stated that it had emanated from contacts of Peter and Mark, as had been indicated by that apostle known to the postapostolic generation as the veteran John.

Luke

The name of Luke does not appear in the notices of Papias on the evangelists that Eusebius has preserved. Yet the Gospel of Luke is alluded to in the remarks of Papias on the Second Gospel quoted above (p. 164). As has been observed, when Papias referred to John in defense of Mark, he used the expressions "accurately" (ἀκριβῶς) and "though not in order" (*οὐ μέντοι τάξει*), and his vocabulary was influenced by characteristic words in Luke's prologue (Luke 1:1, 3): "arrange in order" (ἀνατάξασθαι), "accurately" (ἀκριβῶς), and "point by point" (καθεξῆς). Critics had argued that Mark had produced a meager and loose report in comparison to Luke, offering no parallels to the birth stories and the travel narrative. To defend Mark, Papias quoted John concerning the merely redactional activity of this evangelist. The apology of Papias presupposed that

Mark's critics regarded Luke as the model Gospel. Such appreciation of Luke is also found somewhat later in Asia Minor, for about A.D. 140 Marcion of Pontus declared Luke to be the only normative Gospel.

This alone does not prove that a man called Luke was the author of the Third Gospel. Nevertheless two arguments may be advanced in support of the redactional inscriptio, *Εὐαγγέλιον κατὰ Λουκᾶν*. (1) As was the case with the Second Gospel, no attempts were made to ascribe the Third Gospel to a representative of the apostolic group. (2) The reason why Eusebius did not find it worthwhile to quote Papias concerning Luke may have been just this early appreciation of the Third Gospel which is reflected in Papias's apology of Mark studied above. It would imply that Papias did not find it necessary to explain the origin and background of the Third Gospel, as he had done concerning Matthew and Mark, because no problem was connected with Luke at the time. Consequently the only satisfactory explanation why the Third Gospel, together with the Book of Acts, was ascribed to a person by the name of Luke seems to be historical reminiscences of some kind.

Now if a man called Luke was known as the author of the Third Gospel, it can only be a question of Paul's collaborator Luke who is mentioned in three of the captivity epistles (Philemon 24; Col. 4:10; 2 Tim. 4:11), and in one case is called "the beloved physician" (Col. 4:14). Although the Greek name of *Λουκᾶς* (an Aramaic-like abbreviation of the Latin name Lucius) was not uncommon, there is no reason to presume that some Luke otherwise unknown was the author of the Third Gospel. Since the Book of Acts was produced in direct continuation of the Third Gospel, the interest of its author in the missionary activity of Paul proves that both the Gospel and Acts were produced by a person fitting in with the one who appears in the captivity epistles as Paul's collaborator Luke. To reject their identification leads to unnecessary complications.

Scholars who are accustomed to thinking in Pauline terms deplore the absence of Paul's doctrine of justification in Luke and Acts, although there is a sermon of Paul that ends with a characteristic invitation to justification by faith (Acts 13:38–39). A disciple of Paul, they contend, should be expected to develop the doctrine of justification in a systematic way, and consequently the physician Luke, who is mentioned in the captivity epistles, cannot be the author of the Lukan books. If this argument were valid, then not even the secretary Mark who followed Paul could be the author of the Second Gospel, for Paul's doctrine of justification is also missing here. After all, however, the Gospels of Mark and Luke as well as the Book of Acts were not written to present theological doctrine but to report on historical events (Mark 1:1; Luke 1:1; Acts 1:1). With regard to such ideas that are found in the Lukan writings, but that do not exclusively coincide with Paul's theology, the following circumstances are further to be considered. First, the epistles of Paul were not immediately spread and regarded as normative literature, and therefore quotations from them should not be expected in Acts. Second, the person called Luke in the captivity epistles was not

presented as a young disciple of Paul but as his colleague and collaborator, a notable person known to the readers. Nor did the author of the Lukan writings desire to be only a mouthpiece of Paul, but in the first instance he referred to the witness of apostles and other authorities who had been servants of the word from the very beginning (Luke 1:2). He paid attention to Peter and John as representatives of the apostles (Acts 2:14; 3:1), to Philip as representative of the Hellenists (8:5), and to James as representative of the Jewish Christians (15:13). Third, since the Lukan writings occupy a special position within the New Testament on account of their systematic composition, Hellenistic style, and informative abundance, their author must have been a mature writer, not only a young amanuensis. On the whole, the personal theology of this author is not sufficient ground for rejecting his identification with the collaborator of Paul who is called Luke in the captivity epistles.

Here attention may be drawn again to the greetings from Mark and Luke found in the captivity epistles to Philemon, the Colossians, and Timothy (Philemon 24; Col. 4:10; 2 Tim. 4:11). These greetings are particularly important for understanding the Third Gospel's origin. Since the Pauline background of Colossians and 2 Timothy is not generally acknowledged, while there are no such doubts about Philemon, the subsequent argumentation is only based upon this personal letter, although the two other epistles illustrate the situation of the participants in a corresponding way.

In his letter to Philemon, the apostle characterized his captivity emphatically as a new situation, and in view of this additional distress he appealed to Philemon's mercy toward his slave Onesimus (Philemon 9): "Being what I am, the old Paul, but *now also* a prisoner of Christ Jesus, I admonish you about my child." Consideration of the captivity, to which Paul had recently been subjected, is expected to soften the heart of Philemon. As a measure of discipline, Paul had experienced temporary imprisonment several times (2 Cor. 6:5; 11:23). But only after his arrest in Jerusalem was he exposed to a permanent captivity when he spent the years 58 to 60 as a prisoner in Caesarea (Acts 21:33—26:32). This was the new affliction from which he appealed to Philemon's benevolence. Consequently the letter to Philemon must have been written in Caesarea, and the greetings from Mark and Luke appearing in Philemon 24 suggest an activity of these men in Caesarea while Paul had to stay there in captivity.

This offers a possible explanation for the structural analogies between the Gospels of Mark and Luke as emerging from a concrete personal situation. With the exception of nonimportant details and the so-called great lacuna, the Gospel of Luke contains parallels to nearly all pericopes of Mark, whereas the diction includes considerable variations. No literary theory is able to explain these structural analogies in combination with stylistic differences so well as a reference to a personal contact of the evangelists. Although the letter to Philemon does not mention Mark and Luke as evangelists—because they had not yet become known as such—it shows they were simultaneously among the apostle's collab-

orators in Caesarea and therefore able to share their experiences of the oral traditions. This explains the structural parallelism and linguistic divergence of their Gospels without artificial source theories.

In his prologue the author of the Third Gospel has also emphasized that several persons had recently undertaken to compose a report on Jesus (Luke 1:1). He did not speak of any documents already extant, but of some prepared at the time (*ἐπεχείρησαν*, "they have undertaken"). Among these reports under preparation, there is special reason to think of Mark, because the author of Luke has followed structural lines also found in Mark and vice versa. But the two Gospels diverge so considerably in vocabulary and style that any revision of a written composition remains an unnatural explanation. It is only the personal confrontation of the evangelists and their discussion of traditions available that explain the relationships in a satisfactory way.

Philemon thus discloses a confrontation of Mark and Luke in Caesarea from A.D. 58 on, and this confirms the identity of the evangelists Mark and Luke with the persons carrying these names in Acts and the letters of Paul.

Even the special and Q traditions of Luke without parallels in Mark appear to have been collected by the evangelist in Caesarea. To support this localization, attention may be drawn to the consideration of Hellenistic interests which is so characteristic of the Lukan writings.

In the special and Q traditions of Luke's Gospel the interest is focused on Hellenistic ideas (like *σωτήρ*, "savior," in Luke 2:11) and on Hellenistic countries (Phoenicia and Syria in 4:26–27; 6:17; Samaria in 9:52 e.p.). The predominantly Hellenistic countries of Transjordan are the framework of the travel narrative, the central third of the book (9:51—18:14). In particular, elements of Luke without counterparts in Mark betray a warm interest in the Hellenistic mission. This concern is alluded to in the story of Christ's childhood (1:32) and in the report on his first Galilean activities (4:24–27; 5:10b). Then it extends to being the central motif of the Sermon on the Plain (6:17, 27, 38; 7:9) and of the travel narrative, as demonstrated above (p. 127). Another characteristic of the travel narrative, but intimately connected with the missionary concern, is the numerous descriptions and images that have to do with meals and distribution of food, as was also illustrated before (p. 124). This special attention, paid by Luke to the mission among Hellenists and the celebration of meals, hints at the circle of Christians from whom he took over his single and double traditions.

From the beginning, Luke emphasized his contacts with traditionists who had belonged to the original church (1:2). Apart from Mark, Luke indeed had special contacts with representatives of the early church who combined those concerns for Hellenism and common meals. It is a question of the Hellenists in the primitive church of Jerusalem (Acts 6:1). They were headed by Stephen and Philip, and on both Luke reported at length (6:5—8:2; 8:5–40).

After his activity in Jerusalem, Philip worked as a missionary in Samaria (8:5–13), then on the Philistine Plain and the Plain of Sharon (8:24–40). Eventually

he was active in Caesarea (8:40), where he lived with his four daughters in a house of his own (21:8). The last-mentioned notice is given by a "we" report in Acts, and consequently Luke himself belonged to those followers of Paul who, in the spring of A.D. 58, spent several days as Philip's guests in Caesarea (21:10). On this occasion Luke may have been informed by Philip and his people about traditions of the Jerusalem Hellenists. By calling Philip one of the Seven and the evangelist (21:8), Luke drew attention to the merits of Philip both with regard to the Hellenistic meals in Jerusalem and to the missionary activity in Samaria and on the west coast up to Caesarea. After this Caesarean episode the same "we" report indicates that Luke followed Paul to Jerusalem (21:15). They were invited there by Mnason of Cyprus, one of the Hellenists who accompanied Paul. Since he was at home in Jerusalem and was called by Luke "an old disciple" (21:16), he is to be understood as a member of the early church. Luke thus came into contact with the Hellenists in Jerusalem (Acts 21:16–17) before the company sought contacts with the Hebrew Christians led by James (21:18). This gave Luke a further opportunity to be informed by Hellenistic members of the Jerusalem church. When in the summer of A.D. 58 he came to Caesarea again to work as a collaborator of the imprisoned Paul (Philemon 24, above p. 168), Luke was enabled to interview Philip and his people more thoroughly.

It thus seems probable that Luke composed his Gospel in Caesarea, merging material that he shared with Mark and tradition units that he gathered in contact with Hellenists in Jerusalem and Philip in Caesarea.

Luke concentrated that material by which he went beyond Mark, and which consists of special units and double traditions of the type Q, in three sequences of his Gospel: (1) the birth and childhood stories (Luke 1:5—2:52); (2) the Sermon on the Plain (6:20-49); and (3) the travel narrative (9:51—18:14). Details of the three Lukan complexes reflect the background and movements of the relevant traditions before they were taken up by the evangelist. In this perspective, too, the importance of Luke's contacts with the Hellenists in Jerusalem and Philip in Caesarea will be confirmed.

1. Behind the special Lukan traditions found in the birth and childhood stories (Luke 1:5—2:52) there were messianic expectations in Jerusalem and Judea. The persons acting here represent an enthusiastic piety which corresponds to what Luke has described in Acts as characteristic of the early church in Jerusalem. First among the common topics are the hymns (Luke 1:46–55 e.p.; Acts 4:25–30). There is also rejoicing in view of the present salvation (Luke 1:47 e.p.; Acts 2:46) and gratitude for the possibility of feeding the hungry (Luke 1:53; Acts 2:42). One must further pay attention to the important participation of widows (Luke 2:36; Acts 6:1). The evangelist Luke may have become acquainted with representatives of traditions about these pre-Christian and early Christian ideals and practices when he visited Jerusalem (Acts 21:16). Reminiscences of the women there (Acts 1:14) concerning the mother of Jesus (Luke 2:19, 33, 51) and the prophetess Anna (2:36) can have been imparted to him in Jerusalem or later

in Caesarea. While staying in Jerusalem, Luke was especially in contact with Hellenists such as Mnason (Acts 21:16), so he preferably saw the birth and childhood of Christ as well as the beginning of the church in the light of Hellenistic traditions. In addition, Luke probably inserted reminiscences from Jerusalem offered by Philip and his four daughters in Caesarea. For whereas the father had especially been occupied with meals arranged for the widows in Jerusalem (Acts 6:5), the daughters acted in Caesarea as specialists of prophecy (21:9). These two interests are reflected in Luke's birth and childhood stories (Mary singing a prophetic hymn on Christ according to Luke 1:46-55; the widow Anna praising God and prophesying about Christ in the temple according to 2:38).

2. Within the Lukan Sermon on the Plain (Luke 6:20–49) a single tradition appears in connection with the woes (6:24–26). Otherwise, the sermon consists of double traditions representing the type Q. Although most sayings of Jesus quoted here find parallels in Matthew's Sermon on the Mount, Luke localized the sermon to a plain instead of a mount. This feature is connected with the category of hearers and readers for whom the report of the sermon was meant to be instructive. Among those mentioned as standing on the plain are the apostles (Luke 6:17a), but even more emphasis is laid on a "great many disciples" (6:17b) and on "a large multitude of people from the whole of Judea and Jerusalem and the coast of Tyre and Sidon" (6:17c). By the expression "the whole of Judea" Luke meant Palestine as a whole, because he adopted the official name of the Roman procuratorship with its center in Caesarea; and by "the coast of Tyre and Sidon" he meant Phoenicia. The intention of Luke, or rather of his traditionists, was thus to stress the importance of Christ's teaching on the plain for the population of the entire countries of Palestine and Phoenicia.

According to Luke in Acts, the gospel was spread in these countries during the years between the martyrdom of Stephen in A.D. 36 and that of the apostle James around A.D. 42 (Acts 9:31 mentions Judea, Galilee, Samaria, and 11:19 Phoenicia). The missionary successes were especially ascribed to Philip and other Hellenists. It was in Caesarea, the political capital of Palestine situated on the Plain of Sharon, that Philip had his home. So it becomes evident that Luke's version of the Sermon on the Plain was based on an interest of Philip, or Christians in contact with him, to present a summary of Christ's teaching that should be instructive for the population of countries in the periphery of Caesarea and the Plain of Sharon.

3. In the so-called travel narrative, which forms the central and major part of the entire Gospel, Luke has inserted most of his special and Q traditions. As will be illustrated below, these were adapted to practical interests of the Hellenists in Jerusalem, to whom Philip belonged.

Presupposed is a journey from Galilee to Jerusalem (Luke 9:51). First the Master came in contact with Samaria (9:52), but only for a moment, so that afterward he must have passed through Transjordan (the later reference to

Samaria in 17:11 is only a retrospect on the beginning of the journey caused by the keyword "thankfulness" in 17:10, cf. 16). The warning against Herod Antipas in view of the destiny of John the Baptist (13:31) confirms that Jesus was passing through Perea, where Antipas was the ruler and had arrested John. In Transjordanian countries Jesus sent out seventy (according to a variant reading seventy-two) disciples for the conversion of the people, and Luke explicitly kept them distinct from the Twelve (Luke 10:1). Their mission should be independent of Jewish rules about food (10:7–8), thus referred to Gentiles, and from those pagan regions dominated by demons (10:17) the Seventy were able to win great multitudes of believers who followed Jesus with enthusiasm to Jerusalem (11:29; 12:1, 13; 14:25; 18:43; 19:3, 37). Luke wrote about "myriads" of such followers (12:1), and even if this was a poetic license, the other Gospels also told that Jesus came with a "great multitude" from Transjordan to Jerusalem.

The travel narrative obviously implies that a majority of those following Jesus to Jerusalem were Hellenists. Of the countries belonging to Transjordan, Decapolis was completely Hellenistic and Perea widely so. Therefore the enthusiastic company following the Master into the capital represented Hellenistic people to a great extent. It is not conceivable that all these exulting Hellenistic believers left the city just after the death of Jesus. Several of those who followed Jesus from Transjordan in A.D. 33 must have formed the nucleus of the Hellenistic community in Jerusalem which, in the year 36, had become so important that special administrators of the caritative meals had to be elected (Acts 6:1–6).[8] The leading Hellenists were Stephen and Philip, about whom Luke was able to give detailed reports.

Practical concerns brought these Hellenists in Jerusalem to quote several examples of Christ's teaching in connection with meals during his journey through Transjordan (Luke 10:40 e.p.). Stephen and Philip were known not only for their attendance at the meals (6:3) but also for successful discussion with the Jews and generally for preaching and teaching (6:10; 8:5; etc.). The leading Hellenists of Jerusalem actually combined a "service at the tables" with a "service of the word" (Acts 6:2, 4), and their didactic experience was based on preaching and teaching activity in connection with the meals. It is therefore reasonable to regard material used by them and their colleagues for instruction and discussion as the elements that Luke collected in his travel narrative. Here attention is drawn alternatively to instruction and discussion (Luke 10:1–24 instruction, 10:25–37 discussion, and the same oscillation in the following chapters), and numerous allusions to common meals are included (about eighty-five cases in 10:40—17:32). These particularities of the travel narrative correspond to the activity of the Hellenists in Jerusalem.

8. Reasons for the dates mentioned above, A.D. 33 and 36, are given in B. Reicke, *The New Testament Era: The World of the Bible from 500* B.C. to A.D. 100 (Philadelphia: Fortress Press, 1968), 183–84, 191–92.

By such observations it becomes possible to explain why the Q traditions of Matthew and Luke have been associated with different regions and periods after having circulated for some time as separate units. The majority of the apostles were Galileans and therefore preferred to give the traditions background in the Galilean activity of Jesus, as is noticeable in Matthew's Sermon on the Mount and Mark's concentration on Capernaum. Since several of the Hellenists had followed Jesus from Transjordan, they were rather inclined to connect episodes and sayings with Christ's activity there. The *alibi* analogies in question may sometimes have depended on a similar acting or teaching of Jesus in Galilee and in Transjordan, but in general the apostolic and the Hellenistic preferences respectively for Galilee and for Transjordan explain why the Q traditions are mainly found in Matthew's Galilean report and Luke's travel narrative. It was the Transjordanian nucleus of the Hellenistic circle in Jerusalem which connected several reminiscences of Christ's words and works with his journey through Transjordan, although the apostolic circle traced similar reminiscences back to Galilee.

It must therefore be supposed that substantial elements of Luke's middle section were taken over from Philip in Caesarea. This important representative of the Hellenists had been an experienced administrator of the caritative meals in Jerusalem and a successful evangelist on the missionary field. Being the hospitable leader of a house-church in Caesarea, Philip was especially gifted to convey to Luke such traditions as those found in the travel narrative.

A redactional notice found in Luke 3:1–2 confirms that it was primarily readers in Caesarea and its surroundings whom the author had in mind, among them especially persons of education and rank such as the "most honorable" Theophilus (1:1). For the detailed information of Luke 3:1–2 on political dignitaries officiating in the days of John the Baptist was given such a form that Caesarea serves as the center of the retrospective. The names of the rulers and countries in question were meant to be of interest for contemporaries of Luke living in this region. In the first instance, the emperor Tiberius and his procurator Pilate in Caesarea were mentioned. After this, Luke referred to three rulers of countries known to people in Caesarea. They were all correctly given the official title of tetrarchs: Herod Antipas as tetrarch of Galilee, Philip as tetrarch of Iturea and Trachonitis, and Lysanias as tetrarch of Abilene. In this context Luke was more accurate than Mark, who remained on a popular level and called Herod Antipas a king. But why did Luke refer to Philip and Lysanias, two princes in northern countries that did not have any importance with regard to John the Baptist? The reason was that Philip's and Lysanias's tetrarchies had been taken over in A.D. 52 by the Herodean prince Agrippa II as king of the entire northern Transjordan (Josephus, *Antiquities* XX.138), and this successor of Philip and Lysanias was very well known to the contemporaries of Luke in Caesarea. During the trial of Paul in A.D. 58–60, at which Luke was present according to a "we" report and the letter to Philemon, Agrippa II acted in

Caesarea as an expert on Jewish problems (Acts 25:13—26:32). Luke's special notice on the tetrarchies of Philip and Lysanias appears to be very far-fetched and unmotivated, but it was inserted to the profit of those readers who, like Theophilus, were supposed to converse with official circles and to know about Agrippa II. So the reference to Agrippa's predecessors in the tetrarchies he governed was really apt to illustrate the Baptist's chronology, and the notice thus endorses the orientation of Luke's Gospel to Caesarea.[9]

Chronology

In modern introductions and commentaries the Gospel of Mark is usually dated to around A.D. 70, while the Gospels of Matthew and Luke are referred to the period between A.D. 80 and 90 or even 100. This dating is based on three arguments, which do not endure closer examination.

1. Much too often the common opinion, or in any case the majority of scholars, is quoted in support of such dating. But a mere concord with tendencies of modern scholarship does not warrant a correct answer to the chronological question. What is required is a concord with the witnesses of historical texts.

2. The assumption that Matthew and Luke were produced some ten, twenty, or thirty years after Mark is based on the widespread hypothesis of Mark's priority that goes back to discussions in the nineteenth century (see chap. 1). Serious difficulties are in fact connected with this hypothesis, as is illustrated above. If it cannot be proved that Mark served as the literary source, the only justification for dating Matthew and Luke a few decades later disappears.

3. Fundamentally the habit of dating Mark to about A.D. 70, resulting in dating the other Synoptic Gospels to A.D. 80, 90, or 100, is due to the assertion that experiences of the Jewish war of the years 66 to 70 and the fall of Jerusalem in the year 70 would have influenced apocalyptic words of Jesus quoted in Mark and the other Gospels. Such alleged prophecies *ex eventu,* that is, warnings and threatenings constructed afterward, are said to have been inserted by Mark about A.D. 70 and by Matthew and Luke ten to thirty years later. It is especially the discourse on the Mount of Olives (Matt. 24:1—25:46 with par.) that is used for this late dating. The analysis of the relevant text, carried through above in the study of block 11, has demonstrated that it is impossible to presuppose any such historical knowledge of the Jewish war and the fall of the city. What is predicted are the following occurrences: (1) a Jewish persecution of the Jerusalem church, described in some correspondence to historical events that came to pass in the next years after Christ's death, but not later than A.D. 60; (2) an escape of the Jerusalem Christians to the mountains of Judah, not verified by any documents available; (3) a destruction of the world and a judgment of mankind, described in

9. On the countries that Claudius bestowed on Agrippa II in the year 52, see Reicke, *The New Testament Era,* 201–5.

purely eschatological terms. No prophecy *ex eventu* is implied when the permanence of the temple is denied by Jesus (Matt. 24:2 with par.), for the saying is based on a prophecy of the Old Testament (Isa. 25:2). As far as the apocalyptic chapter is concerned, the destruction of Jerusalem has been treated only by Luke. But when this evangelist wrote about the siege of the city (Luke 21:20) and the punishment of the people (21:22–24), he merely quoted ancient prophecies (v. 20 depends on Ezek. 4:2–3; vv. 22–24 on Deut. 32:35, 41–42; Isa. 3:25; 5:13; 22:5; 63:18; Dan. 8:13; Zech. 12:3 LXX). Since the days of Amos, the destruction of the city and the punishment of the people had been characteristic motifs of prophecy (Amos 9:1–4), and experiences like those under Nebuchadnezzar and Pompey had reactivated such warnings. Luke was critical against disobedient people in Israel (Luke 4:28 e.p.; Acts 7:51 e.p.), and therefore he was prepared to quote threatenings of this kind. If he or his traditionists had already experienced the Jewish war or the destruction of Jerusalem and wanted to construct prophecies *ex eventu* on this basis, they would not have endeavored to obtain accord with the sayings of ancient prophets, but rather with events of recent history. No such concern is found in the Lukan text. The apocalyptic speech of Jesus indicates no familiarity with the political drama of the years 66 to 70, neither in the version of Matthew and Mark nor in that of Luke.

Scholars who prefer a late dating of the Gospels further adduce two Matthean parables connected with the Master's discussions in Jerusalem, and these are the parable of the wicked husbandmen (Matt. 21:33–46 with par.) and that of the marriage feast (Matt. 22:1–14). It is especially the handing over of the vineyard to other workers (Matt. 21:41 with par.) as well as the destruction of the recalcitrant guests and their city (Matt. 22:7) that is regarded as prophecies *ex eventu* in dependence upon knowledge of the Jewish defeat in A.D. 70. To allegorize details of parables in this way, however, is generally regarded as bad taste, and such blunt political allusions can in fact never be found in the parables of Jesus.

In the parable of the wicked husbandmen the high priests and other representatives of the Sanhedrin are explicitly told their vineyard will be taken from them and given to people going to bring the fruits of the kingdom (Matt. 21:41, 43). So the vineyard is not expected to be destroyed but to flourish, and to this purpose it will not be delivered to enemies but will be entrusted to the disciples of Jesus. Therefore the parable of the vineyard cannot have anything to do with the defeat of the Zealots and the destruction of Jerusalem by the Romans in A.D. 70.

In the parable of the marriage feast (Matt. 22:1–14) the point is to illustrate the grievance of Jesus and the apostles caused by the rejection and molesting of the missionaries. This disappointment makes it sufficiently understandable that Jesus threatens the evildoers and their capital with destruction, and no resorting to a pseudo-prophecy on the conquest of Jerusalem under Titus is justified. Allegorical interpolation of the Roman legions is also excluded by the course of events described in the parable. It is the same king who invites the guests to the

wedding of his son (22:3) and punishes the unwilling by the destruction of their capital (22:7). A majestic activity of God is meant in both cases, and it is God as king who sends *his* servants to invite the guests and *his* troops to punish the opponents. In the first case the servants clearly stand for the apostles and the evangelists sent by God, and in the second case the troops of God cannot be identified with the legions of Nero sent to combat the Zealots, but must symbolize angels sent by God to punish the evildoers (cf. Matt. 13:41–42: "he will send out his angels, and they will remove from his kingdom all scandals and evildoers and throw them into the burning furnace"). Moreover, the punishment in fire was a well-known Old Testament topic (e.g., Isa. 9:19). Jesus also threatened Chorazin, Bethsaida, and Capernaum with infernal punishment (Matt. 11:20–23; Luke 10:13–15) because he was disappointed, and in this case no influence of later historical facts is assumable. It is not legitimate to make the parable of the marriage feast depend on the conquest of Jerusalem by the Romans.

A further argument for dating the Synoptic Gospels to after A.D. 70 has been found in the reference to the curtain of the Temple that was torn in two pieces from top to bottom (Matt. 27:51 with par.). By a bizarre allegorization, the curtain has been interpreted as a picture for the destruction of the Jewish temple under Titus, suppressing the fact that besides darkness and other events the splitting of the curtain is said to have accompanied the death of Jesus. Had the traditionists or redactors of the Golgotha report desired to indicate the destruction of the Jewish temple by Roman soldiers in A.D. 70, they would have referred to more substantial parts of the house than the liturgical curtain. The curtain is said to have been parted "from top to bottom" at the death of Jesus, and since this corresponds to the parting of the heavens at his baptism (Matt. 3:16 with par.), the meaning is that at the moment of Christ's death the boundary of immanence was transcended (as indicated by Heb. 9:12, 24; 10:20). No pseudo-prophetic allegory implying Titus and the Romans can be inserted here.

The postwar dating of the Synoptic Gospels is also based on attempts to make the Lukan pericope called "Dominus flevit" a prophecy *ex eventu* (Luke 19:39–44). It contains a lamentation of Jesus on the Mount of Olives concerning a future siege and destruction of Jerusalem by enemies of the people. Here also every reference to concrete events during the Jewish-Roman war are missing. This is even directly excluded by the words about enemies of the city, for to Luke persons of rank in the Roman empire were not at all enemies. One may consider the polite dedication of his books to Theophilus (Luke 1:3; Acts 1:1), and his optimistic pictures of Roman magistrates and officers such as the procurator Pilate (Luke 23:4, 14, 22; in 23:11 the mocking is ascribed to Antipas instead of Pilate), the centurion Cornelius (Acts 10:1, etc.), the prefect Sergius Paulus (13:7), the proconsul Gallio (18:17), the chancellor of Ephesus (19:35), the tribune Lysias (22:29), and the procurator Festus (25:16). A similar aspect is the positive appreciation of Roman citizenship (16:21, etc.). Not the least animosity toward Roman power can be discovered in Lukan reports, and in the pericope

"Dominus flevit" the enemies going to destroy Jerusalem can therefore not be Romans. What the enemies will do has instead been exclusively and consistently described in terms of scriptural prophecies (tears over Jerusalem and its destruction through enemies in Isa. 22:4–5; Lam. 1:3–17; Ps. 79:1; palisades in Ezek. 4:2; trampling on the population in Isa. 3:26; 22:5; 26:6; 63:18; no stone on another in Isa. 25:2; Ps. 79:1). Luke or his traditionists have quoted Jesus in such a way that allusions to well-known prophecies should illustrate his disappointment over the impenitence of Jerusalem. In no point does the pericope indicate the Jewish war of the 60s, and so this text must also have been written earlier.

After all, none of the synoptic pericopes believed to be prophecies *ex eventu* is serviceable for dating Mark about A.D. 70, or Matthew and Luke between A.D. 80 and 100.

Equally unfounded is a late dating of the Synoptic Gospels based on allegedly postapostolic conceptions of high priests, Sadducees, Pharisees, and other exponents of Judaism. Since the high priests and the Sadducees had lost their positions at the Jewish defeat of A.D. 70, their image found in the Gospels is not compatible with the situation during the postapostolic years 70—100. Only the Pharisees were still important, but their scribes are not known to have arranged conflicts with the Christians in that period, so the synoptic reports on the Pharisees did not depend on postapostolic circumstances. It has further been objected that in the Gospels the Pharisees are treated as one uniform group, while in the days of Jesus there were different schools among them. But writings of Paul and Josephus also represent this simplification, without being accused of anachronistic ignorance (Phil. 3:5; Josephus, *Antiquities* XIII.172).

Not even the argument that certain traces of church doctrines, ministries, and institutions are found in the Gospels implies any respectable criterion for a postapostolic dating. All chronological schedules meant to determine the development of religious conceptions and practical dispositions remain free speculation. What the Gospels state about the kerygma, the apostles, the eucharist, and so on, does not indicate they were produced later than, for instance, the epistles of Paul, because it cannot be proved that in the early church the factors in question did not already exist.

However, a real clue to the chronology of the Synoptic Gospels is offered by the final verses of Acts. The church historian Adolf Harnack drew attention to this in 1908 and 1911, although he felt some hesitation in view of the common opinion in Protestant Germany.[10] Nevertheless the arguments pointed out by Harnack have value and can be enforced by further observations, as will be demonstrated here in detail.

10. A. Harnack, *Die Apostelgeschichte. Untersuchungen,* Beiträge zur Einleitung in das Neue Testament 3 (Leipzig: J. C. Hinrichs, 1908), 47–50, 217–21; idem, *Neue Untersuchungen zur Apostelgeschichte und zur Abfassungszeit der synoptischen Evangelien,* Beiträge . . . 4 (1911), 63–95.

The two last verses of Acts deal with Paul's stay in Rome as a prisoner on remand (Acts 28:30–31): "He spent the entire two years in the quarters hired by him. Receiving all visitors who came to him, he preached the kingdom of God and taught about the Lord Jesus Christ in all liberty and without obstacles."

In the fall of A.D. 60, Paul had been brought from Caesarea to Rome by command of Festus, who had recently been inaugurated as procurator in Caesarea (Acts 24:27; 25:12; 27:1—28:14). Accordingly, it was the years 61 and 62 which the apostle spent as a prisoner in Rome (28:30). The soldier who guarded Paul in his Roman lodging (28:16, 23) came from the barracks of the praetorian regiment—as is proved by a similar trial, the process against the philosopher Apollonius of Tyana (Philostratus, *Apollonius* VII.8–33)—and this explains why the whole praetorium was said to know about Paul (Phil. 1:13). Luke has especially stressed that Paul, in his quarters, was able to receive numerous visitors and that he preached the gospel from morning until evening (Acts 28:23, 30–31). The author thus wanted to make evident that Paul, during his whole stay from A.D. 61 to 62 in the lodging mentioned, was treated mildly and permitted to spread the gospel freely.

When writing the two last verses of his report, Luke was therefore looking forward to a continued activity of the apostle. He betrayed no expectation of a coming disaster, such as those which happened in the years after A.D. 62 that were stamped by Paul's martyrdom and other catastrophes.

Neither in the last verses of Acts nor in other parts of the book did Luke indicate any knowledge of the fact that Paul, together with Peter, was killed in Rome at the end of the year 64 or rather in the beginning of 65, a martyrdom which is reflected in various early sources (John 21:19; Asc. Isa. 4:3; 1 Clement V.2–7; Ignatius, *Letter to the Romans* IV.3). Moreover, there is no reference in Acts to the martyrdom of James, the brother of Jesus who, in A.D. 62, was stoned in Jerusalem on the initiative of the high priest (Josephus, *Antiquities* XX.200). Luke produced extensive reports on the activity of James, Peter, and especially Paul, yet he did not allude to the end of their lives in the years 62 and 65, respectively. Seeing that Acts does not reveal any familiarity with these Christian tragedies and that it ends with such an optimistic characterization of the years 61–62, the book must be dated to about the year 62.

Sometimes a farewell speech of Paul, reported by Luke in connection with the apostle's visit to Miletus in the year 58, is adduced in favor of a later date (Acts 20:17–38). This implies reading too much into the text. Paul is merely said to have expressed his fear, based on a revelation, that he would be arrested on his arrival in Jerusalem (20:23) and not be able to visit the churches of Asia again (20:25). In this context not a word alludes to Rome and the death of Paul. His presentiment is exclusively referred to his apprehension in Jerusalem, and this is the only disaster Luke knew of when he wrote Acts. By the reference to his arrest, Paul was meant to appeal to the solidarity of the presbyters from Ephesus to whom he gave the speech. As a rhetorical device, such appeals to solidarity in

view of the apostle's distress may also be found in the Pauline epistles (e.g., 2 Cor. 1:8; 2:4; 4:8). Luke adopted this appeal with regard to Jerusalem, but he did not allude to any martyrdom in Rome, although this would have meant a much stronger argument. Neither the discourse of Paul in Miletus nor any other passage in Acts can be used as a quasi-prediction of the apostle's Roman martyrdom. The optimism expressed in the final verses of Acts remains the salient point in the chronology.

It is also remarkable that Luke has not mentioned Peter's arrival in Rome, which, in view of his martyrdom in the year 65, must have taken place between 62 and 64 (cf. 1 Peter 5:13, "Babylon"). Furthermore there are no traces of acquaintance with the exodus of the Jerusalem church to Decapolis and Pella around 64 (Eusebius, *EH* III.5.3) or with the outbreak of the Jewish war in 66 and the ruin of Jerusalem in 70.

Although several predictions of events later fulfilled occur in Acts (11:28; 20:23; 21:11; 27:34), Luke has not touched upon the martyrdom of James in A.D. 62 or that of Peter and Paul in A.D. 65, nor hinted at the other fluctuations and catastrophes just mentioned. The reason must be that he did not know of them when he wrote Acts. Consequently the Book of Acts is to be dated around the year 62.

Based on textual evidence, this result cannot be avoided by supposing that Luke had prepared a continuation of Acts in which there would be references to events occurring after A.D. 62. No addition to Acts has been indicated by Luke, and the structure of the book is a serious obstacle for any such hypothesis.

In the prologue of Acts the author has referred Theophilus and other readers back to his first book with special regard to its concluding verses dealing with Christ's ascension (Luke 24:50–53; Acts 1:2), and then Luke has reported a second time on this ascension (Acts 1:9–12). According to the Gospel as well as to Acts, the Lord's elevation to heaven was preceded by a conclusive and decisive announcement of his, implying a coming spread of the message from Jerusalem "to all nations" (Luke 24:47) and "as far as the end of the earth" (Acts 1:8). It is this missionary expansion which Luke has pursued in Acts. While the expression "as far as the end of the earth" (*ἕως ἐσχάτου τῆς γῆς*) was based on Old Testament prophecy (Isa. 49:6), it has to be observed that for Luke in Acts this reference to a worldwide expansion represented not only a prediction of the risen Lord revealed to the apostles before his ascension (Acts 1:8) but also a directive of the preexistent Lord revealed to Paul in Holy Scripture according to a passage of the apostle's first sermon quoted in Acts (13:17). No doubt Luke wanted to let the narrative of Acts culminate in the arrival of Paul in Rome.

The missionary world that Paul had in mind consisted of Greek and Roman countries around the Mediterranean (Rom. 15:19–24), and Luke must have shared this view. What the Lord had revealed when predicting a spread of the gospel from Jerusalem "as far as the end of the earth" (Acts 1:8; 13:17) was therefore understood as being gradually fulfilled in the expansion of Paul's

campaigns from east to west. Luke expected his readers to see the final consummation inaugurated by Paul's unimpeded activity in the capital of the west during the years 61 and 62 (Acts 28:31).

One has simply to admit that Acts was meant to conclude with Paul's activity in Rome during the years 61 and 62, and that no continuation of the book was planned. Seeing that Luke did not know about later events when he wrote his second book and dedicated it to a gentleman whom he called "most honorable," Acts has to be dated around the year 62.

Inevitably, the Gospel of Luke must then be given a somewhat earlier date, that is, around the year 60. This coincides with the chronology suggested above in view of Luke's contacts with Paul, Mark, and Philip in Caesarea during the years 58 to 60.

On the other hand, the Gospel of Luke cannot have been written before the Gospels of Matthew and Mark, for its prologue indicates that others had also "undertaken" (*ἐπεχείρησαν*) similar reports (Luke 1:1). The author did not say these others had written gospels which he was reading, but that he knew they were occupied with giving the oral traditions a literary form. At the time in question, several Christians must have begun to feel that available recollections and traditions should be consolidated in script, for more and more the eyewitnesses belonged to the past. Different authors thus decided to set up reports about the events connected with Jesus, as Luke remarked in his prologue. Among the other evangelists indicated by Luke there is special reason to think of Mark as his fellow missionary in Caesarea, but Luke may also have known about the editors of Matthew in Greek.

In any case, since the Third Gospel is to be dated to around A.D. 60, the First and Second Gospels cannot have been composed later, but must rather be dated to about the same time. This is exactly the picture displayed by their quotations of Christ's farewell speech (Matt. 24:1—25:46 with par.), for it was found above that although it contains some allusions to experiences of the community made in the first decades after the Lord's death, there are no hints of the dramatic tragedies of the 60s (pp. 174–77).

A relatively synchronistic origin must therefore be claimed for the Synoptic Gospels. The difficulties of explaining their similarities on the basis of any literary interdependence are enforced by this chronology.

Personal Contacts Involved

As has been emphasized in preceding chapters, the relative parallelism between the Synoptic Gospels is fundamentally due to common traditions of the early church, starting from the celebration of baptism and the eucharist, and especially represented by context-parallel triple units. Luke referred to these living traditions in his prologue, when he declared he would base his report on

what original eyewitnesses and servants of the word had delivered to him as tradition (παρέδοσαν, Luke 1:2). A corresponding use of such common traditions may be supposed with regard to Matthew and Mark.

Yet collective traditions of the early church do not alone explain the complicated distribution of parallels and similarities that appears in the synoptic material. Besides the principal concord, especially found in the 56 or 57 pericopes that form context-parallel triple traditions, considerable differences in the degree of relationship emerge when (*a*) Matthew is compared with Mark, (*b*) Mark with Luke, and (*c*) Matthew with Luke.

To actualize this evidence again, some relevant numbers displayed in chapter 2 are recapitulated here. Within the synoptic material one may count:

a. 105–110 pericopes common to Matthew and Mark, 90–91 of them, or 84 percent, being context-parallel;

b. 95–96 pericopes common to Mark and Luke, 72–73 or them, or 76 percent, being context-parallel;

c. 126–131 pericopes common to Matthew and Luke, 60–61 of them, or 49 percent, being context-parallel, while 31–35 others without support in Mark are generally nonparallel.

Mark is the middle term insofar as 57 of its 115 pericopes, or nearly 50 percent, are contextual parallels to pericopes both in Matthew and Luke, and nearly all other pericopes of Mark find counterparts either in Matthew or in Luke. In sharp contrast to this circumstance, the 31–35 pericopes that are common to Matthew and Luke beyond Mark—corresponding to what is called Q—are never found in contextual parallelism, except a few passages connected with Christ's baptism.

Of course such varying degrees of similarity cannot be explained only by those collective traditions which have yielded a relative concord, especially in the contextual parallels. It has also to be asked which individual factors brought about the different relationships between Matthew and Mark, Mark and Luke, and Matthew and Luke.

The answer to this question is found in various personal contacts between the traditionists and the evangelists. Such contacts have been observed in several parts of the present study, and the issues will be summarized here. On this personal level the flexibility of the material can be explained in natural terms, while any mechanical hypothesis of a literary dependence remains insufficient.

The Relationship Between Matthew and Mark

On closer examination the similarity of the First and Second Gospels is more comprehensive than is evident from the statistical outlines presented above. There are 178 pericopes in Matthew and 115 in Mark, among which 105–110 are common to both Gospels. No fewer than 90–91 of the latter are contextual parallels, including 34 double traditions of Matthew and Mark, and 57 triple

traditions also represented by Luke in contextual parallelism. Thus 95 percent of all pericopes in Mark find counterparts in Matthew, and 79 percent of their total number appear in contextual parallelism with Matthew.

In view of this extensive and impressive correspondence, it seems appropriate to assume that Matthew and Mark were based on traditions developed in the same environment. Admittedly, there is no textual evidence for a personal contact between the evangelist Matthew or his editors and the evangelist Mark. Nonetheless an important feature of both Gospels is the representative function of Peter, and parallel contacts with the preaching and teaching of this apostle may thus be adduced to explain the convergence in several points.

Both evangelists have intentionally and consistently placed Peter in front of the apostles (e.g., Matt. 4:18 // Mark 1:16; Matt. 17:1 // Mark 9:2). In particular, Matthew has emphasized that Jesus proclaimed Peter as the coming leader of the early church (Matt. 16:16) and entrusted him with the keys of the heavenly kingdom (16:19). Peter is also said to have received the Lord's instructions on church discipline (17:24; 18:21). Although the examples quoted are connected with the Galilean scenario, the portrait of Peter has evidently been developed in the perspective of the early church, as the leader of which he acted in Jerusalem for the first ten years (Acts 1:15—12:17). Even the fact that Matthew and Mark have not concealed Peter's momentary insufficiency (Matt. 16:23 // Mark 8:33; Matt. 26:34 // Mark 14:30) confirms their dependence on his own communications. With regard to Mark, two remarkable facts may be recalled here: Peter's house in Capernaum and its neighborhood figures as the center of the whole Galilean narrative (Mark 1:21—9:29), and Luke gives to understand in Acts that Peter entertained contacts with the house-church of Mark's mother in Jerusalem (Acts 12:12). Both circumstances shed light on the indication of Papias about Mark's dependence on Peter. These peculiarities of the First and Second Gospels make it reasonable to refer substantial parts of their common material to the preaching and teaching activity of Peter in Jerusalem.

Starting from such Petrine material, however, the authors of Matthew and Mark did not use it for the same purpose and to the same extent.

The evangelist Matthew, or his editors, represented not only narrative but also didactic interests, and particularly wanted to promote scriptural learning. For this reason he or they adopted several traditions of mainly didactic character and concentrated them on comprehensive speeches of the Lord. Thus it can be supposed that substantial parts of their didactic material was taken over from Peter in Jerusalem, and in this context there is reason to draw attention to Luke's notices in Acts about the preaching and teaching activity of Peter and other apostles in the temple area (e.g., Acts 2:46; 3:11; 5:12). Insofar as the mainly didactic units of Matthew surpass what is found in Mark, they occur either as single or as double traditions. The latter are the elements that are called Q, and the cause of the appearance of similar elements in Luke will be discussed below under 3.

Mark, on the other hand, was more occupied with narrative material and therefore did not include that mainly didactic material which is found in Matthew and Luke as Q. His provenance was the house-church of his mother in Jerusalem, where Peter may be assumed to have taken part in the breaking of bread (Acts 2:46; 12:12). As in other religious brotherhoods, the initiated participants in this and similar meal communities did not so much expect instruction on the principles of discipleship as, rather, edification by interesting narratives. For the purpose of such esoteric illumination Mark concentrated his collection of Peter's discourses on vivid stories about miracles and other episodes. In that mainly narrative context, similarities between Matthew and Mark turned out because of their common dependence on Petrine traditions, which is especially applicable to their contextual parallels.

The Relationship Between Mark and Luke

In the Second and Third Gospels, too, the parallelism of the pericopes covers great portions of the material. Out of totally 115 pericopes in Mark and 186 in Luke, 95–96 are common to both Gospels, and 72–73 are contextual parallels including the 56–57 parallels additionally supported by Matthew. Thus almost 83 percent of Mark's 115 pericopes correspond to similar units of Luke, and 63 percent of the same pericopes even appear in contextual parallelism with their counterparts in Luke.

Under these statistical aspects the distribution of various frequency types in the Gospel of Mark is especially instructive. (1) There are only a few short elements of Mark which are either unique (Mark 1:1; 3:20–21; 4:26–29; 7:31–37; 8:22–26) or to which analogies in the other Gospels appear only in remote contexts (Mark 3:11; 4:24; 6:34; 9:41, 49–50; 11:25–26; 13:33–37). (2) It was stated above under 1 that Mark contains 34 pericopes that appear in contextual parallelism with elements of Matthew without analogies or parallels in Luke. A special case is here a sequence of 8 pericopes (Matt. 14:22—16:12 // Mark 6:45—8:21) to which the Gospel of Luke has no parallel because of its direct transition from the third to the sixth journey of Jesus in the Markan scheme (the so-called great lacuna after Luke 9:17). (3) On the other hand, different sections of Mark contain 15 double traditions which stand in contextual parallelism with pericopes of Luke but to which neither analogies nor contextual parallels are found in Matthew (4 such units in Mark 1:21–38, 1 in 1:45, 2 in 3:7–19, 1 in 4:21-25, 1 in 4:35–41, 2 in 5:1–43, and 4 in 6:6–13; 9:38–41; 11:15–19; and 12:41–44). (4) Largely dominant in Mark, however, are the 57 triple traditions that represent a contextual parallelism both with Matthew and with Luke.

A considerable affinity of Mark and Luke is manifest in these 15 double and 57 triple units which are counted as groups 3 and 4 in the survey immediately above. Even if Mark's parallelism with Matthew is somewhat more extensive because of the 34 contextual parallels referred to under 2, Mark also represents an obvious convergence toward Luke. This parallelism of Mark and Luke is different from

that of Matthew and Mark, for Mark's 34 double traditions with contextual parallels in Matthew and its 15 with contextual parallels in Luke make up two separate networks. Each of them is mingled with traditions representing other types, in all three Gospels with 56–57 context-parallel triple units, in the two larger Gospels with numerous single and double traditions. Nevertheless the 34 specific contacts of Mark with Matthew and 15 with Luke bestow a partial dualism upon the Second Gospel, and in this regard the evangelist Mark is comparable to a Janus with two faces.

How did the evangelists Mark and Luke come to their general concord, which includes 56–57 triple and 15 double pericopes in contextual parallelism?

It may be pointed out again that no appeal to a literary elaboration of available manuscripts can really do justice to what is found in the texts. Luke has mentioned other authors presently occupied with Gospel reports (Luke 1:1) and oral traditions delivered to him (1:2) but has not indicated any written source used by him. Considering the very uneven distribution of the context-parallel triple traditions on different text blocks, the bizarre consequences of the utilization theories have been characterized several times in preceding chapters. Another drawback is the constant and obstinate variation of the diction found in Luke's and Mark's parallels. Furthermore, no exclusive priority can be claimed by one Gospel alone, neither by Mark nor by Luke, when pericopes common to both are compared. Each case has to be treated individually, and the priority is not always found in the same Gospel. Thus, for instance, Mark appears to be prior to Luke when telling of Christ's departure from Capernaum in 1:35–38, for here Mark has a reminiscence of Peter's reaction, while Luke's contextual parallel in 4:42–43 includes no personal details and is quite vague. On the contrary, however, Mark's unmotivated description of the crowd and the boat in 3:7–10 cannot possibly have influenced Luke's pertinent reference to a similar crowd in 6:17–19, where the crowd logically functions as the audience of the Sermon on the Plain in 6:20–49, to which Mark has not the least analogy. Such an oscillation is found several times and does not fit with general theories of literary dependence.

These and similar imbroglios are overcome when a personal confrontation of the evangelists Mark and Luke in the same environment is supposed to have been the fundament of their convergency. Scriptural evidence for such a contact and collaboration in Caesarea has been indicated above in several connections, and the data may be recapitulated here.

Mark is mentioned the first time in Acts because of his mother's house-church in Jerusalem which Peter visited (Acts 12:12), and then is found as the assistant of Barnabas and Paul on their journey to Cyprus in the year 47 (13:5). Furthermore, three captivity epistles of Paul quote Mark together with Luke among the collaborators of the imprisoned apostle (Philemon 24; Col. 4:10, 14; 2 Tim. 4:11). As has already been emphasized (p. 168), v. 9 of Philemon ("now also a

prisoner") proves that it was in Caesarea during the years 58 to 60 that Mark and Luke belonged to the company of the apostle.

In the latter situation the evangelists Mark and Luke were obviously able to develop personal contacts and to increase their familiarity with traditions about "the matters which had taken place" among the believers (Luke 1:1). At the same time, both evangelists will have been able to consolidate and coordinate or eventually to enlarge and revise their material on the basis of collective and individual traditions represented in Caesarea by the entire community and important disciples. Under all circumstances, the assumption of a personal exchange of experiences and mutual information during the symbiosis of Mark and Luke in Caesarea offers a natural and profitable explanation of the parallels between the Second and the Third Gospels.

The Relationship Between Matthew and Luke

A substantial harmony between Matthew and Luke together with Mark is formed by the 56–57 context-parallel triple traditions, which are forcibly accumulated in the reports on the baptism and passion of Christ, but gradually reduced in text blocks preceding these reports.

Without being shared by Mark, a further correspondence between Matthew and Luke is established by 31–35 pericopes spread on different contexts of the two larger Gospels, and in the present study these double traditions of Matthew and Luke are called Q. Here the number of pericopes to be counted varies unusually much, because several elements are united in one Gospel and separated in another. The total number of Q units is actually much higher, since many pericopes consist of shorter elements also forming double traditions, among which are several logia of Jesus. But on the level of such details the situation becomes so intricate that no exact statistics can be displayed here, and the approximate number of the pericopes gives at least an idea of the proportions between the Q material and other synoptic categories.

To a great extent the Q traditions are based on logia of Jesus and represent didactic interests, as is the case with the Sermon on the Mount (Matt. 5:1—7:28). But this fact does not justify talking of a "logia source," for the Q traditions also include narrative pericopes such as the story of the centurion's servant (Matt. 8:5–13; Luke 7:1–10). Moreover, no evidence for such a written source has been found.

Often accompanied by single or triple units, nearly all of these double traditions of Matthew and Luke are stamped by a complete lack of contextual parallelism, so that one can only speak of *alibi* analogies.

Apparent exceptions are two or three context-parallel elements of Matthew and Luke which surround the context-parallel triple tradition on Christ's baptism (Matt. 3:13–17 with par.). On the one hand, the authors of these Gospels have permitted the reports on the baptism of Jesus to be preceded by examples

illustrating John's preaching (Matt. 3:7–10 + 12 // Luke 3:7–9 + 17) and, on the other hand, to be followed by details about Christ's temptation (Matt. 4:2–11a // Luke 4:2b–13). As was pointed out in the analysis of block 2, these elements of Matthew and Luke are not Q pericopes in the sense of double traditions not found in Mark but are parts of a triple sequence abbreviated by the latter. In contextual parallelism, short Markan analogies to both reports are still found (Mark 1:7–8, on John's preaching; 1:12–13, on Christ's temptation), and they are obviously fragments of a common tradition represented more adequately by Matthew and Luke. Thus what Matthew and Luke have preserved beyond Mark in connection with the triple tradition on Christ's baptism cannot be counted among the Q traditions as long as these are defined as textual units without support in Mark.

Concerning the actual Q traditions, the fact remains that not the least contextual parallelism is to be discovered among them. Their localization always shifts, and it thwarts all scholarly endeavors to reconcile Matthew with Luke in a synopsis. In different ways combined with single or triple units, most of the Q traditions have been presented by the evangelists Matthew and Luke within nonparallel textual agglomerations characteristic of each. Matthew has concentrated his Q traditions in six comprehensive speeches of Jesus (Matt. 5:1—7:28, the Sermon on the Mount; 9:37—10:42, the commission speech; 13:1–52, the parable speech; 17:24—18:35, the discipline speech; 23:1–39, the anti-Pharisaic speech; 24:1—25:46, the apocalyptic speech). Luke's use of Q elements was more summary, for after having quoted some of them in the Sermon on the Plain (6:20–49) and subsequent pericopes (7:1–35), he combined plenty of them with single units in his travel narrative (9:51—18:15). It is not possible to see any contextual parallelism between Matthew and Luke in connection with Q traditions, not even in the Sermon on the Mount and the Sermon on the Plain which are comparable as totalities but appear in widely different contexts and quote the logia of Jesus in a clearly diverging order. The whole Q material of Matthew and Luke consists of *alibi* analogies, and this is true not only of the 31–35 pericopes as units but also of the shorter elements included.

Because the Q material of Matthew and Luke is characterized by such complete disharmony in the order, all speculations on changes made in a written source are contestable. Whether one Gospel is believed to have been the source of the other, or an unknown document like the so-called logia source is made responsible for the similarities, the literary manipulations presumed must seem absurd. A normal person would not cut out such a great number of text pieces from a book on his desk and then shuffle the cards in order to get all pieces distributed on completely different parts of his manuscript.

This odd consequence of literary source theories on the Q material of Matthew and Luke can be avoided if the reason for their analogies in content along with differences in context is sought in the affiliation of the evangelists with groups of believers representing living traditions of similar and yet different kind. On the

basis of preceding observations, the probability of such affiliations can be demonstrated. It will not be a question of direct contacts between the evangelists Matthew and Luke, for in any case no proof of their personal confrontation is available in the documents. What can be demonstrated, however, is that Matthew's and Luke's reports involved double traditions originating from parallel groups of disciples in Jerusalem. These personal factors can actually explain the profound mixture of similarities and divergences in the Q material.

As was observed with regard to Matthew (above, p. 182), the apostle Peter generally plays a central role in the First Gospel, and especially within its didactic parts which mainly include Q units and single traditions. Matthew has repeatedly placed Peter in front of the disciples who are permitted to hear the instructive speeches of the Lord (Matt. 4:18 + 5:1 e.p.). This indicates that Matthew or his redactors have taken over several didactic traditions of the Q type from Peter and the apostolic circle in Jerusalem, of which he was the leader during the first ten years after Christ's death. In the retrospective of Luke in Acts the teaching of Peter and the apostles has explicitly been localized to the temple area (Acts 2:46 e.p.). A primary source of the didactic Q units and single traditions found in Matthew may therefore be discovered in the didactic activity of the Petrine group in Jerusalem and particularly in the temple.

With regard to Luke, the foregoing analysis of its middle section in block 8 (pp. 118–25) has pointed out the Hellenistic character of the rich didactic material found in Luke's travel narrative (Luke 9:51—18:14), which consists of numerous Q units besides single traditions. The entire material was meant to exemplify Christ's instruction of disciples and discussion with opponents. In the analysis of block 8 the frequent references to meal scenes have also been underlined (p. 124), and this phenomenon was used to argue in favor of ascribing Luke's material in the middle section to contacts with the Hellenistic group of disciples in Jerusalem that was foremost responsible for the charity meals (Acts 6:3). Communications stemming from the Hellenistic circle were furthermore supposed to have been conveyed to Luke by Philip in Caesarea (p. 170), that leading member of the Hellenists in Jerusalem who became a successful preacher and teacher in Hellenistic areas. Having been among those whom Luke referred to as "servants of the word from the beginning" (Luke 1:2), which means in Jerusalem, Philip was apt to become a main authority for Luke when collecting the material of his travel narrative. A similar orientation may be claimed for Luke's Sermon on the Plain (6:29–40), which has also been presented in a Hellenistic perspective (p. 171). Luke's supply of didactic Q units and single traditions may thus essentially be traced back to the activity of Philip and the Hellenists in Jerusalem, primarily at the charity meals.

Under these circumstances two separate but adjacent backgrounds of the Q material found in Matthew and Luke can be supposed. On the one hand there was the preaching and teaching of Peter and the apostles and on the other that of Philip and the Hellenists. Both activities originated in Jerusalem, though not

exactly among the same people and for the same purpose, and in both cases reminiscences of Christ's didactic logia were fundamental.

The difficulty of explaining why the Q material represents that intricate combination of similarity in the content and diversity in the context has always been a stumbling block. A reference to living traditions supported by the two Jerusalem groups in question helps to clear up the problem. In conclusion, the fundamental circumstances may be summarized as follows:

1. The notorious spread of all Q pericopes and their elements on different parts of Matthew and Luke was a consequence of their preliterary use by two groups of traditionists with somewhat different orientations.

a. As must be supposed with regard to most parts of the synoptic material, the double traditions of Matthew and Luke without support in Mark were originally isolated units circulating in the community before they were organized in more comprehensive structures. And corresponding to what Papias indicated about Mark when he referred to expositions of Peter (διδασκαλίαι) given according to occasional needs (above, p. 161), the nucleus of each Q tradition in Matthew and Luke, too, was a practical subject to be treated. This is demonstrated, for instance, by the Lord's Prayer (Matt. 6:9–15; Luke 11:2–4). After having first been quoted freely, such traditions were later adapted to comprehensive structures and written texts just according to which theme had to be illustrated.

b. Most analogous traditions of the Q type are found in the Galilean section of Matthew and in the Transjordanian block of Luke (Matt. 4:18—18:35; Luke 9:51—18:14). This was due to Matthew's dependence on apostles with a background in Galilee and Luke's on Hellenists who had come from Transjordan (see, e.g., pp. 121–22).

2. In spite of their constantly different context in Matthew and Luke, the Q traditions consist of pericopes and shorter elements that comprise internal similarities in both Gospels. Two important factors have brought about this correspondence.

a. On the preliterary level, the Q traditions were developed either for apostolic or for Hellenistic teaching, but in both cases they were based on reminiscences of Christ's works and especially his words. In their present form not all of them may retain verbally what Jesus did and said, for inevitably the reminiscences were exposed to individual adjustments, and probably a translation from Aramaic into Greek was involved. A priori, one must nevertheless have the right of presuming a relative correspondence between the experiences of the eyewitnesses and the reminiscences of the traditionists. Common roots in essentially similar recollections can thus be understood to have caused that internal similarity of form and content which is found when individual traditions of the Q type in Matthew and Luke are compared one with another.

b. Although two different groups of traditionists are discernible behind the Q traditions of Matthew and Luke—on the one hand the apostles and on the other the Hellenists—they were both active in Jerusalem and did not live isolated from

each other. Possibilities of personal contacts and mutual influences were doubtless offered and exploited. It may be supposed that these contributed to a substantial assimilation of the reminiscences and traditions in question.

In order to elucidate the roots of the synoptic traditions, emphasis has been placed on concrete historical circumstances reflected in the extant texts. The author has endeavored to concentrate the analysis on what can be established as to empirical conditions and personal contributions of the traditionists and the evangelists. It seemed necessary to avoid two antithetic extremes, which have led to a polarization of theological judgments on the Gospels today. One of the poles implies a dogmatic rejection of human factors, and its advocates remind one of people telling children about the stork which brings a baby from heaven. The other pole is represented by a mechanical criticism of the written documents without concern for the life setting of the material, and this limitation makes the development of the Gospels resemble the procreation of a child in a retort. Here the ambition of the author has been to discover the living roots *and* human factors involved.

Index of Ancient Writers Quoted as Witnesses